JUN 2006

Rock Island Publi
401 - 19th Street
Rock Island, IL 61

D0836162

HELLO, I'M SPECIAL

HOW **INDIVIDUALITY** BECAME THE NEW CONFORMITY

by Hal Niedzviecki

CITY LIGHTS ✦ SAN FRANCISCO

© 2006 by Hal Niedzviecki
All Rights Reserved

First published by Penguin Canada in 2004. First City Lights edition, 2006.

Cover design: Yolanda Montijo
Book design: Elaine Katzenberger
Typography: Harvest Graphics

Library of Congress Cataloging-in-Publication Data

Niedzviecki, Hal, 1971-
    Hello, I'm special : how individuality became the new conformity / Hal
Niedzviecki.
        p.   cm.
    ISBN-10: 0-87286-453-7
    ISBN-13: 978-0-87286-453-5
    1. Popular culture.   2. Individuality.   3. Conformity.   I. Title.
    HM621.N515 2006
    306—dc22

Take the Conformity Challenge:
www.helloimspecial.com

Visit our website: www.citylights.com

City Lights Books are published at the City Lights Bookstore, 261 Columbus
Avenue, San Francisco, CA 94133.

ACKNOWLEDGMENTS

I gratefully acknowledge the Canada Council for the Arts, the Ontario Arts Council and the Toronto Arts Council for providing financial assistance toward to the writing of this book.

I am grateful to the following people for their suggestions, advice, encouragement, and assistance: Brian Davis, Emily Schultz, Chris Frey, Hilary Clark, Andrew Blauner, Natasha Danemen, and Bruce Westwood.

Thanks to my editors Diane Turbide, Cheryl Cohen, and Elaine Katzenberger for their enthusiasm and hard work on this book.

Grant Shilling let me tag along with him on his delivery/surfing route and introduced me to a whole bunch of great people who patiently answered my questions. He made an invaluable contribution to this book.

En Route Magazine sent me to Florida, and, along with the *Globe and Mail* and *This Magazine*, let me use their esteemed pages to try out some of the ideas found in this book. Thanks to those publications and their editors.

A keg-sized thanks to Darren Wershler-Henry for helping me develop the title and cover of this book, plus his ongoing suggestions and input.

My parents Sam and Nina Niedzviecki can be counted on to provide rebel-friendly greeting cards (with checks in them) plus unflagging support.

Rachel Greenbaum gave me ongoing valuable editorial feedback and critique, plus books and articles instrumental to developing the arguments herein. She was a constant in the writing of this book - supportive, insightful, patient. I can't thank her enough.

Finally, gratitude to everyone and anyone who took time out to email me an article, check a fact, recount a movie plot, or sit down for an interview. *You* truly are special!

Particularly vivid inspiration and information was gleaned from the following books and writers: Stuart Ewen's *PR! A Social History of Spin,* Michael Bracewell's *When Surface Was Depth*, Ulrich Beck and Elizabeth Beck-Gernsheim's *Individualization*, Juliet Schor's *The Overspent American*, Benjamin Barber's *Jihad vs. McWorld*, Carl Graumann and Serge Moscovici's *Changing Conceptions of Crowd Mind and Behaviour*, Wendy Shalit's *A Return to Modesty*, the writings of Georg Simmel and Michel Foucault, the reporting of Warren St. John in *The New York Times*, and finally *Habits of the Heart* by the scholars Robert Bellah, Richard Madsen, William M. Sullivan, Ann Swidler, and Steven M. Tipton.

For all the special little ones, but especially
Dov, Talia, Erez, Jared, Aden, Jonah, Jordan, Cooper,
and little Elly.

I AM SPECIAL

(to the tune of "Frère Jacques")

I am special,
I am special,
Look at me,
You will see,
Someone very special,
Someone very special,
It is me,
It is me.

—Popular song found on many primary school education resource
websites

CONTENTS

INTRODUCTION

"MOM, DAD, I'VE GOT SOMETHING TO TELL YOU . . ."

DISCOVERING THE NEW CONFORMITY

FLASH BACK TO THE MID-EIGHTIES. Ronald Reagan has just capped the ascendancy of the conservative age with his victory over a hapless Walter Mondale. The Maryland bedroom community where my family resides boasts one of the highest concentrations of retail outlets in the world. My father works for the World Bank, an ominous-sounding international organization known for its conservative fiscal policies. My mother is social coordinator at the Canadian embassy—not an institution known for its wild parties. Conservative people living in a conservative era, working in a conservative city at conservative establishments, and at the end of their conservative day, driving their conservative cars back to their comfortable conservative suburban domicile.

Like so many suburban teens, high school Hal is bored. Through the veil of his teen angst, he sees nothing but shopping malls and hypocrisy. Clearly the scene is rife with opportunity—opportunity for a rabblerousing whipper-snapper to lift his leg and mark his territory.

Teen Hal definitely intends to do his best.

I come home after disappearing for an entire weekend. I stink of tequila and sick. Dad takes me aside and tells me I should "stick to vodka." I "borrow" a Visa card and spend my parents' credit with abandon. Dad yells at me. Mom slips me a twenty. I deliberately fail classes in Hebrew school, in the process acquiring a large stack of conduct referrals and detentions. I forge my mom's signature on the mailed slips and almost get away with it. The parents sigh and transfer me to the local public high school—where I hone my ability to ingest intoxicating substances, blare depressive Euro alt-rock, and spend profligately on non-Jewish girls I make a habit of inviting to Passover Seders.

The parents laugh. They tell me I'll grow out of it. Dad takes me aside and gives me a fistful of condoms. I'm the one who blushes.

Fast-forward to my university days. I decide to become a writer. I announce I have no chance of ever making a living. Mom rushes off to tell the neighbors that I'm an *artiste*. Dad slips me a twenty.

Now I'm in my thirties. The parents still revel in my "radical" tendencies. Not only do they seem to encourage my idiosyncrasies, but they go out of their way to make sure I know how proud they are of my nonconformist status.

Take the birthday cards they give me. For my thirtieth birthday, I got a Hallmark card depicting a crowd scene—dour grey men in suits, hats, and overcoats. Superimposed on the picture is the announcement: "Conformity—proudly serving painfully boring people since time began." Inside it says: "Happy birthday to a non-conformist."

For my thirty-first birthday, I got a card showing a delicately painted landscape: blue tree and purple sun. The front of the card said: "The challenge is to be yourself in a world that is trying to make you like everyone else." Inside: "Happy birthday to a one-of-a-kind you!"

The parents are delighted with the cards, which, as far as they're concerned, represent their open minds and understanding natures. But, perched as I am on the edge of the abyss known as middle age, the cards have an unintended effect. They depress me. They confirm something I've long suspected but have never wanted to acknowledge: My primary behavior pattern is, essentially, obsolete. In a world that craves Hallmark greeting cards about overturning the grey-suited enemies of individuality, the nonconformist has lost his identity. Far from being weird and rebellious, he becomes normal and placid. On my thirty-first birthday I realized that my nonconformity is not merely tolerated, but replicated and accepted.

This is obvious from the reaction of the family, who revel in my every "bad boy" antic, but also from the way society as a whole has scooped me into a warm, fuzzy, loving, be-yourself embrace. How can nonconformity be rebellious when a Hallmark birthday card practically begs you to *go for it?*

And yet, being considered a nonconformist—a free thinker who challenges trends, ideologies, accepted patterns of behavior—is an important part of how I define myself. If I'm not a rebel, what am I? Or maybe the question should be: If I'm a rebel sanctioned by society, encouraged by my parents, and cheered on by Hallmark, what is left to rebel against?

On the morning of my thirty-first birthday, I turn over my card, unable to face its soothing, brush-stroked message. The back of the card contains information about its origins. The maker is Brush Dance in Sausalito, California. I read that the name *Brush Dance* comes from "a Yurok Indian healing ritual. . . . Being true to yourself is the one and only Yurok Indian law." Not only does the entire world now encourage my rebellion, but Native spiritualities co-opted by card companies have even legitimized self-obsession. Once upon a time, being "true to yourself" was the siren song of the beer-swilling punk, the footloose beatnik, the Left Bank absinthe-guzzling, orgy-seeking, perpetually unemployed painter. Once upon a time, adopting the philosophy of being true to yourself was considered hedonistic and self-indulgent. Today, the principles of moral self-indulgence are trumpeted on the backs of New Age greeting cards given to cranky cynical sons as an enthusiastic acknowledgment of their "one-of-a-kind"-ness.

Brush Dance has a website, of course, where I came upon the Brush Dance manifesto. It proclaims:

> A powerful movement has begun. We are in the midst of a major shift as individuals, as a culture and throughout our planet. . . . We are becoming more "spiritual," more conscious

and more caring as individuals and on a global level. We are becoming a community of seekers, joined by our intention to deepen self-understanding and increase the vitality and meaning of our lives. We are drawn to what is deep and true above what is fleeting and easy. We are utilizing this vitality by seizing the opportunity to act as change agents and healers on a local and global level.

Ay Carumba! as nonconformist imp superstar Bart Simpson might say. It's worse than I thought. Not only has my stance as a nonconformist been co-opted to sell cards, but it has been turned into a wishy-washy philosophy that, horribly enough, encompasses most of, if not all, the attributes once identified with the domain of nonconformity. Brush Dance invites us to be "change agents" and asserts that there is a revolution in which individuals seek to "deepen self-understanding and increase the vitality and meaning of our lives." This is, essentially, a kind of New Age hedonism, a permissive individualistic life code adorned with quasi-religious rhetoric and couched as a "major shift." The Brush Dance manifesto comes down to: Be yourself, make yourself happy, "deepen" your "*self*-Understanding," and, hey, in the process you'll be acting as some kind of "change agent" or "healer." It's a philosophy that says: The world needs to be reconfigured—according to my specifications. The best way to get the world to realize this is by doing exactly what I want. I have no need to ever modify my behavior at the behest of others. I am deeply spiritual, you see, and my quest for "self-understanding" and desire to "increase the vitality and meaning" of my life actually benefits the world; people simply have to observe my example in order to better themselves. This, naturally, does not involve me doing anything more than going about my business precisely as I feel like it.

Isn't it wonderful? I'm an *agent of change* just by doing exactly what I want! So it is that the Brush Dance manifesto and my own nonconformist mental latticework sound horribly similar. All this, of course, forces me to wonder: How did the central ethos of my rebellious ways end up on a New Age birthday card bought by my parents in some sprawling North American mall offering thirty different takes on khaki?

I'm not about to complain that corporations have co-opted nonconformity. It's undoubtedly true; huge companies like Hallmark have always tried to give themselves a veneer of rebellion in order to better appeal to everyone, from glue-sniffing teens to paunchy mid-life-crisis types longing for their edgy university days. But Brush Dance, with its dedication to recycled paper and soy inks, is hardly part of an evil empire. This is a painfully earnest outfit that practices what it preaches, seeks to do good in the world, and, with its inky landscapes, lives far, far away from the terrain of cool that giant companies are always stumbling into, which sends hipsters fleeing to the hills. Hallmark co-opts cool by mass-producing cards that exude irony toward the so-called mainstream. By contrast, Brush Dance is in the malls not for its teen-pleasing cool, but because it represents some aspect of the mainstream—not a corporate trend, but a genuine shift to believing in the transcendent possibilities of anything-goes individualism. The company's existence, and the message of benevolent self-obsession it conveys, reflects a change in the value system of North America and the greater Western world. Brush Dance isn't sexy, hip, or ironic. Strip away the layer of New Age blubber and you get Brush Dance preaching that nonconformist individuality is a "major shift" sweeping the land. Couple that with the fact that my parents bought the card for me in one of the many malls they obsessively frequent—thrilled to have found something that represents the cantankerous world view of their Hal—and the nonconformist has a problem. A whole lot of people have a problem.

WE NOW LIVE in the age of the individual. We are free to determine and undertake diverse and conflicting agendas. We can flaunt our sexuality and infidelity on cheesy temptation game shows, run up huge debts hiring plastic surgeons to give us the look of lizards, devote our lives to collections of serial-killer memorabilia.

These days, not only are you allowed to chart your own path

toward life, liberty, and the pursuit of happiness, but you are seemingly *required* to do so. Even within the realm of the heretofore ordinary—work, family, church, bureaucracy—one is expected to express individuality.

Conformity is no longer about adhering to strict social practices meant to preserve and uphold the sanctity of the family, the church, the nation-state. Today, conformity is about doing whatever you feel like, whenever you feel like, so long as what you are doing is all about the new you. Individuality is the new conformity. Institutions take a back seat to our personal quest to *be ourselves*. Religion has lost meaning, family is fragmented, and nations are judged on their ability to foster an environment in which the individual has the opportunity to attain the kind of revered status once held in reserve for monarchs, religious leaders, and the rare genius.

Nonconformity is now the accepted norm of society. As a result, traditional community is changing, which means our relationships to government, family, religion, and employment are in flux as we seek new meanings and institutions that can embrace the all-pervasive nonconformist ideology. This flux has given rise to what some may view as positive developments in society: a more fluid relationship between work and play; a dramatic increase in time spent on various kinds of creative endeavors; and a reassessment of traditional institutions that have dominated the lives of previous generations and led us down the path of environmental degradation, mass depression, and unsurpassed greed.

And yet the rise of individuality and the subsequent crumbling of tradition are also pushing us down a slippery slope. Obsessed with celebrating our individuality and finding ways to rebel against traditional structures, we find ourselves hurtling down "Mount Me," careening in strange directions, out of control.

THIS BOOK IS NOT ABOUT ME. But it is a general rule that inserting oneself early on in the argument creates a personal connection with the reader. (Is it working?) In starting this book with my own travails, I have used a standard, even what some might call a conformist, structure. I did so unintentionally, but there it is. A book about the rise of conformist nonconformity begins by demonstrating just how difficult originality has become.

Is there anything I can do that will show myself to be a definitive rebel exuding anti-establishment tendencies? Somewhere around my thirty-first birthday I realized that being a rebel is harder to pull off than it seems. My own brother—just a year and a half my elder—took a sudden turn to the religious some years back, and though it wasn't of Taliban-like proportions, the minutiae of his orthodoxy and the bizarreness of his switch from pop-culture liberal to near-fanatic still haunts me. Is he the rebel now, having embraced old-style religion and cast aside Brush Dance assurances of moral self-actualization? Has he, in one all-encompassing lifestyle change, bested my lifetime attempts to embody the nonconformist?

I've skated through the night in a hockey marathon; braved the frigid whitewater of Scottish rivers in the course of pretending to know how to kayak; written a book of obscure short stories focusing mostly on masturbation; ingested many an intoxicating substance while on the payroll pretending to perform some part-time task; and started a magazine of underground culture in which I deliberately published the sickest stuff I could find, including an article about a male stripper who sticks a barbecued chicken up his, uh, rear. All these things I have done at least in part to proclaim my individuality, my iconoclastic status, even as my formerly disaffected pot-smoking brother drifted toward Orthodox Judaism and a career as a corporate lawyer. And yet nobody really considers me a rebel, and it is my brother's adherence to traditional values that causes the most friction in the family.

Perhaps my brother's conversion is the flip side of my own antics. Both of us grew up in the cradle of pop's promise—"Just do it, superstar!"—and came of age confused and conflicted by the era of intense greed that served as a backdrop to our adolescence. Did we both seek to rebel, and simply take two opposing yet parallel paths? One a cultureproducing bohemian hedonist and the other an ultrareligious family man? These days, which is more individualistic?

Whatever the answer is to these questions, I do know one thing. It's time to shove those birthday cards into the back of a desk drawer and get on with the business of figuring out what and who I want to be. In a previous book called *We Want Some Too,* I wrote of a world of independent cultural creators determined to find some way to rebel against corporate culture. I believed that I was one of those rebels, a pop-influenced semi-slacker determined to reinvent mass culture to serve individuals and communities in an era of expanding global commonality and shrinking locality. But, looking back at that book and what I've since seen happening in our world, I realize that I was far too optimistic. How much of what I thought of as fruitful rebellion was really narcissistic I'm Specialness? How much of my own work has been about exuding a pretense of cool as opposed to truly challenging institutions and norms?

It's time to face up to the whirlwind of conflicting expectations, crumbling traditions, spiritual agendas, and pop-culture-inspired fantasies that make up my fragile consciousness. I'll start by visualizing the way I can do things differently on my next birthday. Instead of anxiously ripping the envelope off my card and pretending not to immediately search for the inserted check while the parents look on in proud expectation, I might just have to pull the folks aside and have a little heart-to-heart talk.

Mom, Dad, I'll say in the hushed whisper reserved for family scandal. I hate to disappoint you but, you see, I'm not a nonconformist any more. Now hold on. Don't panic. Let me finish. What I mean is, I am, but I'm not. What's that? You don't get it? Well, you see, if *everyone* is a free-thinking, deepening-the-self-understanding rebel, then I'm just like everyone else. A nonconformist conforming to nonconformity. Talk about a loss of identity. Do you still love me? Am I still me? Mom, quit trying to hug me! Dad, c'mon, this is serious—I'm not asking for money—will you put your wallet away?

PART ONE

WHERE WE ARE NOW

1

1

HELLO, I'M SPECIAL

THE RISE OF NONCONFORMITY

Hot, sunny day in the backyard. A six-foot, wood-slatted fence encloses a cropped square of emerald-green grass. I sit on the raised patio: plastic chair, shade cast by a protruding deck umbrella. I gaze languidly out at the scene on the lawn in front of me.

A guy gets punched in the face.

Guy moans, shakes it off. Tries to get loose. But his arms are being held behind his back by a fellow in a gaudy Hawaiian shirt who looks like a cross between *Fantasy Island* hosts Tattoo and Mr. Roarke. The victim—a lanky, golden-haired fellow who, like all the combatants, is in his late teens—struggles furiously. His three assailants show no mercy. Taking advantage of the captive's collared arms, two of the attackers repeatedly slam their fists into his stomach and face. One of the attackers, his tender white skin pinked by the sun, wears shorts, a white tank top, basketball shoes. And a *Friday the 13th* Jason-esque goalie mask. His partner, face exposed but locked in a savage grimace, starts kicking.

Suddenly the fellow taking the beating breaks free, somehow managing to knock all three of his tormentors down. On the patio we watch as chairs are thrown, stepladders are swung, and the fence's durability is tested to the limit when the fighters slam heavily into it—some of them using the wood as a springboard, some of them crumpling against the swaying planks.

Then, a surprising outcome: Mask Guy is manhandled into the air and lands heavily on his back. He is pinned, while his confederates lie splayed around him, beaten, unable to get up. A kid, his barely pubescent appearance accentuated by black-and-white-striped referee shirt, bangs the count out on the grass and pronounces the match over.

The guy perched on the roof of the shed slowly climbs down, carefully guarding the digital movie camera strapped around his neck.

Everyone springs up and shakes hands.

The Backyard Wrestling Federation Friday Night Massacre taping is done.

Until next week.

I COULD BE IN almost any backyard in North America, if it weren't for the chatter about pain, new wrestling holds, data uploads, digi-camera angles, and next week's title bout. Instead, I'm in the nexus where pop culture meets reality, where implanted passions to be somebody translate into amateur histrionics that both parody and transcend mainstream culture.

I'm in Mississauga, Ontario. It's a forgettable spread of malls and subdivisions located between Toronto and Buffalo. I'm in a suburban backyard, temporary headquarters and current arena for the little-known but culturally virulent Backyard Wrestling Federation (BYWF). Believe it or not, at the time I stopped by, they were the most famous amateur wrestling league in the world.

Between five thousand and seven thousand viewers were tuning in to watch the website broadcast of each Friday Night Massacre around the time I visited the set. The number of viewers once spiked as high as fifteen thousand, after USA Today sent a reporter and photographer to Mississauga in 1999. The resulting story ended up on the front page.

Far more important than the specific antics of the BYWF "performers" is what these young men represent: a new approach to asserting individuality in a mass-culture age. Backyard wrestling is just one of the ways that growing numbers of people, no longer content to be simple observers, are putting themselves forward as participant-performers. They are announcing themselves to the world as individuals dedicated to the establishment of their own fleeting narratives and recorded legacies. By regularly pursuing activities that function primarily as channels to proclaim difference, mixing ongoing performance with their everyday responsibilities, and deliberately seeking a place for themselves in global mass culture, backyard wrestlers are intentionally signalling their specialness. This is the new conformity: part sociological phenomenon, part (pop) cultural practice, part challenge to the old orthodoxies of institutional expertise, and part expansion of a me-first agenda long promised by the abundances of techno-capitalism.

The BYWF (as fans know it) is a deceptively simple idea. In 1998, a core of three guys started filming matches, concocting roles and dramas, and uploading a weekly installment every Friday evening to their website. Dumping stuff on the net is hardly an exciting concept these days, but there's a first time for everything, and in 1998, the revelation that you could have your own wrestling federation, find an instant audience in the thousands, and still lead a so-called normal life sent shockwaves through the millions of fans who have grown up devoted to one of the most inexplicable but enduringly compelling pop-culture phenomena of all time—televised "professional" wrestling.

Mind you, that's not the way the BYWF participants see it. They are refreshingly free of jargon and conceptual baggage. They just want to make a wrestling show. They leave the ruminations to the pansy writer who can't help shuddering when a body hits the grass, thinking "I know it's pretend, but that's *got* to hurt." The BYWF triumvirate manages ten to twenty wrestlers in their fluctuating roster, and the one thing they do care about is spectator numbers. They talk among themselves about their stats and about the fans who email in with comments, suggestions, and appreciation. "I do it just because it's fun," says Kris Verri (a.k.a. Dylan Foxxx, the victim and eventual winner of the match I observed). But fun is not enough to sustain a multi-year tradition. When the group gathers to talk about editing the Massacre and getting it ready for upload, fun is in the background, like a snapshot of some really good time you've pinned to the billboard so you don't forget about it. The fans make it real, elevate it from kid stuff to the serious business of mass entertainment.

Keeping an eye on the action, I chat a bit with a former backyard wrestler turned sideline showgirl whose stage name is Jasmine. She tells me of the post-*USA Today* explosion of interest and how she suddenly began getting fan emails from around the world. Some of them like her moves on the grass. Others want to marry her. These days, Jasmine prefers to appear on the sidelines, tramping about in a tight outfit that displays her charms and Dylan Foxxx's championship belt. In reality, Jasmine is shy, speaks of the embarrassment she felt when her restaurant co-workers discovered the site, cringes when recounting some of the emails she's gotten. But during the shoot, she goes to the trouble of applying makeup, fixing her hair, and slipping into a gaudy outfit just to walk up and down the sidelines—efforts that will make up a minute of footage on the Massacre, at best. It isn't hard to detect a fierce pride as she paces the periphery of the action or tells me about being razzed at work. Why shouldn't she have fans or dress up for the camera? Jasmine enjoys her spot of fame, and defends it with an embarrassed but enthusiastic grin. Like Kris Verri, she doesn't do it for the money. And she has no illusion that backyard wrestling will bring her fame or fortune. But as Verri has said: "Every single one of us has had or has a dream of maybe one day becoming a WWF [World Wrestling Federation] superstar."

BACKYARD WRESTLING spreads from suburb to suburb, site to site, and continent to continent as new generations of expert amateurs seek attention through pop performance. Although the BYWF is now defunct, its legacy continues. There are now hundreds, if not thousands, of amateur internet wrestling leagues—not to mention the other amateur extreme sports sites that depict everything from skateboarding off rooftops to undergrads scaling the 20-story university library, to snowboarders, surfers, and more, all willing to put life and limb on the line and online. Ken Flatt has been a backyard wrestling fan for about two years and tells me in a cyber intimacy that he first came to the pastime by stumbling across a website called Scrambled Wrestling Association. He thought it was cool. "I later found the BYWF, which totally blew me away," he explains. "FULL SHOWS! I really admired the creativity these Canadian kids put on."

Not long after seeing the BYWF, Flatt was inspired to start his own wrestling troupe. "I am working on my own federation as we speak. I have been getting lots of advice on how to go about doing things and getting shows up together. My friends and I are having a lot of fun just acting and being in front of the camera."

In the fake-real world of pop, Flatt has chosen a character called Corporate Ken, whom he describes as "the company's biggest heel." Flatt's alter ego is a straitlaced business type that the other, cooler wrestlers love to mock and torture. Not long ago, the businessman was an admired symbol of success. Today, conforming nonconformists cut him down to size. The businessman is a loser, an anonymous cog. He has not reclaimed his identity, announced his specialness. In my last email from Flatt, whom I initially contacted based on comments he had posted in an online wrestling chat room, he told me he was twenty-four, and a student living in Bristol, England. Flatt wrote: "The main aim and goal at the moment is to get the shows we've filmed put together and edited and finally uploaded. If I were to succeed sometime soon we would be noted as the only active wrestling federation in the UK, even if we are a Backyard Circuit."

We can see the way these ideas spread, from backyard to backyard, community to community, country to country. As the rising tide of nonconforming conformity crests into a tidal wave, the roles that once symbolized respectability and normalcy (e.g., the corporate team player) become targets of ridicule. As a result, almost everyone is an aspiring celeb "bar chef," remixologist, or rap star biding time on the tradingroom floor. All the while, the creators of this kind of amateur pop culture insist that it's "just for fun," with Ken Flatt stating in email conversation with me that despite what appears to be his urgency to "succeed" and his frequently posted enthusiastic comments, "I would not say that it is an important aspect of my life. I suppose it is like a hobby." (Flatt would send me a follow-up email several days later asking if I needed any pictures of Corporate Ken in action to go with his "profile.")

The Normal of Special

The BYWF supposition—that just about anyone can "be" an entertainment-style wrestler—emerges naturally from mass-media-inspired dreams of becoming a superstar. Millions of otherwise "normal" citizens of the Western world harbor the notion that fame of some sort awaits them. In that sense, the creators of the BYWF are fascinating as much for what they aren't as for what they are. They aren't artists, philosophers, punks, anarchists, actors, activists, or intellectuals. They are normal young men and women conforming to the suddenly normal idea that they should, could, and will be *special*.

Essentially an imitation of a TV spectacle (a spectacle that is, itself, an imitation of a sport), the BYWF suggests the nature of the new conformity. More and more people want to be special and noticed, and we want to create bigger, better narratives, but our approach is to imitate established practices like televised wrestling. In that sense, the BYWF participants articulate the kind of specialness that characterizes the new conformity, regardless of age, perspective, and nationality: a genuine desire to articulate genuine individuality that is nevertheless mired in cliché and convention.

Consider the case of Gary Stone, one of thousands of Elvis impersonators who reside in the United States. "I am 50 years old," he explains on a website, "married and a national account executive for a large corporation. I live in Cincinnati, Ohio, and I am a Sunday

School teacher and deacon at a local church. I impersonate an older Elvis Presley to bring some enjoyment and happiness to various groups of people."

Gary Stone inhabits very traditional worlds. That someone living what appears to be a conservative life feels free to impersonate a pop star who died from drugs, drink, and excess certainly hints at just how deep the ethos of individualism permeates our culture. And it also suggests that even a figure like Stone, with his church, good job, and presumably a happy marriage, longs for something more. The old-style institutions don't embody him, can't contain his spirit, won't speak to who he is the way, oddly enough, doing Elvis impersonations does.

Elvis-impersonator associations, conventions, clubs, newsletters, websites, guide books, and, yes, protocols abound. The Elvis Presley impersonation cult(ure) appeals to Gary Stone because, in an age when business and religion are no longer seen as institutions capable of fostering individuality, he appears to find true community, shared values, and a place to express benevolent personhood in Elvis Presley impersonation. You might argue that all Stone is doing is dressing up and making, say, sick kids laugh. (It's not hard to imagine Stone working the wards in the local hospital.) But if Stone just wants to do his thing, then why have a website? Why put his picture and biography up for all the world to see? And, more importantly, why not become a clown or some other generic figure of fun? Stone is not just someone who does Elvis impersonations. He is part of the culture of Elvis, the *community* of Elvis impersonators. Like the backyard wrestlers, he is conforming to the crowd's pop-inspired rules and regulations, so that he can manifest a more urgent, free, and active identity than his roles as churchgoer and businessman allow. When Gary Stone puts on that Elvis outfit, he is tapping into a new world of non-traditional structures that has come into existence solely to serve the needs and desires of people like himself. No longer just another churchgoer, family man, middle manager, Gary Stone is now a new conformist—an "I'm Specialite" using the precepts of mass culture to reshape his own life.

In *The Organization Man,* William H. Whyte's 1956 ground-breaking sociological study of office life, a company president advises a group of aspiring executives. "The ideal," he tells them, "is to be an individualist privately and a conformist publicly." But in the era of the new conformity, the ideal is reversed: Figures as diverse as Gary Stone and the backyard-wrestling crew seek to capture the *outward appearance* of specialness, despite their essentially conformist, conservative lives and convictions. Outer individuality obscures inner conformity. As the need to proclaim oneself an individual becomes more urgent, it is no longer sufficient to simply be a deacon and an account executive. One must, always, be more than what one is, constantly reinventing, constantly announcing. Once, it was enough to be recognized in your community, to be somebody in your own small town or neighborhood. Those days are over. As Gary Stone shows us, people now crave a different sort of authenticity. Increasingly, we are submitting ourselves to a different sort of authority—the mercurial world of fabricated, mass-produced, instantaneous stardom.

IF THERE IS a single constant in the emergence of individuality as the new conformity, it is the ubiquitous presence of celebrity. Celebrity doctors treat celebrity adventurers who date celebrity zoologists who lunch with celebrity art critics and celebrity entrepreneurs. (They eat at the famous diner presided over by the famously crotchety waitress who, famously, had a bit of a stint on *Letterman* and doesn't give a fuck who you are.) It is no coincidence that the I'm-Special shift coincides with an explosion in the number of celebrities announcing themselves in the virtual realms of cyberspace and TV-land. Not only do we have more celebrities than ever in the interlocking spheres of sports, pop culture, and the arts, but new categories of celebrities seem to be constantly emerging.

Consider the celebrity chef, once unheard of, now a regular phenomenon, appearing everywhere, it seems, except restaurants. These ubiquitous creatures spend more time hawking their seasoning lines or flying to strange places to eat monkey brains (on camera, of course) than they do in the kitchen. The Iron Chefs descend from their podiums to do battle with challengers in the "Kitchen Stadium," a scene as deliciously surreal as it is popular with hipsters and straitlaced dads alike. The celebrity-chef trend became so oppressive that, at one point, *Time Out New York* actually did a story singling out great chefs who *aren't* celebrities. Hot on that trend's heels is the phenomenon of the celebrity bartender. With their signatures featured prominently on fancy cocktail menus, and hyped-up names for drinks of their own invention, celebrity bartenders will soon, no doubt, be mixing their own Food Network specials, flying off to the ends of the world to dilute absinthe with crocodile blood in a coconut shaker—a memento from a previous adventure tending bar for a tribe in the Amazonian rain forest.

"One should either be a work of art or wear a work of art," wrote Oscar Wilde. Wilde followed his own advice, prancing down London's Kings Road in what Wilde biographer Richard Ellmann described as "a brown suit with innumerable little buttons that gave it the appearance of a glorified page's costume." Wilde was accompanied by his wife, Constance, who wore "a large white picture hat, with white feathers, and a dress of equal flourish." Figures like Oscar Wilde glided through their environs dispensing *bons mots* and exuding carefully crafted charisma. Wilde was followed by the Dadaists and Surrealists, and, eventually, the seventies punks (who performed his life better than Sid Vicious?). The arrival of art star performers like Andy Warhol and the presence in pop culture of enigmatic figures like David Bowie, Michael Jackson, Madonna, Marilyn Manson, and Anna Nicole Smith (whose reviled reality TV show was the first of a genre to epitomize the notion that everyday life is an ongoing act) have fully ushered in the age of celebrity devoid of any particular talent or accomplishment.

In his book *The Nineties: When Surface Was Depth,* English writer Michael Bracewell documents the process by which our pop figures appropriate the celebrity concept by demanding and attracting attention not so much for their work as for their everyday personas. Commenting on former Smiths front man Morrissey, Bracewell writes that the singer "represents what is known in modern

European philosophy as 'the will to self-create'; another term for this would be 'auto-fact.' What both of these mean is the ability within individuals to realize themselves as a mythology."

Today, using performance as a way to get noticed has moved from the realm of artists and performers into everyday life. Many of us are starting to feel the pressure to "realize" ourselves as a "mythology." From the suburbs to the ghettos, from the fringe to the mainstream, the notion that we must always be shaping and telling our special tale of ascendancy has become pervasive. Furthermore, identity "creation" has become almost compulsory. It is those who are *not* in some way performing roles who seem old-fashioned, of a different era. Those who seek to adhere to the old tropes of society—stay-at-home mom, successful businessman—are ignored or derided by a society that is mesmerized by toddler pop stars, business bad boys, and pierced pretend radicals.

EVERY TWIST AND TURN of fate is, these days, accompanied by the creation of a newly crowned celebrity culled from the ranks of the ordinary and given the opportunity to literally recreate who he or she is. Remember Sherron S. Watkins, the Enron vice-president who emerged as a heroine for having tried repeatedly to warn her bosses about the fuzzy math that might soon catch up with the energy company? This suburban manager and former sorority girl was portrayed in the media as a heroic whistle-blower, even though at Enron she did nothing more than send internal memos warning of potential problems resulting from bogus accounting. Watkins followed the new-conformity trajectory. In this myth, you go against the grain and are ultimately rewarded with the Holy Grail of achievement: instant celebrity. Watkins found herself meeting President George W. Bush, receiving the Court TV Scales of Justice Award, becoming *Time* magazine's Person of the Week, signing book and movie deals, and commanding large fees for her speeches. In public appearances, she addressed the employees of large corporations on the need to be more themselves at work, to be undaunted by foolish bosses and fraudulent bureaucracy. Despite the fact that her warnings went unheeded by her superiors and many people lost their life savings in the Enron debacle, Watkins has become the poster girl for the kind of success you can reap in the era of non-conformity. Even the illusion of dissent is enough. The whistle-blower will be rewarded, the Corporate Ken derided.

Will we soon be seeing a rash of babies named Sherron in tribute to the supposed Enron rebel? These days, experts and their books and websites circle expectant parents like vultures over carrion, ready to swoop down at a moment's notice and feed off Mommy and Daddy's desire to choose a hip individualistic name that will set baby apart from the crowd. In true new-conformity spirit, these names are often culled from the world of pop culture, where celebrities or the characters they play give us children named Trinity (from *The Matrix*), Madison (sudden eighties boom after the Daryl Hannah vehicle *Splash*), and Keanu *(The Matrix Reloaded)*. In the popular book *Cool Names*, potential names are divided into sections such as Hot Cool, Pre-Cool, Safe Cool, and Cool Cool. Whatever. As long as you're cool, right? How do the cool-name gurus select monikers to recommend? Explain the co-authors: "We look at movie stars' names and what they're naming their children. We look at names that cut across several trends at once. But after that, it's just instinct."

So what's the next cool name? I've got one for you. Dusty. Why? Because our man Dusty is a burgeoning celeb specialite whose twisted accomplishment—having sex with his teacher—will surely lead to cultural adulation from horny teens worldwide. Where once scandal might have embarrassed those involved, today it is welcomed as a way to get noticed. Dusty Dickeson is a twenty-one-year-old Sechelt, British Columbia-based self-styled bad-boy rapper. You might remember him as the seventeen-year-old student whose widely reported affair with his twenty-nine-year-old high school teacher shocked the community. At least, Dickeson is counting on you to remember him that way. His CD is called *Teacher Scandal:* "Sunshine Coast / Teacher scandal," raps Dickeson, backed up by his band Straight A's. Not to be outdone, after completing her ten-month sentence of house arrest for having sex with a minor while in a position of authority, the ex-teacher, Heather Ingram, wrote a steamy account of the affair, complete with sentences like: "My sexuality, almost fully buried, has awakened and whipped itself up around me like a tornado." Apparently the former lovers are now collaborating on yet another book about the affair, this time from the perspective of Dickeson, even as Ingram juggles bids to make a movie about her story.

This obsessive marketing of one's "individuality" as celebrity can be found not only in North America but also in Europe and Asia. Thai massage parlor king Chuwit Kamolvisit has been riding high after his arrest for, among other things, "procuring underage girls for prostitution." Chuwit responded to his arrest by going public about the $2.5 million in bribes he has paid over the years to various police and government officials. He leveraged the ensuing media frenzy into a hit talk show, *Chuwit, Alone and Shabby,* and a bestseller, *Golden Bathtub*. He spent a month in jail in 2003, but less than a year later announced his official candidacy for the August 2004 race to become the next governor of Bangkok.

Meanwhile, it was France that produced Jean-Marie Messier, the former Vivendi/Universal executive dubbed "France's first rock star CEO" by *Fortune*. Messier wrote a book called *J6M.COM*. Apparently the six *M*s are meant to signify something like Jean-Marie Messier, Moi Meme Maître du Monde (loosely translated, Jean-Marie Messier, Master of the World). He tells us in this modest tome, "Never having to answer to a higher authority, that is what guided me. I have been lucky. At each turn in my career, I have succeeded in increasing my independence." Not long ago such crass egotism and dismissal of the idea that there might be a higher authority than the successful CEO would have been shocking. But in the age of new conformity, he's just very special.

BATHED IN THE GLOW of our celebs, awash in the cologne of perpetual reinvention, millions are searching for ways to join the permanent party of special.

Sometimes the quest takes strange forms. Sonya Thomas is a thirty-six-year-old woman from South Korea and an unlikely star in the American "competitive eating circuit." Thomas ate an impressive twenty-five hot dogs at what has been described as "the World Series of competitive eating." Asked by a reporter why she does it, she said: "Before, I was just normal, like everybody. Now, I'm special."

This is essentially the mantra of the New Age of the New Conformity. Find some way to be yourself, but better. *"Before, I was normal. Now, I'm special."* Consider the case of 29-year-old Johnny Lechner. He's turned what would otherwise be a pathetic 12th year of college into an impressive brand. What's so great about Lechner? Nothing except his canny marketing ability. He sold himself as a laid-back party animal in a website he created with a friend. When the Wisconsin State Journal responded to his emails about the site with a profile, an entertainment industry feeding frenzy began that included appearances on Letterman and Good Morning America, and ended in potential TV and book deals currently being peddled by the William Morris Agency. *National Lampoon* is paying his tuition and Monster Energy drink delivers thirty cases a week to the house where he lives, billing themselves as "the offical energy drink" of his 12th year. In another time, Johnny would be a forget-table failure. In the age of special, Johnny's a canny self-promoter with a bright future as the ultimate slacker.

It's no surprise that talk shows liked Johnny. In fact, talk shows actively seek out everyday figures they can elevate to momentary celebrity. So much so that TV talk show producers are now eager to cast not only the hottest celebrity guest, but also the most enticing, interesting, special audience members. On The Ellen DeGeneres Show, audience members are encouraged to dance wildly at the start of the program. When Ellen took a fancy to the way a 74-year-old woman in her audience made a face and covered her ears while a loud pop song blared, she turned the willing retired teacher into a momentary star by continually replaying the clip and having the teacher back as a guest six times. Meanwhile, Martha Stewart's new show is also utilizing the newfound desire of the specialite to invigorate the daytime talk show model. Members of the audience, says a producer of the show, should be "prepared to participate without notice." There is a plan for one episode of the show to populate the audience with people who have knitted their own copies of the poncho Stewart wore on her way out of prison. Another episode will give audience seats only to women who go by the name Martha Stewart. The idea, with television as with life, is to blur any distinction between us and them—we're all special, we can all knit a celebrity poncho, we call have the name of a celebrity, be on the celeb's show, maybe even be a celebrity ourself.

These days even busboys and diners seek specialness. A reality-TV show set in a New York City restaurant and called *The Restaurant* attracted one thousand potential celebrity waiters, bartenders, chefs, and maître d's, all hoping to be hired by celeb chef Rocco DiSpirito. Apparently the producer who sold the show to NBC convinced the network that "restaurants are the new theater." Even diners were cast for the show—those seeking reservations applied on NBC's website and were asked to state why they thought they deserved a table.

There's a reason reality TV has become the new model for entertainment. Reality TV pulls us even further into the dreamy world of externalized perpetual performance and internal normalcy that is the hallmark of the new conformity. Here, ordinary people are themselves but better. They are ultra-self-aware versions of the ordinary, über-facsimiles of themselves in the same way that online personals are *recreations* of self constantly tweaked for maximum response and effect. Watching *The Restaurant* is watching people trying very hard to pretend that their chosen pose is who they really are. The new conformity, like reality TV, is about acting as though you are not acting. The process is excruciating, squirm-worthy, familiar to anyone who has subjected themselves to the likes of *Extreme Makeover, Who Wants to Marry My Dad?* or *Survivor*. It is all artifice and fakery, from those supposedly spontaneous professions of love to the tears of heartbreak, surrounded by TV cameras and lights. Reality TV introduces a new level of artifice into personal presentation; steeped in the fakery of special, both those participating and those passively observing cannot help but think in marketing terms—the value-added me; myself *plus*.

With its array of celeb busboys, brides, plastic-surgery supplicants, and even nannys, reality TV further spreads the ideology of new conformity. Everyone could and should separate from the crowd, be more than themselves. Losers are those who are content to stick with the crowd. Winners are those who reinvent themselves to stand out. The message is clear: With a little tweaking, you, too, can be a more and better you.

This conformist blueprint for individuality is replicating across all spectrums, from the backyard wrestling pit where Dylan Foxxx reigns supreme to the ivory towers of higher education to the office towers of high commerce. Thomas Homer-Dixon, author of *The Ingenuity Gap*, notes that celebrity is becoming increasingly prevalent in all aspects of life. "A star system has developed in many elite universities, whereby a few scholars and researchers are paid astronomically high salaries compared to their colleagues," he writes. "The same trend is visible across most industries and occupations in modern economies." For a great many people, it's no longer enough to be simply very good at what you do. One also has to be a public figure, noticed, and celebrated, and preferably televised.

This star system has infiltrated the minds and expectations of new generations. With Nike bestowing $1 million on a thirteen-year-old soccer player, Mountain Dew signing up a thirteen-year-old snowboarder, Lego and Jones Soda harnessing the skills of a six-year-old skateboarder, and Reebok running commercials featuring a three-year-old-basketball wunderkind, the message of superstar normalcy becomes abundantly clear. "Any child," an acerbic commentator noted, "can grow up to be famous enough to be a brand-image enhancer." So it is that few students today anticipate their lives as middle-class drudges. *The Wall Street Journal* cited a poll of college seniors: Fully 74 percent expect to one day become millionaires.

Prefab Special

We can't all be millionaire executives or have the good luck to turn sex scandal into notoriety or a skateboarding hobby into a multi-million-dollar enterprise. As a result, we are a people in constant need of prefabricated ways to announce our difference and specialness. Just take a look at what's on sale these days.

One of the hottest things you can sell on the net is yourself. Internet dating ranks in the top five uses of the web in the United States and probably Canada. Indeed, in the first half of 2003, Americans spent $214 million on dating sites, nearly triple what they spent in all of 2001. Why are these online sites so popular? Well, at least partly because they allow people to redesign themselves, to articulate their pseudo-individuality, to shed roles and adopt new ones while still holding on to a core conservatism, a willingness to pretend, but not actually be. The founder of one service, Nerve.com, says that people turn their ads into "constantly evolving marketing channels" by regularly tweaking their sites, updating photographs, and changing text to refine their pitches. Others create multiple ads. As a twenty-six-year-old lawyer and online-dating fan says: "You could be the cocky guy in one, and a humble, thoughtful guy in another. You're hitting a much broader target audience. Getting someone to write you back affirms your ability to market yourself." The goal, it seems, is not to make a real connection, but to get a response, to be noticed for being somebody special—anybody special.

As it is online, so it is in the local mall. There is an increasing interest in buying products that articulate special. These days, the trend is toward *not* sporting giant corporate brands on one's outfits and products.

In 2002, only 10 percent of Gucci merchandise carried the company logo, down from 40 percent the previous year. In 2003, Tommy Hilfiger announced that it was reinventing its brand after being battered by less logo-conspicuous clothing brands. Its stock plummeted from $41.06 in 1999 to $5.73 in 2003. It closed thirty-seven of its forty-four special shops, and its new lines no longer feature the trademark gigantic red-white-and-blue Tommy logo splashed all over the front of a shirt or pair of shorts. Brand names are out, notes *The New York Times,* citing "a return to individuality in fashion." Comments consumer critic Juliet B. Schor in the article: "It's tied to a larger resistance to branding strategies and connected to individuality, to rejecting the corporate definition of who you are." A retail analyst agrees: "[Teenagers] don't want to look like anybody else and they don't want to have somebody's name plastered on their things." One is tempted to couple this evolving demand for logo-free mass-produced items with the runaway success of Naomi Klein's treatise *No Logo,* which was a bestseller in Canada and Britain, and popular in the United States. Its Canadian cover featured publisher Knopf's familiar leaping-dog logo crossed out on the spine. The popularity of the book, and the way the *No Logo* logo has itself become a recognizable icon, again suggests the new-conformist craving for *products* that evoke freedom and personal identity (pants, book, whatever).

These new conformists are spending more and more time trolling malls and box stores for semi-individualistic purchase. They're looking for outfits and accessories that can make them who they want to be. They don't want prepackaged. They want *special.* And yet they generally have little interest in making their own clothes or doing anything other than buying a look. Here, the conformity of individuality is obvious. It's no coincidence that, as the logo fades, the single trend in fashion these days is custom-made. You can now get Gap jeans custom-stained, -bleached, or -torn. In London and San Francisco, Levi's stores offer on-site custom denim garments. To meet the demand for jeans that speak to individual personality, Levi's developed a "new vintage" program in which limited editions of jeans are made to look like an exact replica of a pair of 1920s denims. Comments one style writer: "Replicas provide idiosyncratic clothes without the hunt for them, evidence of a lifestyle without the effort involved in a life." Nike has offered a customized shoe service—you pick the color combos and get your name stitched on the side. One ambitious youngster ordered his shoes emblazoned with the words *sweat shop*. Meanwhile, livery operations that specialize in making custom suits and shirts report that business is suddenly booming. "Might our present decade be remembered as a backlash decade where individual style—or individuality—wakes up from a long slumber?" asks a fashion writer.

There's an analogous trend in booze consumption, where greasy-haired, underemployed hipsters have adopted low-end beer brands such as Pabst Blue Ribbon. After steadily sinking since the 1970s, sales of Blue Ribbon rose by 5.3 percent in 2002. In 2003, supermarket sales of the brand were up almost 10 percent. Who is drinking Blue Ribbon? The brand attracts middle-class twenty- and thirty-somethings because they do little advertising and project a blue-collar image that seems cool. In other words, it's the alcohol equivalent of logo-free, custom-made: a brand that seems authentic, a brand that can stand for anything for anybody. Pabst, desperate not to screw up the revival, is now struggling to figure out how to market to this disparate hipster generation without actually appearing to be marketing. According to one marketer, Blue Ribbon's relative scarcity and cheapness, coupled with its low profile as a brand, is what has turned it into an "underground darling." A commentator writing about the Pabst resurgence notes: "It's very much a politics of individual freedom, of rejecting overt pitches and elite tastes."

The trend to "personalization" in beer and fashion mirrors a broader trend in everything from license plates to the rise of portable technologies. We want our stuff to be just for us. Giant cereal maker General Mills put up a website in 2001 that at the time allowed people to customize their cereal box by mixing and matching their various products. At mycereal.com you could mix Lucky Charms with Cheerios or double up on colored marshmallows. Tower Records is offering consumers the opportunity to make their own mix CDs in-store; Sony is releasing the portable net surfer (keep in mind that the original Walkman has sold more than 250 million units worldwide!); and digital video recorders that let you pick and choose your own nightly lineup from the seemingly vast offerings of cable are now making serious inroads. The most well known of these, TiVo, reported over 4 million subscribers at the end of 2005. MP3 players—like the now ubiquitous iPod—let you customize your musical preferences and hear only the songs you really like. These slim gadgets have replaced the Walkman and completely revolutionized the way we listen to and buy music. In her book *The Overspent American,* Juliet Schor notes that, at least among the relatively well-off, "individuality and differentiation are essential. Why? Because mass-produced goods are too homogenous, too common. Everybody has them. This makes them incapable of conferring distinction." The rise of conformist individuality on a larger scale is confirmed by the plethora of "individualized" goods that seek to cater to our burgeoning need to communicate specialness. In the absence of any uniqueness test or other definitive way to ascertain how special the person standing next to us might be, most of us turn to pre-established signs and symbols that can project a sense of our individuality. Essentially, in our ongoing bid to demonstrate that we are special individuals, we require an endless supply of limited-edition, handmade, one-time-only products, contests, and events capable of conveying at least some partial sense of our uniqueness to everyone from co-workers and friends to people we pass on the street.

FLORIDA-BASED PROFESSOR James B. Twitchell argued in his book *Living It Up* that the ability of more and more people to afford luxuries like cellphone-digicam-web browsers and custom clothing actually increases our individual dignity and happiness.

But such dedication to having what you want the way you want it can turn ugly. As any nutritionist will tell you, there is a dark side to this be-yourself attitude. You will be left with more than just a hangover if you drink too much Pabst (actually a brew produced under contract by Miller and reviled in its original hometown, Milwaukee, after Miller shut down its brewery operation and tried to screw workers out of their pensions). The other prevailing fashion trend is for bigger and bigger sizes, due to the obesity epidemic in Western countries. The United States leads the charge, with a staggering 64.5 percent of its citizens clocking in overweight, and a shocking 31 percent of that crowd actually considered medically obese. Other Western countries can claim to be slightly leaner, though countries like Canada and Britain do only marginally better: In Canada, 32.5 percent of the population is overweight and 14.9 percent is obese. Even France, slowly being colonized by fast food and salty snacks, is becoming concerned because its obesity rate recently topped 10 percent for the first time.

In the age of individuality, the overall trend is not to encourage people to lose weight, but to make people feel good about their extra-large bodies. Ralph Lauren and Tommy Hilfiger, the Gap, and Old Navy all now offer plus-plus sizes. Teen mag *Seventeen* has started a new section: "Curvy Girl." The debut issue of *Teen Vogue* sported this headline on its cover: "Making It Big: How Curvy Girls Are Changing Hollywood's Stick-Thin Standard." Says *Teen Vogue* editor-in-chief Amy Astley: "I spend a lot of time in focus groups and a lot of time talking to teenagers. They really don't want to be told that they have to change."

A news release tells me the story of a fourth grade teacher who "carries the message of self empowerment to the nation." Apparently DeLores Pressley, an Ohio schoolteacher, is also "founder of a movement in this country that has made society realize that not everyone was born to be thin, that we are all special, just the way we are!" Pressley's "movement" consists of her new career as a plus-size motivational speaker, a modelling agency called Dimensions Plus (presumably to help Gap and Ralph make their biggie sizes look sexy), and producer of the Plus USA Woman Pageant. In the age of individuality you can be beautiful any way you are, never mind that Pressley's message of "self empowerment" is also one of mass delusion: In an age of unnaturally bloated bellies, in a country leading the way with 65 percent of its residents overweight, Pressley might just be doing a bit too good a job convincing us that it's okay to be chunky.

Many factors contribute to the obesity epidemic in the West: office work, eating at McDonald's, the prevalence of cars, and too much time spent watching TV, for instance. The very world we live in actually makes us fat. So why should fat be a stigma? In the new conformity, the answer isn't to change our world or ourselves: It's to change our story. Throughout the nineties, an array of feminist indie culture periodicals from *Bust* to the *Heavy Girl* zine challenged patriarchal notions of stereotypical beauty and advanced the idea that there are many ways to look and feel that are positive and healthy. But that positive I'm-Special message became corrupted by the new conformity. What begins with an empowering not-for-profit indie magazine or a support group ends, invariably, with a glossy magazine, a website, a consultant, and a whole new language of "curvy" and "plus-size"—all meant to make the overweight feel happy and represented. And, of course, they are encouraged to keep buying. Never mind that obesity poses serious medical problems. The relentlessly positive individualist message of special allows for a world where nobody is ever ugly or sick; nobody needs to change an unhealthy lifestyle; all you have to do is find the right story to tell, the right image of yourself to reflect back through your mind's eye.

For those who don't like those extra pounds, the rise of pseudo-individuality has nicely dovetailed with the rise of cosmetic surgery. There is no longer the slightest social stigma in having your tummy tucked or your stomach surgically shortened so you eat less. The number of cosmetic surgeries increased by 48 percent in the United States from 2000 to 2001. Non-surgical procedures are also popular: Botox injections were up 45 percent in the same time, chemical peels up a staggering 116 percent with 1.4 million done, and collagen injections trailed just behind—1 million injections given, up 85 percent. Sites like breastimplant.com and breastaugmentation.com battle it out to be the ones to refer you to your local cosmetic surgeon.

This is surgery in the name of looking better and younger. But it is also surgery in the name of easy reinvention, a way to retell the story of your life to convey a new aura of specialness. Cosmetic surgery in the name of individualism isn't limited to Western countries. Indeed, in China, a country experimenting with capitalism and pseudo-individualism, people are submitting themselves to a risky, painful, and expensive operation to add inches to their height. In a country where height is associated with status, and where institutions often use stature as a criterion for hiring (males must be at least five foot seven to apply to the Chinese foreign ministry), people are undergoing a lengthy procedure designed forty years ago by a Russian doctor looking for ways to straighten deformed limbs. One woman told *The New York Times* her reason for having the treatment: "I'm confident," she said, "that the operation will pay for itself many times over. I'll have a better job, a better boyfriend, eventually a better husband."

Back in the West, there are people—mostly girls—who are busy doing equally horrible things to their bodies: cutting themselves, starving themselves, and making themselves throw up. There are websites on which young women encourage each other and share tips on how best to purge themselves of food. The clubby aspect makes me wonder how much of this activity is, again, about asserting one's individuality, conforming to the idea that "I'm Special."

"If I was at my ideal weight I'd feel really in control of my life," says a college anorexic to a researcher. Another student anorexic proclaims: "I think my issue was wanting to control my life." The Toronto-based *Globe and Mail* restaurant critic Joanne Kates discovered her daughter had a serious eating disorder. After three hospitalizations, the turning point didn't come until, as Kates writes, "She decides to take charge of her life. . . . I see now that she had to leave me in order to do this. If her illness is about control, then leaving home and entering an adult program may be the only way to get out from under." In the article, which features writing by both mother and daughter, Kates's daughter makes it clear that her illness had a lot to do with being special, with standing out. She writes of her first visit to the hospital: "I am jealous of the deathly ill patients. They must be more self-disciplined than me. It is like a competition of who's the best anorexic." These young women have a need to resolve their sense that they are not in control of their own narrative. Beauty and thinness and celebrity and self-determination all seem to go together; in our conflicted times, the idea that slimness represents the ability to control your life and articulate your "specialness" almost seems to make sense.

I'm not arguing that women and girls actually resolve their problems through an eating disorder (any more than the *StarWars* collector's obsession ends with the discovery of that final missing bit of Yoda memorabilia). And not all eating disorders can be explained by the need to be special. But the stunning rise in such phenomena as eating disorders and cosmetic surgery suggests our belief in our right to do as we please, to justify any behavior or decision as a mechanism to turn our inner disruptions into an outer narrative that, if nothing else, sets us apart from the crowd by conveying that essential "I'm Special" mantra.

It seems contradictory to point out rising rates of anorexia, cosmetic surgery, *and* obesity as symptoms of the new conformity. How does obsessive craving for celebrity (from chefs to bartenders) coexist with the reclaiming of the role of celebrity for ordinary people à la Elvis impersonators and backyard wrestlers? And yet, all these trends exist concurrently because they are consistent with the prevailing conditions in which the urge toward individuality has become paramount. So it is that a national newspaper article speaks of the "inevitable—if counterintuitive—marriage of North America's twin obsessions of fast food and dieting." Sensing the mood of individualist conformity, fast-food outlets are falling all over themselves to offer low-cal meals while displaying nutritional charts fully disclosing the carbs and calories of their menu items complete with helpful advice for those watching their weight (e.g., skip the hash browns; drink water instead of Coke). The results, predictably, mirror society's increasingly contradictory message preaching both indulgence *and* abstinence in the name of self-invention.

Like the paradox of the new conformity, fast-food diet food serves merely to reinforce the perception that there are no longer any rules to get you where you want to be, or even any rules about where you should want to be. What now predominates is a painful and all-consuming desire to be exactly and only who you want to be. This involves taking the wheel of life and steering that sleek sports car or engorged SUV wherever we damn well please. And if there doesn't happen to be a road? Make one. And if your road happens to go directly through someone else's park? This is about you, not them.

Intuitively, it makes perfect sense. In a society where recognition in any form has become a primary goal, who is going to set the rules about what you should or shouldn't do? What authority remains to guide us? If we want to promote ourselves as plus-sized paragons of health and encourage others to be big and beautiful, who is left to tell us we're wrong? Certainly not the televised celebrities who equate success with equally unhealthy, equally narcissistic, impossibly skinny bodies. Certainly not parents, police, teachers, doctors, or priests—those are constricting roles requiring you to wear someone else's uniform and tell someone else's story. They are all variations on hapless Corporate Ken. Many still seek the comforts of such structures. But more and more people, particularly those of the pop-culture-defined generations of boomer, X, Y, and the coming Z (the generation that will be post-millennial, post-*Barney,* post-Pokémon), are seeking to emulate role models whose primary attribute has been to cast aside old definitions and reinvent themselves at every turn. The result is totally contradictory and yet completely contained within the framework presented here. Welcome to the land of Special. Welcome to the new conformity. Here are your brochure and tourist map. Now run along and find your own way.

The Experts Weigh In

A whole host of sociologists, philosophers, novelists, singers, anthropologists, psychologists, and professional thinkers have touched on various aspects of the rise of individualism as a new kind of conformity. Many have noted how, over the last few decades, individuality has changed from "a given" to "a task." Ulrich Beck, a German sociologist, writes in his book *Individualization:*

> There is hardly a desire more widespread in the West today than to lead a "life of your own." . . . It would be only a slight exaggeration to say that the daily struggle for a life of one's own has become the collective experience of the Western world.

Beck's fellow sociologist Zygmunt Bauman concurs. In the foreword to Beck's book, he writes: "Needing to *become* what one *is* is the hallmark of modern living."

Is this the need that compels figures as ordinary as Gary Stone and Ken Flatt (a.k.a. Elvis Presley and Corporate Ken) to adopt personas and narratives seemingly so far removed from their ordinary lives? The authors of *Habits of the Heart,* a sociological text examining the changing values of the American middle class, conclude that "the meaning of one's life . . . for most Americans is to become one's own person, almost to give birth to oneself."

Few of these commentators sound happy about the rise of individualization. In his book *Rugged Individualism Reconsidered,* anthropologist Francis Hsu attacks America's traditional image as a country founded by independent-minded entrepreneurs (a mythology that has been successfully exported as a model for the rest of the world). This, he argues, has led to a steady increase in structures and practices meant to uphold and cater to the individualist notion, creating institutions that propagate a harmful blueprint version of "Special." He writes: "It is no accident that in America intelligence tests, which purport to reveal individual differences, and psychoanalysis, which deepens and intensifies the feeling for self, have both achieved great popularity." In other words, you must do well on the SATs because you must be special. You must undergo therapy, because therapy will help you restate the narrative of your life and set you on the path to specialness.

But even psychoanalysis is in flux, grappling with the new role of individualism in contemporary life. Therapist and author Ron Taffel points out that traditional therapy must change if it hopes to overcome the problems of institutionalized individualism. He notes that in past decades it was assumed that teenagers in therapy were struggling to rescue their individuality from "overbearing parents." The role of therapy, then, was to create spaces in which the young people could come into their own. But in the present day, writes Taffel, "teens and adults are already so isolated from each other that it no longer makes sense to build ever bigger walls between them."

As conforming specialness spreads, our problems as a society change. No longer are we trying to escape the confinement of restrictive parents, religions, and communities. Instead, growing numbers of us are trying to find situations in which we can replicate a sense of belonging in nonrestrictive ways. We want to be noticed for being who we are and we want to be told, gently, who we should be.

"One forlorn fifteen-year-old boy," writes Taffel, "told me that he hated to go to a parent or guidance counsellor seeking advice only to be asked: 'What do you think you should do?'"

Academics and therapists aren't the only ones who have begun to grapple with the implications of the new conformity. Within pop culture itself, "I'm Specialism" is a recurring theme.

In the late seventies the Kinks sang about everybody being a "star," everybody wanting to be in the movies, regardless of "who you are." "Deviate from the norm," ordered geek stadium rockers Rush on the early eighties classic *Vital Signs*.

By the mid-eighties, David Byrne was directing the quirky film *True Stories*, in which the fictional town of Virgil, Texas, is caught up in preparations for a local "Celebration of Specialness." Byrne peoples his town and festival with ordinary people who have ordinary problems stretched to grotesque proportions. The Laziest Woman in the World, the perpetually lonely Louis (played by a charmingly oafish John Goodman), and the Lying Woman all make appearances as Byrne demonstrates that behind the most ordinary facade is a unique and special personality.

In Byrne's movie, the phenomenon of special remains embodied in the quaint desire of the ordinary to be recognized as somebody. But a decade later, Chuck Palahniuk's dark novel *Fight Club* shows how this quaint naive desire is transformed into an all-encompassing demand by ordinary people to be recognized not for who they are but for who they *think* they should be.

Palahniuk relentlessly satirizes the attempt to express uniqueness. His protagonist attends self-help groups peopled by those struggling with addiction and disease just so he can *feel* something, anything. *Fight Club* uses bare-knuckled boxing as a metaphor for the desire within each of us to break out of the comfortable apathy of middle-class existence. Essentially, Palahniuk argues that Western society no longer allows for true emotional catharsis, for real danger and excitement and emotion. We are unable to truly express ourselves as individuals. "Nobody had left much room for adventure," he writes in the later novel *Choke*. "Except maybe the kind you could buy on a roller-coaster. At a movie. Still, it would always be that kind of faux excitement. . . . and because there's no possibility of real disaster, real risk, we're left with no chance for real salvation." Arranged, monitored, controlled, we cannot find real elation, real excitement. And so, even as vast numbers of us turn within through pseudo-therapy, we seem to keep coming back to the outward indicators: What can we do or buy that will make us special? The result is the faux individuality articulated, as Schor argues, through customized consumer products or through the pseudo-carnage of a secret society like the Fight Club (or the BYWF). These contrivances allow us to project the message of special. As the Irish-American novelist Michael Collins writes, wittily adapting Warhol's adage on fame, "In the future, everybody will be ordinary for fifteen minutes."

Mass media, consumerism, and the American myth of the rugged individualist continue to propagate the I'm-Special idea, inviting the question: What comes next? What are the implications of ever-increasing numbers of people clamoring to turn their lives into sitcoms, reality-TV specials, underground video epics, confessional comic stand-up routines?

Reading an article about people left behind after a Rhode Island nightclub fire that killed ninety-seven people, I am struck by a mother's description of the life of her son, who was twenty-seven and working at Wal-Mart before his death. "He went to those rock shows to see what the musicians did so he could copy them," she explained to a reporter. "He had big plans. He wasn't going to work at Wal-Mart all his life. He was going to be a rock star." Her son didn't die indulging himself in yet another pointless rock show—he died studying the intricacies of mass entertainment, planning his inevitable ascent to the stage. With his life redefined as a noble quest for fame, the victim becomes more than just son, friend, anonymous worker—he becomes a potential superstar cut down before he had a chance to realize his plans. Even in her grief, his mother senses that his life didn't add up to much. It requires a bigger, better narrative. Clearly, this narrative comforts her. And, as much as it encapsulates the new conformity, there is something redemptive and egalitarian about it. In the I'm-Special world, nobody needs to die just a regular guy. Everybody can go before their time, just about to achieve their pop dream, just on the verge of mounting a startling comeback.

But where does all this leave us? Are we actually happier than we were when our roles were clearly defined, when success was represented by a four-room bungalow and a couple of cars? Are we leading better or worse lives?

We are no longer born into a web of social strata and expectations that, essentially, define and determine every major aspect of our lives, from birth to marriage to work to children to death. In these days of perpetual reinvention, we members of the Western world can be anything, at least theoretically. We are always just another uniform or hobby away from a brave new world, one decision away from a better new me. On the one hand, the potential to reinvent one's life, to determine one's narrative, is a positive, liberating development. On the other hand, the need to constantly reinvent—the feeling of perpetual anxiety that one hasn't come up with a good enough storyline—sows the seeds of fear, depression, and even insanity.

BUT I'M GETTING AHEAD of myself. In the backyard suburbs, they've got Dylan Foxxx in a choke-hold. He's soon to shake off his oppressors, get loose, stand triumphantly on the green grass holding a cardboard-and-tinfoil champion's belt over his head. For a moment, he is a hero, a winner, a star. He isn't Kris Verri, college student and part-time employee—he is something more and better than himself. In colonizing his fantasy and making it real, Verri inspires thousands of others to do the same. These young people are moving out into the world, getting jobs, praying at halls of worship, voting in elections, starting families. How will their semi-articulated fantasies of special change society?

2

ALONE TOGETHER

THE NEW CONFORMITY CHALLENGES TRADITION

F RIDAY EVENING in affluent suburban Atlanta. The Sabbath is ushered in by the ritual prayers of Jews following traditions thousands of years old. I'm sitting in the back of one of the
fastest-growing synagogues in North America. A Vietnamese
woman stands at the podium. She has just completed her conversion to Judaism, a transformation precipitated by her recent marriage. Temple Kol Emeth's Rabbi Steve Lebow blesses her,
welcomes her and her husband to the Marietta, Georgia, congregation, then steps back to allow her to read a prepared speech.

She speaks in stilted English of her great respect for the Jewish
people, their history as "entertainers" and achievers. She is, of course,
referring to the Semitic tradition of immigration and success, of hard
work and self-reliance. As she begins to thank the rabbi and the congregation and her husband, she breaks down and starts to cry. The
scattered audience of 150 or so faithful also dab at their eyes. Many
don't know this woman, or have only recently met her. But her relief
and gratitude are obvious. This is, one senses, the completion of a
long journey—from Vietnam to Georgia, from Buddhist temple to
synagogue, from the poverty of her Asian country to the affluence of
the West. As she struggles to hold back her tears and finish her

remarks, I wonder: What brings people like this young woman and her husband here, to this sanctum, to this tradition?

Speech over, hugs offered, handshakes and memorabilia bestowed, the young couple take their seats. Next, the rabbi calls up the head member of the temple brotherhood to lead the service, an honor bestowed on him for his commitment to the synagogue community, helping with everything from charity drives to the softball league. The rabbi makes a joke, something along the lines of how every congregation should have an ex-Mormon in its ranks. Everybody laughs, including the brotherhood president, who encourages male congregants to join the brotherhood (there is an equivalent sisterhood to be honored, no doubt, on some coming Friday) and then awards a plaque to a long-time congregant in recognition of his years of service. I'm following the activity, but I keep looking around, can't help wondering—who else in this congregation comes from another faith, another tradition? It is, of course, hard to tell. Though my grandmother claimed to be able to immediately recognize a fellow Jew, I don't have that skill, or maybe it's just that times have gotten far more complicated. Today, it seems, a Jew can be from Vietnam, can be an ex-Mormon, can even be a Vietnamese ex-Mormon. In my grandmother's day, Jews came from Eastern Europe, spoke Yiddish, and liked boiled meat. Very, very boiled. Conversion was rare. Who would sign up to be persecuted and slaughtered? At any rate, the Jews have never had a history of the kind of proselytizing that the Christian faiths pioneered and the Mormons raised to a compulsory art form. While it may be common to have various races and ex-religions represented at a born-again Baptist ceremony, at traditional Jewish services you rarely encounter a convert or meet a non-Caucasian worshipper.

With the help of several members of the brotherhood, we move through the service. Songs familiar to me from my aborted tenure in Hebrew school are folked-up, accompanied by the cantor's acoustic guitar. Other prayers are read responsively in English, the Hebrew on the page eliciting instant memories, though the translation sounds oddly stilted, unfamiliar, church-like. Long on speeches and community recognition, relatively short on prayer and the word of God, the service ends crisply after an hour.

We spill out into an adjoining hall to celebrate the arrival of the Sabbath by partaking in soda, chips, and cookies—really just an excuse for a weekly informal post-service gathering, a reason to pause before heading back to our separate cars, homes, television sets, and kiddie bedtime stories. I find myself in conversation with a man who turns out to be the brotherhood president's sibling, a tall husky blond with several silver teeth. Turns out he too was a Mormon, but left the religion as a young man, choosing the army over a compulsory stint as a missionary. He hasn't really been part of a faith since, he tells me. He's visiting from Arizona, staying with his brother while he looks for a new house in the Atlanta region so he can move here with his wife and five kids. Until three weeks ago, he says, he hadn't really given faith much thought. Three weeks ago was the first time he accompanied his brother to the temple's Friday-night services. "I felt the presence of God that night," he tells me. "I hadn't felt that since I was a kid."

As his brother's children and their friends jump around us, the ex-army former Mormon explains how, since that moment, he has come to feel an absence in his life. He's thinking about converting to Judaism. But he hasn't mentioned it to his wife—a non-practicing Catholic. "Hell," he says, "until my brother did it, I didn't even know you could convert." He leans down to ask me a question: When does the collection plate get passed around? I explain to him that Jewish congregations pay a set annual fee rather than a donation every Sunday. He nods. It makes sense to him. I say, well, do you think that this is a good way to choose a religion—you just show up and check it out? You can choose a religion the way you choose a band, he says. You show up and listen. If you like what you hear, you buy into it. He notes that most religions really aren't all that different; you make a choice from options that are all pretty much the same.

The Oneg Shabbat is winding down. I shake hands with the brotherhood president's brother and we wish each other luck.

RELIGIOUS AFFILIATION is dwindling and with it the social mechanisms of order and control that conflict with the conforming individualistic agenda of modern society. I have felt that dwindling in my own life, but I have also felt the pull toward something greater, a need to feel less alone, that desire to travel the well-worn paths of my ancestors. If tradition is fading away, though, why are Temple Kol Emeth's ranks swelling so noticeably? I wanted to find why and that meant talking to Rabbi Lebow.

I meet Lebow in his expansive book-lined office. He moves aside a Bob Dylan CD so I can take a seat on the couch. The rabbi is bald, smooth-shaven, dressed in baby-boomer casual style. He looks nothing like the rabbis of my childhood, imposing men with wild grey beards as perpetually dishevelled as their out-of-style suits. This rabbi does not speak with a Yiddish accent, and does not cite the Old Testament. He speaks in the contemporary language of business. He has a talk-radio show and plays guitar.

"We live in a society permeated by opportunities to do secular activities," he tells me. "People are constantly exposed to images of other lifestyles. We have to compete, otherwise we will lose. Judaism has been losing—only one-third of all Jews are actually affiliated with a synagogue. So we're dropping the ball if we're not doing something about it."

Lebow tackled the attrition rate head-on. He launched an advertising campaign.

"We ran ads, we've done billboards. Look, we started out as the smallest synagogue in Atlanta and now we're the third largest. We saturated the market. It's a very unusual thing for a synagogue to do, but churches do it all the time. It's considered now either brilliant or outrageous and in poor taste. But we all compete in North America in the marketplace of ideas."

Sounding more and more like a public relations executive, Lebow explains how he "constructed a message for what we wanted to do different than other synagogues. What we give them is a more exciting, more vibrant synagogue. There are social activities, an art auction, bowling league, baseball league, youth groups. We formulated a message, researched our niche: families with kids, interfaith families, the disaffected. How do you get to them? Through the media. We took this message and honed it, and we've been able to stay on message. We've been able to bring people in that otherwise might not have joined at all."

Temple Kol Emeth's growth also came from a unique presence in the Atlanta media. Explains Lebow: "We're the only congregation that televises all the High Holiday services on Atlanta cable. It occurred to me that there are people who can't make it on High Holidays, because they don't belong to a synagogue or they're sick. Unaffiliated Jews watched it as well as non-Jews who had never seen a Jewish service before. There's almost no downside to using the media this way other than this narrowminded approach, *'Well, we've never done it that way before.'*"

Televising the High Holidays is a natural for a rabbi who has had his own talk-radio show for years. "It's an entirely different congregation to preach to," he enthuses. Lebow started out on a small station doing a show from a Jewish perspective. He quickly discovered that, in the Christian-dominated South, "the vast number of listeners were not Jewish, and they would say, 'I listen to your show every week.'" This encouraged him to take his show to a bigger venue, moving to Talk Radio 1340, one of the largest such stations in Atlanta. Now he has a Monday-afternoon time slot covering general religious issues.

With all that media exposure, it's no wonder that Temple Kol Emeth has grown from its early beginnings as a 50-family fringe congregation to an 850-member congregation that, with its liberal, non-confrontational values, has come to represent the "I'm-Special" mainstream. Indeed, the temple's growth mirrors a demographic trend as aging baby boomers, confronted by the needs of family, the deaths of their parents, and even their own possible demise, have sought religious institutions that can do two things at once: speak to the individualism of their media-infused, sixties-inspired youth and provide the rites of passage and community comforts they increasingly yearn for. "This congregation started out on the fringes of the counterculture," Lebow explains. "Ex-hippies—they became yuppies—had decided there might be some worth in their Judaism. They looked for a rabbi left-wing enough, but also conforming enough. There were fifty families at the start. So I tried to bring them together, give them organization. They wanted a rabbi, but having a leader, it was a struggle for them."

Over the years, many have left the temple, accusing Lebow of being too conservative or too liberal. Some objected to his radio show, others to his public stance in support of gays and lesbians at the congregation. But far more came and stayed, finding plenty of room for their brand of conservative liberalism in the array of services and neo-traditions that Lebow presides over.

"People might come because they are lonely. They don't want to go to bars; they don't have a healthy way to meet other people, other adults. It offers the potential for networking. Churches have become supermarkets for services that people need . . . there are twenty support groups at Kol Emeth."

Lebow knows Judaism has to compete with other faiths, other congregations, and the secular attractions of the MTV marketplace. If that means offering conversion services to a wider array of interested parties, he's willing.

"In the last fifty years, conversion to Judaism has taken off. We try to discourage people doing it to please in-laws or because the spouse insisted. But people do come to us out of their own sincerity. There are people who are just religious seekers; I tell them that they can take the classes but they don't need to be Jewish. You don't need to be Jewish to get into heaven," he says. "Others are completely sincere, and they have different stories to tell—a Jewish person in their background, or they felt some affinity for an ancestor. I had someone convert a few weeks ago who had many Jewish friends and was influenced by Judaism. There is the perception that the U.S. is ultra-religious, but the largest number of people is unaffiliated, and many of those people do feel that they are looking for some deeper meaning in life."

Kol Emeth may have begun as a congregation joining together

a small group of like-minded Jewish ex-radicals settling into the middle-age comforts they once rejected, but it has grown to encompass a far wider swath of people whose own process of conforming individualism mirrors the hippie-to-yuppie pattern. The search is not so much for God or tradition, but for a loose framework of support groups, community recognition (brotherhood plaques, etc.), and perhaps most of all, as the rabbi puts it, "a natural tendency to want to feel part of the greater whole."

THE JEWISH TRADITION has never encompassed mixed-race marriages, large numbers of converts, and guitar playing. After talking to Lebow, I realize that what the Kol Emeth congregants, and so many others, are looking for is no longer an adherence to a tradition but the feeling that tradition used to provide: a sense of belonging that is bigger than ourselves, the feeling that the ex-army fellow calls "the presence of God." We want that feeling, but we want it on our own terms.

In searching for tradition without the strictures that tradition used to entail, our society is altering the religious institutions we created to give meaning and order to our lives. Can we have a sense of tradition without *traditional* tradition? The new conforming individualists want exactly that. They want religious institutions to adapt to their needs, ambitions, and desires. As a result, Temple Kol Emeth opens its doors to gay couples, to converts, to variations on the traditional service, to those Jews who want to worship on a Friday night but violate every other religious law concerning what one should or should not do on the Sabbath.

Kol Emeth is just one of many religious institutions meeting the needs of new generations of individualists who want to *feel*, but not necessarily *be*. It is growing in leaps and bounds because its rabbi fosters an environment of equality and equal opportunity; a combination community center and place of non-judgmental worship. You want to come here to pray? Fine. The temple takes credit cards, takes deferred and partial payments, offers all possible postmodern worship conveniences, including daycare, marriage counseling, sports, and participation in feel-good programs from Bible study to building a house for the Christian non-profit Habitat for Humanity.

Call it tradition-lite, but don't take it lightly. The dimmed lights of the sanctuary still illuminate the ancient Torah scrolls, and the podium is still a place where marriages, conversions, and funerals are performed according to Jewish ritual. What *has* changed are the participants: Jews and Jewish converts who choose to make this non-judgmental, semi-traditional congregation part of their daily lives. Why? Not because they are compelled to by any rule or obligation; more than half of North American citizens identify themselves as unaffiliated. No, they make this choice because they want to. The individual congregants are the buyers of a service, and the successful rabbis and priests are the ones who have figured out how to supply a barely articulated demand for a community united not by age-old restrictive tradition, but by something as fleeting as the desire for a feeling.

And so another Friday night at Kol Emeth ends. We walk out the door into a Georgia night that smells of exhaust and fallen leaves. Car doors slam, engines rev. We go home feeling just a little bit less alone.

The Death of Religion?

Despite the growth of institutions like Kol Emeth, and despite what seems like a deeply traditional all-pervading Judeo-Christian cultural ethos, religion, especially organized religion, seems to be in big trouble. A City University of New York study in 2001 concluded that participation in organized religion in the supposedly ultra-religious United States is declining by 1 percent per year. "No religion" is the fastest-growing demographic identifier, ranking third just under Catholics and Baptists. This study also tells us that the proportion of the US population that can be classified as Christian has declined from 86% in 1990 to 77% in 2001. A 2002 *USA Today* poll concludes that 50% of Americans consider themselves religious (down from 54% in 1999) and 33% consider themselves "spiritual but not religious" (up from 30%).

More recently, The Barna Group, a survey company that focuses exclusively on chronicling religion in America, has produced several interesting and telling studies. These include the announcement that despite the hype, the number of people who call themselves evangelical Christians remains at 7% of the adult population, a number that hasn't changed since the Barna Group started charting that statistic in 1994. Meanwhile, a Fall 2005 study by Barna notes that "for a rapidly growing number of Americans, a local church is no longer the place to go as their primary religious meeting place." The survey explains that while many Americans still engage in some form of worship, they are changing the way they worship, replacing traditional congregations with a wide variety of more personal options including online churches, home churches, and worship groups located in malls and at the work place. As many as 50 million people, or 22% of the population, are turning away from traditional faith institutions in favor of what the Barna Group calls "a variety of divergent faith models."

Internationally, the Roman Catholic Church, beset by pedophile priests and an ultra-conservative leadership, is one of the hardest-hit religions. Even in once staunchly Catholic Ireland, attendance at Sunday mass has hit new lows. In a *New York Times* article, one observer described how a cavernous Dublin church has split its space in half: "Now the front end provides a more intimate setting for the sparse congregation, and the back end is used for self-esteem classes and aromatherapy sessions intended to make people feel better about themselves and their faith." In Ireland in 2000, fewer than 100 people entered into the priesthood, whereas the annual average in the 1960s was 1,400. Clearly out of whack with the increasingly secular, high-tech prosperous Ireland, the Church is scrambling for a new role in the community not unlike the one that Temple Kol Emeth now fills. And maybe that's not such a bad thing. Notes Kevin Whelan, a scholar of Irish culture: "All you are seeing is the breakdown of a hierarchical, topdown type of church. What I see is the possibility for spiritual renewal."

Will aromatherapy and support groups bring about this "spiritual renewal"? Or will it simply precipitate the decline of the only institutions that might be able to provide solace from the fragmentation and confusion that dominate everyday life? The Pope is still a hugely popular figure. A study of Canadian Catholics indicated that 81 percent of those surveyed approved of Pope John Paul II's performance as leader. But almost half—42 percent—disagreed with his views. In other words, they liked his celebrity power, but didn't like the way his dogma cramped their lifestyle. It's reasonable to assume that the 42% turned off by conservative authoritarian views will not find Pope John Paul's replacement Joseph Ratzinger much to their liking. In fact, with the arrival of a new hard-line pope even more determined than his predecessor to maintain traditional hierarchies, it's hard to imagine how "spiritual renewal" will emerge out of the institution of the Roman Catholic church

As the Barna Group reports suggest, Catholics and others are already moving on: to more personalized home churches and online congregations, or to places like Kol Emeth where a celebrity preacher's laissez-faire soul-searching more accurately meshes with the new conformist lifestyle. When Pope John Paul II came to Canada for World Youth Day in 2002, the crowd, estimated at 200,000 participants, looked enormous. But, really, the crowd was tiny. At the previous World Youth Day 1995 in the Philippines, the participation was estimated at 4.5 million. In 1993 in Denver, 600,000 turned out for the Popemobile.

Organized religion has always shifted with the times, re-evaluated the needs of its faithful, and found ways to adjust rituals and rules to accommodate new priorities and lifestyles. At the same time, the churches, temples, mosques, and synagogues of organized religion have never before faced such dramatic demands. Increasingly, survival means massive reinvention. A haven for nonconforming conformists, Temple Kol Emeth is at the pinnacle of this reassessment: It is a success within the context of the new marketplace for religion.

Religious institutions are changing to respond to the call of the marketplace and the demands of individuality. But, in the process, they are leaving themselves open to the possibility that they will no longer be able to provide the sense that God is present. If everyone can join, if every ritual or rule is re-evaluated in a quarterly report or a congregation vote, what will be left of tradition? And if tradition is absent, how will religions foster the sense of holiness and continuity that delineates them from community centers or groups of like-minded science-fiction fans? In other words, it is quite possible that by allowing themselves to become part of the media marketplace of signs, symbols, and entertainments, traditional faiths are inevitably signing on for their own demise.

We are already seeing evidence of this decline, even as the numbers of those of us who want to be associated with spirituality and religion may very well be growing. A recent survey of Canadians parallels what is happening to religion in the United States. The survey found that 78 percent believe in God, with 66 percent identifying themselves as Christians. And yet, over the past ten years, despite a 13-percent increase in various kinds of conversions to Christianity, there has been a 19-percent decrease in weekly church attendance. The authors of the survey dubbed these non-participatory converts "Customized Christians"—people who "hold Christian commitment with the individual right to self-design."

The conservative alarmists claiming the death of religious tradition through neglect have it wrong. Though traditional organized religion seems to be steadily declining in Western society, it is, ironically, conformist individualists searching for a faith to belong to who may well end up killing religion as we know it—not by rejecting it, but by embracing it.

SINCE THE EARLY EIGHTIES advent of New Age spirituality with its array of crystals, dream catchers, incense, and prayer-wheels, piecing together a tradition that is right for you has become an accepted and predominant phenomenon. With it, of course, comes criticism: While religion has previously been about submitting yourself to a higher power, New Age faith tends to be the opposite—the world submits to *your* sense of what you want and how you feel. Critics of

New Age faith see narcissism and instant gratification instead of sacrifice and commitment.

Which is all very well, except for the fact that people *want* condemnation-free spirituality, not cant and long-winded history lessons. Organized religions that refuse to meet the age of I'm Special halfway are having more and more difficulty filling seats and raising funds. The exception to this is the small minority of mostly fundamentalist religions that are actually growing. Those attracted to fundamentalist religions tend to believe in the literal words of the Bible; they find themselves frighteningly adrift in an era of choose-your-own-adventure existence. Terrified of being forced to constantly decide who and how they want to be, they choose an all-encompassing fundamentalism.

There is a huge divide between traditional faith and the overriding morality of contemporary society, which says you can be who you want, do what you want, and the only rule is that you have to take personal responsibility for your actions. Organized religion takes the opposite approach: Do what *we* want, and *we* will take responsibility for your actions, absolve your sins. But new conformists want yoga and self esteem, not sin and forgiveness; the freedom to reinvent narratives, not the constrictions of a narrative written thousands of years ago; and, most of all, we/they want recognition, celebrity, specialness. Today, any institution that wishes to submerge individual destiny into a complicated hierarchy and the will of God is in trouble.

Churches are experimenting with ways to make religion feel more modern and hip as well as create appealing celebrity preachers like the Rock and Roll Rabbi – preachers who can draw a crowd and keep the collection plate full. Evangelical Reverend Steve Munsey of the Family Christian Center in Munster, Indiana likes to rev up the congregation filling the 5000-seat chapel by driving his motorcycle across the pulpit. The pulpit, by the way, features a replica of biblical Jerusalem complete with, as Munsey puts it, "a very lifelike cave depicting the tomb where Jesus was lain." The motorcyle is a custom-made Harley. It's named the Passion and is custom decorated with a crown-of-thorns paint-job.

A Winnipeg company has developed an electronic tithing kiosk that does away with the collection plate in favor of a bank-machine-like booth that can instantly process cash, checks, and credit cards, and provide a tax receipt adorned with a prayer. For worshippers who can't make it to the church, the machine also offers online services like volunteer coordination and, no doubt, web donation. "We're not just brazenly sticking this thing in front of the door to get your credit card," said Mark Blanchard, director of develop-ment for the Roman Catholic Diocese of Baton Rouge, Louisiana, which uses one of the machines. "It's one of the benefits, sure, but there are other things we're offering here as well."

As if church bank machines weren't enough, an Episcopal church in Fort Lauderdale, Florida, has launched a monthly service aimed at pets and their owners, complete with doggie treats at communion time. In Newmarket, Ontario, a former Anglican priest recently celebrated the one-year anniversary of his Christ the King Graceland Independent Anglican Church. Rev. Dorian Baxter—who goes by the name Elvis Priestley—attracted 175 people for the anniversary service, despite being dismissed from the traditional Anglican church *and* excommunicated from the Collingwood Elvis Festival, which made it clear the impersonator was no longer welcome at its annual gathering after Priestley per-formed Elvis funerals for deceased fans.

With tithe machines, communion for dogs, cable-TV broadcasts of services, and Elvis congregations, is it any wonder that religion is increasingly being treated as a joke? Church kitsch has been all the rage in stores like the hipster-oriented chain Urban Outfitters. The plastic Jesus Action Figure, nun salt and pepper shakers, key chains dangling miniature Bibles, Jesus night lights, and Virgin Mary tank tops. Similarly, hipster Jews can read an obnoxious magazine called *Heeb,* quaff He'Brew Genesis Ale, watch the blacksploitation parody movie *The Hebrew Hammer,* and sport a T-shirt emblazoned with "Shalom Motherfucker." Is Grandma's religion funny? Yes, it is. The rise of religion as a subject of kitsch to be sold to hipster thirty-five-year-olds suggests the way that religion is not only being trivialized and fetishized, but also becoming a nostalgic part of our past that we yearn to reclaim without being undermined by such blatantly uncool things as belief or dogma. "Can religion as a fundamentalist driving force survive its domestication and commodification and trivialization as something akin to a fun fiction?" Benjamin Barber asks in his book *Jihad vs. McWorld*.

The answer: Sure it can, if it follows the Kol Emeth model. After all, today's disenfranchised I'm-Special hipster is tomorrow's hungover, I-need-meaning-in-my-life middle manager. The big question, of course, is what will we find when we finally get back to the sanctuary? The sociologists Robert Bellah, Richard Madsen, William M. Sullivan, Ann Swidler, and Steven M. Tipten who wrote the book *Habits of the Heart* tell us that liberalized versions of traditional biblical morality tend to rank themes of divine authority and human duty below the essential goodness of human nature, while stressing the power of human choice and the possibility of self-acceptance. As a result, the unfolding of the universe "reassures us of our freedom to choose our own God, our own labors, and our own ultimate ends, whatever they may be."

Conformist individualists will get back to church only to find that church no longer fulfills the comforting functions of yesteryear. Instead, the faith institutions seem to be saying: "Okay, have it your way. This isn't about God or a higher power, it's about you. It's all about YOU!" Even our holiest of customs and institutions are changing, conforming to the conformist individuality. "The less attractive aspect of organized religion," notes Rabbi Steve Lebow, "is that a fairly high value is placed on conformity with regard to practice. My personal opinion is that it is okay to have religious standards, but it is better to be judgmental to yourself."

Birth-School-Work-Death No More

When they finally choose to return to traditional infrastructures, boomers bring with them their own self-styled values. But if boomers began the breakdown of social consensus and the disintegration of tradition, they won't be around to finish what they started. Distrust of institutions, lack of interest in anything but the developments that directly affect them, obsessive belief in the power of the self—these boomer traits have been passed on to the next generations. While we might argue about which generation is the most uninvolved, it is clear that all generations since the boomers have been disengaging from traditional structures.

Here, the statistics tell a clear story. The United States is the Western country where the trend toward so-called unconventional families and childhoods is most dramatic. In 1960 there was one divorce for every four American marriages; by 1994 a full half of all marriages failed. By 1998 only half of all children lived in a conventional two-parent married household. In 1976 there were 1.6 million "latchkey" children in the United States; by 1994 there were 12 million. Every Western country has a rising divorce rate and a falling birth rate. Writes Ulrich Beck:

> When birth rates began to fall sharply after the baby boom of the 1950s and early 1960s, in Germany as in other industrially developed countries, it took demographers completely by surprise. . . . Even today . . . in nearly every country belonging to the Council of Europe, the birthrate is lower than required for the population to remain the same.

Beck argues that the trend is paradoxical: Why are the richest, most comfortable countries producing the fewest babies? He notes that in the former East Germany, after reunification, the birth rate plummeted by a staggering 60 percent between 1989 and 1994. Attributing the drop to a wider range of lifestyle possibilities, he writes:

> The greater people's options and demands for a bit of "a life of their own" and the greater the attendant risks, uncertainties and demands, the more does having children cease to be a natural part of life and become the object of conscious planning and calculation, hopes and fear—in short, the more it becomes "the question of children."

Restated one might say: The more we conform to the primacy of individuality, the more traditional structures and behaviors decline.

If the rise of the new conformity in Western countries has paralleled a vast decline in the making of babies, it's logical to conclude that conforming self-obsession will eventually lead to extinction. Without immigration, most of the world's stable and affluent countries are shrinking in population. I live in Canada, which has consistently been rated by the United Nations as one of the best countries in the world as far as quality of life goes. But its birth rate is one of the lowest in the world, with 13 babies born for every thousand people. By contrast, the African country Niger has a rate four times higher, with 53 babies per thousand being born. And yet, babies born, if they survive, have a life expectancy of only 45 or so years and a GNP per capita of a mere $220 In Canada, babies can expect to live till 80 and share in a GNP of $20,000 per person.

Reluctance to give birth runs parallel with a growing reluctance to tie the knot. This dynamic also prevails across the Western world: fewer marriages, and an increasing number of children born out of wedlock. In 1999, 31 percent of all U.S. births involved children born out of wedlock. In 2001, 1.2 million couples were living common-law in Canada, up 20 percent from 1995. In Western Europe, the number of babies born out of wedlock ranges from 31 percent in Ireland to an astonishing 62 percent in Iceland. Both the United States and Canada have think-tanks aimed at encouraging people to get married and stay married. Despite decades of family-values rhetoric from government, nothing seems to be working.

My point with this barrage of numbers is this: In the post-boomer era, and without the first-hand inspiration of the sixties pseudo-revolution, every aspect of traditional social life—from marriage to childbirth to religious belief—is up for redefinition.

BUT PEOPLE STILL GET MARRIED, have kids, face the death of loved ones. As my conversation with the ex-Mormon from Arizona indicated, even those who have had negative experiences with constricting religions seek the sense of a higher purpose and meaning that religion imbues us with. As religious tradition collapses, contemporary I'm-Special society faces a dilemma: how to manufacture meaning?

Well, one answer is to do it yourself. Just as more and more people are making their own rap CDs and staging their own wrestling extravaganzas, more people are making their own God. In *Habits of the Heart,* the authors incredulously discuss a woman who had created her own solitary religion and named it after herself. "Sheila Larson," they write, "is a young nurse who has received a good deal of therapy and who describes her faith as 'Sheilaism.'" The accordion-playing comedian Judy Tenuta, who has been preaching something called "Judyism" for years, has managed to turn her comedic instincts into a book called *The Power of Judyism* and a Grammy-nominated CD, *In Goddess We Trust.* Judy laughs about it, but others take it all too seriously. More and more people have come to think of themselves as their own kind of religion. "I'm not a religious fanatic," Sheila Larson explains. "My faith carried me a long way. It's Sheilaism. Just my own little voice."

Sheilaism permeates our individualistic conformity and continues to demand that our institutions dramatically change to accept us as we want to be. A few years ago a friend of mine told me that he was going to New Mexico to marry a couple he had known since college. You mean, I said, you are going to their wedding. No, he jovially responded, I'm marrying them. Apparently he had been ordained as a minister by a website that provides an online ordination service requiring little more than name and address. The thought of this pal of mine performing a wedding ceremony is strange— he flits through causes and careers the way a teenager flicks through cable, and simply lacks the kind of gravitas most us think a minister should possess. But clearly that was the point for his engaged pals. They wanted someone who had known them both at the early stage of their relationship, and they saw no need to have their union blessed by any kind of authority figure. Maybe they even saw my friend's random lifestyle as a way to communicate that the marriage was not going to change their own laid-back, anti-authoritarian, We're-Special! approach to life.

Online ordinations, offered by several different operations but most commonly from the 43-year-old Universal Life Church, are skyrocketing. At the Universal Life Church (popular because it's free and you get your ordination document via email) ordinations doubled, from fifty-one thousand in 2001 to one hundred thousand in 2002. And while there may be questions about the legality of a marriage performed by a minister who was ordained online, most of those who sign up are more interested in the symbolism than in any sort of formal power conferred in the name of the state. "If you have no church, then you create your own authority figure. You choose the person who has the most authority in your relationship," says one 37-year-old groom quoted in an article on the rise in numbers of the online-ordained. Of course, in creating an authority, you are dispelling the myth of authority held by church and state. By acknowledging that a friend holds more authority for you than a priest or government official, you are, quite obviously, undermining institutional authority. But the new conformists aren't interested in political implications. They just want what's best for them. A 34-year-old groom notes: "It's not like we're anti-authority. It's just that we didn't want a fake authority . . . It wasn't like 'la-la-la, you're married and here are some flowers.' [Our minister] treated the situation with the gravity it deserved." Still, an Episcopalian priest asked to comment by a reporter clearly sees such marriages as a challenge to authority and institution-based religion. He says: "It's short-sighted. It shows a lack of respect to a heritage that goes beyond just my own generation."

COMPARATIVELY FEW COUPLES are turning to an internet-ordained pal to marry them. Many—including those who are not affiliated with a place of worship and are distinctly secular in their lifestyle—still want some kind of tradition to be present at their wedding. Non-affiliated I'm-Special people can turn to an array of non-denominational ministers who perform "authentic" marriages while operating outside traditional religion.

Joyce Gioia is a Greensboro, North Carolina consultant who

calls herself a "multi-faith minister." Gioia, whose last name evokes Gaia, the New Age term for life force or earth, performs fifteen to twenty weddings a year—down from a high of fifty when she was based in New York City. "I work outside of any particular religion," she tells me. "I tailor the wedding to who they are and what their beliefs are. Because I've performed over four hundred weddings, I have a vast database of different prayers and readings, and when I find out who they are, then I identify from my database what I think they're going to want, and most often I'm right. Most couples come to me because they are looking for a spiritual and not very religious ceremony and because they want to have an opportunity to have a significant input to what gets said and what gets done at the wedding. Most clergy have a standard wedding ceremony that they do, come what may. I have a totally different attitude—my attitude is what you want is what you get, and I will work with couples to craft just the right wedding for them."

Gioia's services come with a price tag—at least several thousand dollars for consultation, the design of the "unique" wedding service, and the performance of the ceremony. But most of the middle-class couples don't flinch at the news. After all, if you're spending, say, twenty grand on catering and flowers, the least you can do is invest in the most important part—the ceremony. Nevertheless, it would be cheaper and easier for couples to simply sign up their local priest or notary public. So why don't they? Gioia explains it this way: "They're saying I believe in God, I want to have a relationship with God, but I don't necessarily want to be beaten up by this particular religious organization. Religion has an opportunity to speak to people's value systems, and in many cases what happens when you go into a church is that you are given, in one form or another, the dogma and you either believe it or you don't. And if you don't choose to believe it, they're not particularly interested in having you be part of their church. And people are feeling a connection with a divine power that is almost to some degree blocked by the insistence that they adhere to the format and the form of what that particular sect expects."

In the vacuum created by the demise of traditional religion, people like Gioia are happy to step in. They provide something resembling meaning without commitment. You don't have to join, you don't have to think about your spirituality, and you still get the comforts of a carefully designed ceremony. You'll choose the service the way you choose the band, from an array of possible styles — classic jazz, light jazz, dancey jazz, soul-jazz, whatever you want. Almost as telling as the process that Gioia offers is her description of what people want out of faith now — a connection "with a divine power" that isn't "blocked" by dogma. Gioia better watch out. Rabbi Steve Lebow and Temple Kol Emeth have also figured this out, not to mention churches offering aromatherapy and doggie treats.

Most of us seek a connection with a higher power at crucial moments in life — marriage, divorce, birth, death. But many would also like incremental doses of spirituality in between. The weekly Kol Emeth Friday-night service does the job for some, keeping loneliness and despair at bay with a handshake, a plastic cup of orange pop, and a folksy version of a traditional prayer. But many religious institutions haven't yet made the full transition and compromises necessary to precipitate the return Kol Emeth is experiencing. So where are the new legions of nonconformists finding that higher power?

Some are turning to a variety of spiritual counsellors to give their lives the kind of meaning that organized religion once provided. Charmaine Semon is a "spiritual counselor." She works out of her home in the upscale urban Beaches neighborhood of Toronto. With piercing blue eyes, chicly conservative designer outfits, and a perfectly coiffed mane of blond ringlets, she conveys an image of confidence and authority. Semon, who goes by first name only in the course of her professional capacities, describes her role as "a confidante, a personal and professional confidante, which is rare today. I'm a catalyst for personal change, and a leadership mentor." Semon works with upper-class power-brokers undergoing crises of confidence. "I teach people rituals, help them develop an internal support system. My niche in the marketplace is to help people achieve a quality of life that's sustainable. We work in a series of eight four-hour sessions, plus I provide support in between those sessions. I introduce them to breathing techniques, help them become present in what they're doing, living in the present, connecting with themselves. They're in the future all the time, they don't know how to stop and celebrate."

Semon's clients are usually middle-aged or older, and at a point in their career where they are realizing the extent to which corporate achievement has taken its toll on their personal lives.

"The first session, they just share for two and a half hours, anything and everything they want," says Semon. "I'm someone who can be totally present for them 100 percent, someone who can truly listen to them. They need to be heard, they're isolated. I'm someone they can trust with a high degree of confidentiality. When people are troubled they want someone they can be intimate with who will be totally private and personal. Confidants provide so many different services that friends, wives, don't offer. I help them define what success is to them, bring a deeper meaning of success. Emotionally, they're not managing their lives very well."

So why can't they find deeper meaning in their lives at, say, a church? Why don't they confide in religious figures? "People are losing faith," explained Semon. "New churches are being born today as traditional churches are losing their following. People want a spiritual relationship, not a traditional one."

By the time a client has left Semon, he or she will have spent between six thousand and fifteen thousand dollars learning how to "remove themselves from an ego-dominated reality. . . . how to manage relationships between ego self and higher self." Semon's mixture of confessional New Age spirituality, psychology, and common sense is intended to help her clients develop "a quiet place to go where they can honor their rituals. Where they can create an altar, whatever their faith is. People need rituals. Culture is losing its sense of the spiritual. So I invite people to design a set of rituals that support them on a daily basis, to keep centered and grounded and connected. You need those twenty minutes of meditating. People should have an altar in their office or cubicle."

In her book *Altars,* Denise Linn advises readers on how to create a personal altar and claims that if you spend regular time in front of your altar, "you may find that many unexpected and happy coincidences begin to occur in your life." Like the altars Charmaine Semon helps her clients create, such portable places of worship can contain anything of meaning to the worshipper—photographs, dolls, seashells, candles. What they rarely contain are the traditional trappings of organized religion: These altars are Star of David- and crucifix-free.

Alienated from religious institutions, desperate to become more ourselves, to determine the narrative of being a better me, some of us are turning to spiritual entrepreneurs like Semon and Linn. Why? Because they understand that we want a connection to meaning and spirituality, but that we want it to be about us specifically.

Just as Joyce Gioia reinvents the wedding to tell the seemingly unique story of a couple she's never met, people like Charmaine Semon are helping the upper-middle class invent a new version of their story. Semon talks about her "niche in the marketplace" helping people find a way to "sustain their lifestyles." Though she also talks about transcending the ego, she doesn't advocate a commitment to charity, or giving up the SUV, or even taking a less demanding job. Instead she shores up the self, provides new-conformity I'm-Special "coping strategies," helps people to become more themselves by rewriting the terms in which they see their lives. The goal here is not to examine and change, but to find a story that makes individuals comfortable with who and what they are. With a regimen that is less about substantive change and more about staying the same but different and better, Charmaine Semon and her ilk preach the aura of specialness and individuality without demanding the requisite levels of responsibility and self-reflection that traditional therapy depends on. My story isn't working for me any more . . . how do I rewrite it?

Special at the Office

There is another aspect of Western tradition that this troop of narrative revisers, multi-faith wedding ceremony consultants, personal confidants, and spiritual advisers are helping to dramatically change in order to better accommodate the new conformity. The rise of the conforming individual is altering the traditional business model of treating your employees like . . . employees. Today, consultants insist that to succeed, employers must treat employees as friends. Ask them how they feel, what they want, and make sure that they can grow on the job. Not long ago, it was assumed that an employee would come to work, do a good job, and take home an honest day's pay. Now a decent salary isn't enough to guarantee that employees will care about what they are doing—unless they can reshape the narrative of their working life around their own sense of worth and identity. New Age consultants are telling corporations to start telling their employees a different story: This isn't about profits and company success, it's about . . . YOU!

Both Charmaine Semon and Joyce Gioia have strong connections to the business world: Semon counsels business executives and was herself the founder of a company. When not performing marriages, Gioia is president of The Herman Group, which bills itself as a "futurist" think-tank whose clients are primarily corporations searching for the next trend they can profit from. Both believe that the culture of business is sick, though hardly terminally ill. Both believe that the cure for what ails corporate life is a healthy dose of the I'm-Special formula.

Gioia once worked as a consultant with a company that faced disaster because it couldn't retain its employees. She says that she was able to help reduce employee turnover from more than 300 percent to less than 25 percent in less than five months. She performed this remarkable feat by explaining to company execs the new realities of working life: Corporate loyalty is dead; everyone is looking out for number one. As a result, the only way to retain employees is to make them feel that their jobs aren't just jobs but opportunities for personal growth.

"What we have to do is to help the company provide that enlightened self-interest to the individual," she explains. "One of the key values that people have these days is to stay marketable. So if I can get the company to offer training and development to the individuals, I can get the people to stay, because there is a perception, 'Why should I leave if I'm growing?'"

Charmaine Semon also sees change on the horizon in business and employee relations. "Corporate culture is starting to bring in support systems for leadership because it's affecting the bottom line," she says. "The twenty-first century is all about transforming the corporate culture, so people are operating from a more soulful place. I was a president of a company, I had my own brokerage firm, and I did extremely well because of my humanity. What's happening is that people are bleeding, their souls are bleeding in the workplace, people are suffering in the workplace, before they even leave the front door. Companies are realizing that what's affecting the bottom line is the attitude and discontent of their employees. Now there is a much more positive approach, more consciousness around how leaders are managing their people."

"In the future we will see more focus on the individual and away from companies," predicts Joyce Gioia. "What's driving that is that the Gen-Xers are accustomed to being independent, getting things done on their own by themselves. The baby boomers had lots of company—we used to play outside, our mommies were at home during the day. Gen-Xers had to play inside because there was nobody to watch them. So they got used to working independently, and the millennials are even worse. We still need to get things done as a team, it's just that we need to help people feel comfortable as a team."

In the quest to conform to the age of nonconformity, the company gives the employee even more confidence to assert his or her independence and personality. Employees, in turn, begin to want even more freedom from the corporation. As a result, writes author Michael Lewis in the *New York Times Magazine,* "The worker who is willing to subordinate his identity to some giant corporation is so deeply unfashionable that, for cultural purposes, he might as well not exist." Lewis cites several changes in the corporate environment that account for the shift from autocratic, faceless institution to friendly, You're-Special idea incubator. These include the decline of corporate loyalty, the rise in distrust that the corporation is actually doing what it does for any reason other than to enrich its investors, and, in the age of rampant lawsuits and freelance lifestyles, the demise of the boss as a figure who can tell you what to do. In fact, notes Lewis, the boss now understands his role is not to oversee, monitor, and keep control, but to "turn the wage slaves who report to him into whirling dervishes of innovation." Echoing our New Age consultants, Lewis notes that a "new corporate language has been invented to support people's need to believe that their work is actually an endless quest for originality."

Lewis reports that the phrase *thinking outside the box* has become so popular in corporations that it has actually become "itself a kind of conformity." He writes: "Working at home in the nude is no longer evidence that you are an interesting person, or even a happy one."

The narrative of corporate life is being rewritten to cater to the new ideas-oriented, individuality-obsessed worker. We see this reflected in the weird little details of corporate life. For instance, at the headquarters of conservative public relations firm Hill and Knowlton Canada, a cart loaded with boozy beverages trolls the halls on Friday afternoons. In fact, offices around North America are now hosting regular semi-mandatory drinking sessions. And the rationale is always the same: The kids (a.k.a. junior employees) like it! Not only that, but it's an opportunity for them to loosen up and informally exchange ideas with their co-workers. In the process, the employees feel noticed, wanted, recognized—*special*. Along not-dissimilar lines, a human resources consultancy noted in a recent annual survey of businesses that the number of companies offering flexible working hours (flex-time), employee wellness programs, and fitness programs is at an all-time high.

THE RISE OF THE PSEUDO-INDIVIDUAL and the semi-collapse of tradition create ever more uncertainty and even disaffection. Where once we may have been relatively content with our status in the middle, living a life within a mostly predetermined nexus of family-church-work, now we crave more, better, faster. What are we looking for? Increasingly, we are searching for an opportunity to articulate our narrative on our own terms—a chance to inject ourselves into the media sphere and become special.

It's easy to make these claims in the abstract, particularly when most of us (me included) would probably claim to be living pretty "regular" lives. Far more of us are working freelance than ever before, but most of us aren't basing our career options on the frequency of the arrival of the beer cart. Nor are we hiring (or becoming) spiritual employment counselors, or doing much of anything that seems to definitively connect to the I'm-Special world. And yet the new conformity has touched our lives and perceptions, whether we know it or not.

Tall and charismatic Matthew, aged thirty-two, is the co-founder and co-owner of a Toronto-based graphic design company. From the outside, he seems to be a relatively conservative sort following in a tradition of entrepreneurship lauded all over the world. But internally he is a mass of contradictions, many of them emerging directly from the influence of the new conformity. Matt's company has six full-time employees and has been around for five years. It was, at the time of our interview, profitable enough to ensure Matt an extremely respectable living by the standards of North American life. So things sound like they are going great, right? You start your own company, slog it out, do things faster and better and smarter than the competition until the point when you are an established entity with an impressive list of clients. But Matthew doesn't see it that way.

"It was more exciting four years ago," he says. "Back when a three-thousand-dollar account was amazing. We've built it up now, so we could step out of the picture. Now the days are a bit longer for me." Matthew had more fun and found things way more exciting when the company was struggling. He is frustrated by the restrictions placed on creativity when clients have aims other than good design.

"We deal with clients who don't have any vision. There is so much competition and saturation. All our clients care about is getting it out next week, being first to market. They don't look at what we're doing closely, they just want to get it out first."

To counter the doldrums of everyday work under the thumb of companies who really don't care how interesting or creative the design is, Matthew is in the midst of developing an ambitious project for his firm. He wants to create a hip men's magazine devoted to the much-coveted eighteen- to thirty-five-year-old market. He's been developing the idea and looking for corporate investors for more than a year. "We have really talented guys in our office, and this would be an opportunity for us to showcase our design ideas. I'm hoping to grow it into a custom-publication branch of the company. I'm trying to create something where we don't have the limitations a client puts on what we do."

Matt is already his own boss, but more than that, he wants to control his own narrative. He describes a previous job in which he was constantly being told to do things for no particular reason. "I would wake up with a knot in my stomach and I thought, well, this is what it is, this is what a job is." In response, he left and went out on his own. "If I'm going to be stressed, I want to know why, I want to be accountable—if I fail, I want it be my failure. I don't care if I succeed or fail, but I want to know that I've tried. My mom always bugs me about my tattoos, says that I'll come to regret them. But I think I'd rather regret things I've done than things I didn't do. You only get one shot at things."

Matt's seize-the-day new-conformist attitude is different from the old-style entrepreneur whose goals were clear-cut: Develop a successful business; *become* the corporation. In contrast, Matt wants more than just a competitive start-up that pays out good salaries. He describes a meeting with his business partner, who co-owns the company. "He came to me and said that we have to decide if we want to have fun or make money. But I don't believe those are the only options." Like many new conformists, Matt wants it both ways, which is probably why he is channelling his energies into a formulaic magazine that might offer some opportunities for design experimentation, but is hardly to be considered a radical expression of creativity.

Work defines who Matt is and what his values are. As a result, any upgrade of the story of his life requires a change in his work focus. In starting the men's magazine, Matt becomes the maverick workaholic who makes good by starting up a hip, new, irreverent—and ultimately profitable—magazine.

Successful, intelligent, married, and blessed with two healthy young children, Matthew is seemingly the embodiment of the good life. Yet he bristles with unfulfilled expectations, with the desire to do something else, to establish the narrative of his life in creative ways that can never be attained through the traditional channels of corporate power. At the same time, like most of us, he isn't prepared to reject the comforts of disposable income. Independent yet reliant on conservative corporations for the success of his company, Matt yearns for a true freedom that really doesn't exist. Like so many of us, he has redefined success in terms of a conformist individuality that centers around the mythical properties of creativity and freedom. He is happy, well-off, and lucky. But he is also frustrated, agitated, and unsure of what he might be doing next year or even next month. He is a man seemingly rooted in institutional roles—business, marriage, fatherhood—even as he seeks to limit the narrative power of those roles and clings to the ability to reinvent himself at any moment. Caught up in the era of specialness, he embodies all the contradictions and possibilities of the new conformity. Should we feel bad for him? No more than we should feel bad for our own lost selves, perpetually trapped between dream and reality, significant achievement and the way mere achievement tends to pale in the spotlight of recognition and celebrity.

The Self-Reliance Fantasy

We are increasingly hell-bent on standing out, announcing ourselves as special. We refuse to have our lives subsumed by antediluvian tradition. But the more we strike out on our own, the more we feel truly alone. On our own, we are less able to find meaning in what we do and be satisfied with who we are. Thus, a continued flirtation with traditional structures. These institutions, despite our mistrust of them, are our strongest link to a sense of purpose and meaning. Recognizing this, the traditional structures are trying to adapt by countering our suspicions and acting on our need for meaning and stability. They are tired of being rejected. So they are reinventing themselves as flexible institutions that can accommodate the fluctuating needs of individuals who seek both the comforts of convention and the freedom to shape convention into new narratives of self-definition. And so the new conformity gives birth to tradition-lite. Tradition without responsibility. Tradition without involvement. Tradition without requirement. The huge numbers of people who want tradition-lite are altering—some might argue hollowing out—institutions. The institutions themselves are increasingly willing to exchange rigid ritual for warm bodies in the seats.

This leaves us in an interesting position. When we turn to traditional social institutions to give meaning to our lives, we also demand that those institutions change to give us the room we need to discover our I'm-Special selves. And yet, when our institutions change, they may no longer be capable of giving us meaning, or educating us, or governing us, or guaranteeing us jobs. Thus, we are thrown back on our selves and have to decide if we should be inventing new traditions, trying to resurrect old ones, or just forget tradition, community, and continuity altogether.

At the same time, we are seldom prepared to go it alone: The vast majority of us still want to be recognized in business, noticed at church, redeemed by marriage. But we want only the recognition and success—not the confinement of responsibility. Like Matthew, we want to work for the company, but we also want to be able to deny that we work for the company. In the end, we are chronically dissatisfied because the kind of freedom we idealize and internalize in our everyday lives—a freedom from all institution and authority that nevertheless is able to provide connectivity, order, and higher meaning—does not exist.

At the heart of the new conformity is a fantasy about success and self-reliance and narrative projection of those values. This fantasy has altered our relationship to work, family, faith, education—almost every institutional structure that exists. Where before many struggled against the yoke of restrictive institutions that tried to tell us how to pray, work, marry, even love, today many struggle to find forms that will tell us how to do these things without compromising our powerful desire to manifest total and absolute individuality. There's nothing to say that tradition-lite is any more or less self-deluding than all-encompassing faith in tradition. But, where before we could project our frustrations and dissatisfactions on the corporation, the government, the church, today all of our frustrations are internalized: I'm not my own person; I'm letting some religion I don't even really believe in tell me how to get married; I'm successful in business but not known as the rebellious adventurer I think I should be. The fantasy of total freedom seems to constantly undermine our lives to the extent that a successful entrepreneur and family man like Matthew is always dissatisfied, convinced that to move forward he must be more creative, bolder, willing to completely reinvent his life today, tomorrow, next year, or next month.

The rise of the new conformity changes our relationship to the institution, and the institution changes in response, hoping to woo us back with new permissive structures. Suddenly the institution that not long ago provided stability and meaning in exchange for unquestioning acceptance has become subjective, flexible, flawed, debatable, relative, *up to you*. As a result, many of us are finding that the traditional institutions are unable to fulfill their mandate and provide us with structured mechanisms for deeper meaning and a sense of direction. We are, increasingly, seeking venues for deeper meaning *and* recognition of our specialness elsewhere, particularly in the fantasy world of pop culture that underwrites the new conformity.

PART TWO

(RE)CREATING THE INDIVIDUAL: POP-CULTURE CONFORMITY

2

3

EVERYONE'S A STAR

POP CULTURE INVENTS THE NEW
CONFORMITY

THE SCENE IS thousands of youngish pop-star wannabes corralled in a gravel field awaiting their thirty seconds with the judges. We could be almost anywhere in the Western world. The image is certainly familiar. A mortgage broker croons tremulously; a mother keeps a tired watchful eye on her tattooed, belly-button-pierced sixteen-year-old daughter; a twenty-something secretary fingers her crucifix, closes her eyes, and imagines, just for a second, what it would be like to *make it*.

As I said, we could be anywhere. But this is Canada in 2003, and the place is the first ever *Canadian Idol* tryouts in Toronto. Young people, ages sixteen to twenty-six, have turned up at the Metro Convention Center to audition for the show, a spinoff of the popular American talent-search show (itself a spinoff of a British version). They have come in droves, in numbers that surprise everyone and leave the organizers struggling to accommodate a mass congregation of pop supplicants. They start arriving on Saturday morning, prepared to sit in front of the building until the Monday-morning tryouts begin. And they keep arriving. All day Saturday, a mass influx Sunday night, and a final staggering swell—spurred on by news reports—Monday morning. To wander through the anxious corridors of pop-star wannabes lining up behind plastic barriers and watched over by a flotilla of private security guards, cops for hire, and *Idol* factotums is to encounter a veritable herd of new conformists. Here is the "I'm Special" sameness in all its contradictory glory. Here are thousands of young people planning on singing interchangeable pop songs, and they all share the same dream: Each believes that he or she is a unique individual soon to be singled out and led to the altar of stardom. This is a new-conformist coming-out party, a where-were-you-when moment for a generation of perpetual teens searching for that elusive feeling of specialness.

"Anyone can become what they want to be," says sixteen-year-old Brooke. "If it doesn't happen, you can't give up, you gotta keep going." Delilah, twenty-six, has been waiting since 4:30 Sunday afternoon and works for the Salvation Army. "I've been singing since I was very small. It's a dream of mine to go further with that." Ben, a university student studying theater, is twenty years old and showed up around 3:30 A.M. Monday. "I'm looking for my break. I'm doing it for the experience, for the pressure. I want to be a rock star."

Everyone I speak to says exactly the same thing, regardless of age, ethnicity, what part of Ontario they have trekked from or how many hours they have been standing in the crowd. All of them think that they have a good chance, that they have what it takes to be famous, and that singing is their dream. When I ask what makes them different from the ten thousand people patiently waiting beside them, they simply reiterate that they want it more because it is their dream and passion. When I ask them how they might feel if they are summarily dismissed by the judges, they are ready for that too. The kids in line are so steeped in the myth of instant stardom that they are already figuring out how even rejection will benefit their bid. Afrodhasia, twenty-three-years-old, explains that even if you don't make the final cut, "you get seen and maybe picked out for something else in movies, or singing or dancing." Mark Albay, seventeen, insists that I use his last name in anything I write. He tells me that it doesn't matter if he gets on the show, it's all about the marketing. "I see myself as a singer. I'm doing this for the publicity, to get myself known." Billy, a twenty-year-old house painter, hadn't even planned to try out; he just accompanied friends. But the infectious attitude got to him, so now he's prepared to sing a song the title of which he can't even remember until a pal prods him. No matter, "I'm confident I can make it. I don't want to have regrets that I didn't try. If you really want to make it there's always a way. If you don't have your dreams, what do you have?"

Inevitably, there are those who emerge from the other side rejected and dispirited. There are complaints about the poor organization, the lack of any kind of consideration for those trying out. I speak to people as they come out of the pre-audition tent having waited twenty-plus hours in order to sing for thirty seconds. About one-third emerge wearing wristbands that confer upon them the honor of coming back the next day for a real, two-minute tryout. (Much later in the day, these wristbands are bestowed like candy on all the people still left in the gravel parking lot, mainly so that they will disperse and the security guards can be sent home.) The two-thirds who emerge without wristbands somehow have to face up to the impossible: failure. And yet even these rejects manage to cling to the pop dream: Bianca, a young woman, exudes confidence despite her disappointment. "It's still a dream. This isn't the last of me. I know I'm going to be a star. The only person who can make your dreams not come true is yourself."

The young people at the *Canadian Idol* tryouts seek freedom. They seek the freedom that they think comes from attaining the dream of pop stardom. To them, celebrities are liberated from the drudgery of school, family, work, everyday life. Celebrities are lifted out of the grind of normal. They are noticed, unique, special. Even Denham, a twenty-five-year-old mortgage broker who is smart enough to know that his chances are slim, makes no move after telling me he's going to give up and go home. The dream remains, difficult to relinquish. "I wish I'd started singing earlier," he sighs. "I wish I'd thought about it as a talent from early on."

At the *Canadian Idol* tryouts I find thousands of bright, funny, interesting, horribly deluded people, new conformists every single one of them. They all share the same dream and pursue it in exactly the same way. Coincidence? Human nature? I don't think so.

Introducing the Pop Theme

Pop culture comes with a message that is suspiciously similar to the ideology of new conformity: It's the story of you.

In her song "Vogue," Madonna tells us we are all superstars. Nike exhorts us to "Just do it." These are catchy summations of the grand pop-culture theme that bombards us every day. Each and every manifestation of pop culture purports to be telling the story of how the individual transcends obstacles and the masses to earn recognition, success, happiness. Though the plot may be about a sultry maid from the wrong side of the tracks working for a repressed rich guy (nineties sitcom *The Nanny* or Jennifer Lopez's feature *Maid in Manhattan*), the story is really concerned with how all of us ordinary people can transcend our limitations; the story is really how *you* feel, work, live, love.

The purveyors of popular culture want to connect an audience to the character, song, or message they have created. Of course, this is economics: The more people who connect, the greater the number of tickets bought or copies sold. But it's also something intrinsic to the way pop culture functions. It is, after all, the only mass-produced product that makes us cry, laugh, momentarily rethink our lives. Does your lawn mower do that? Does your new hat? Pop culture gets inside us in ways that the old-style arts never could.

Adolescent psychologist Ron Taffel notes in his book *The Second Family* that teenagers now often attach more importance to the world of commercial pop culture and peer relationships than they do to their real families. "While our real-life friends still matter," writes Juliet B. Schor in *The Overspent American,* "they have been joined by our media 'friends.' We watch the way television families live, we read about the lifestyles of celebrities and other public figures we admire, and we consciously and unconsciously assimilate this information."

What is the "information" we are assimilating about our new pop culture pals? They are (or at least pretend to be) secretaries, doctors, janitors, divorcees, hen-pecked husbands, and disgruntled daughters. The message of pop culture is one of transcending ordinary life by combining adventure, heightened excitement, and, inevitably, success (fast-food combo order of everlasting love, luxury, and life purpose). Every pop-culture narrative tells us that, despite ordinariness, you too can be special, super, noticed, discovered, successful. You too can alter the narrative of your life, make a dramatic U-turn, become a better person, become more you. The message of pop culture is always that of the triumph of the ordinary person who, in the process of following his or her heart, bucks the system and becomes the exception, a larger-than-life but still completely regular it-could-happen-to-you hero.

While art forms like the epic poem, the play, and the novel laid the groundwork for the omnipresence of these narratives, it took Hollywood to iron out the ambiguities and perfect the instant connection between the audience and the inevitably triumphant "regular" movie star. Novels, let's face it, allow for too much distance, too much abstraction. The movies are immediate; they seem to put you right into a parallel reality, show you a person who could be you. *Pretty Woman* and *Erin Brockovich* (both starring Everywoman Julia Roberts) are about working women whose status is elevated when the rich and powerful recognize how really special they truly are. In *Patch Adams* and *Dead Poets Society* (both starring Robin Williams), unlikely rebels challenge the strictures of an ossified education system and "seize the day." In *Rocky* and *Rambo* (both played and written in whole or part by Sly Stallone), not-too-bright muscle-bound heroes succeed even as society and a proliferation of evil types stack the odds against them. And, of course, in the blockbuster *Star Wars* and *Lord of the Rings* trilogies, the lonely farm boy stuck on the planetary equivalent of Idaho turns out to be none other than the last hope for the world as we know it.

The theme of the solitary individual conquering adversity has been the bulwark of Hollywood movies since their inception.

Consider the films of Frank Capra, best known for his *It's a Wonderful Life* (1946). In Capra's *Mr. Deeds Goes to Town* (1936), a suddenly rich Everyman must struggle to reclaim his average-Joe status. The film was remade as *Mr. Deeds* by Adam Sandler, whose only contribution was to make the "I'm Special" premise even cornier and more obvious: Money doesn't matter; what's inside you is what counts; we're all important in our own special way. Almost seventy years passed between the two films, but the theme of the Hollywood movie rarely changes—exceptionally ordinary main character overcomes adversity in order to become a much better person (but also a richer, more famous, more loved person).

This, of course, contrasts with the prevailing ethic of previous years, when hubris and vanity were punished, not celebrated and raised up as the ideal. From the Greek dramas to Shakespeare to Hans Christian Andersen, relentless self-absorption and concern for one's own happiness and status led to insanity and tragedy— not redemption and reward.

Those times are long past. Now, each mass-cultural product is carefully tested to ensure that audience accessibility and enthusiasm is in no way diminished by as piddling a problem as depressing content. At the same time, pop culture's overarching theme of the normal individual who overcomes abnormal circumstance is becoming more and more persistent in our culture. Even as Frank Capra was giving us the archetypal pop-culture plot, mass culture was moving out of the movie theater and into our living rooms. Television quickly became the perfect medium to preach the pop theme of the exceptional individual. TV features recurring characters whose lives are at once more exciting, triumphant, and difficult than ours ever could be, despite seemingly humble and unpromising jobs and situations. The very nature of its repetitive ubiquity makes it the perfect medium to articulate a world of the exceptionally mundane. Everything from *The Dukes of Hazzard* (two good old boys fight the system) to *The A-Team* (rag-tag misfits help the unfortunate) to *M*A*S*H, ER, NYPD Blue, Letterman, Cheers, Buffy*, the aforementioned *Idol* spinoffs, and a whole host of shows we haven't heard of yet all assert the specialness of the ordinary individual while implanting in us entire decades of made-up memory.

Ah, what memories! Mass-market tales of a motley crew of losers, school kids, secretaries, orphans, servants, bartenders, cops, convicts, waiters, and hillbillies who fought the law, the boss, the administration, the vampires. How many hours have we spent with these characters, plots, situations? And how little has television's central pattern changed over the years? Even the plots of the videos on MTV convey the message of overcoming authority or adversity or a bad breakup. Writes one disapproving critic: "MTV . . . offers blips savoring freedom and disdaining authority." And so the seemingly rebellious and edgy MTV joins its peers in preaching incessant selfhood, a recipe for individuality that calls for just the right amounts of rebellion, free will, style, and, ultimately, acceptance.

Trapped in a Theme World

John Conte plans to play the piano continuously from Christmas Eve to Boxing Day. It's a fifty-hour stint that he hopes will earn him the world record in non-stop piano playing. But, a few weeks before the December 2002 attempt, the thirty-nine-year-old classical musician seems oddly, well, unenthusiastic. "If it advances my career, that's fine," he says. "But it's a pretty dubious achievement. I'm not sure in what way it will help."

Playing fifty hours straight onstage at the Cornelia St. Café in Greenwich Village is not something one simply does out of the blue. The obvious question is: If Conte isn't doing it for his career, why is he doing it? "We're shooting a documentary of this event," Conte explains. "Everything leading up to it, my preparations. And we've got this radio show from Jersey City that's following our progress week by week."

What is the relationship between these chronicles of the event and Conte's decision to try to break this obscure record? Conte says that he is doing it to help an independent production company. He has written the score for two of the company's films, which so far have not been picked up for distribution. The director decided to put a stunt together that might earn his company some quick attention. "It started out as a much bigger plan," Conte says. "We were going to try to get several of us to break a record of some kind and we were trying to synchronize it. But I'm the only one who was left."

So he's signed on to help out the director's career? Not exactly. Says Conte: "We were just trying to find a way to get some attention for these two small pictures. We thought this might do it." The plan is to sell the documentary to something like the Sundance Channel and, in the process, turn the buyers on to the other films. In other words, the stunt is less about the director or the world record attempt than it is about the fate of the two movies.

Who is John Conte and what does he want? He's a classical piano player with an interest in the avant-garde. He's a twelve-year veteran of a "fantastic" orchestra that, by his own admission, "just can't seem to break through." He acknowledges that the record-breaking stunt will do little for his career as a musician, but at the same time tells me that he itches to "try to do something different." He's ambivalent about the feat that looms before him, and admits that there's a good chance he might not succeed. "We'll still have a movie," he is quick to add. "It might even be better."

Conte represents how far pop's reach extends—pulling the most unlikely figures into a world of fairy-tale fakery and radical restlessness. Incidentally, he set a new world record for "longest keyboard marathon": He played non-stop for 52 hours, 20 minutes.

He is hardly alone in his attraction to the allure of the special.

Ken Hechtman is a Montreal database programmer who spent six days as a Taliban prisoner after wandering through the southern Afghanistan front lines in search of a story for an alternative weekly newspaper. With war-correspondence experience consisting, as one Canadian newspaper put it, "largely of reading *Soldier of Fortune* magazine," Hechtman headed off to Afghanistan. What was he looking for?

In a nutshell, Hechtman wanted to be noticed. In his reports on being held captive and very nearly executed, he seems pleased with the outcome of his antics. And why not? What better scoop is there than: "I Was a Taliban Prisoner!"? His commentary—which appeared in the *Montreal Mirror* and the online magazine www.straight-goods.com—is oddly jocular. "Mistake #4," he jokes, describing his attempts to explain away a notebook full of information about Taliban troop movements. "Nobody wants to hear that all their military secrets can be compiled in an afternoon of net-searching and the Taliban is no exception." In Afghanistan at the time, people were dying, families were starving, hundreds of thousands were displaced, but Hechtman, well, Hechtman was Hechtman. He's lucky he made it out of there alive, but it's obvious from his delighted reports that Hechtman would do it all again in a second.

Unlike Conte, with his ambivalence and reluctance, Hechtman is a type that everyone can understand. After all, what is he but a slightly more extreme version of your average Idolite? Here is a pop-culture-fed, *Soldier of Fortune*–reading data programmer willing to risk his life to claim the pop mantle of individuality. Did Hechtman get rich from this stunt? No. Did he get noticed? Oh yes. All over the world and, most particularly, in his home country. And yet the usual denouement is absent. In the movie version, there would be a family to rescue, a George Clooney-led *Three Kings*-like refugee situation to resolve. In real life, there's only Hechtman to rescue, Hechtman reporting on . . . Hechtman. His actions, triggered by neither financial gain nor altruism, create a kind of vacuum. Hechtman is a lot more like John Conte than he is like a movie hero. Hechtman, Conte, and the Idolites all seek to insert themselves into pop culture to overcome the dullness of their everyday lives. They all seek to be something more, something bigger. And all end up in a shadowy zone of ambiguity, doing things not for the sake of doing them, but for the sake of creating a narrative about having done . . . something.

This is more than a matter of fringe individuals pursuing weird cultural antics devoid of meaningful consequence. In the case of Hechtman, death was very nearly the outcome. And in the case of Conte, his decision constituted a potentially wrenching and certainly radical break from a high-art aesthetic that eschews fame. The number of people across North America and the world who have tried out for *Idol*-like shows and their spinoffs in the past five years (let's not forget *Junior Idol!*) surely reaches the hundreds of thousands. What makes people willing to risk life and limb, willing to stand in a hot gravel parking lot for twenty-four hours, willing to toss away a lifetime of artistic conviction?

Conte's stunt illustrates how far the pop-culture dream permeates contemporary thinking. It is no longer restricted to the lives of suburban teenyboppers, but also the thoughts of an experienced classical musician. Hechtman and the Idolites do not necessarily recognize the conformity of their actions. *(Note to self: Quit job as a programmer and pursue childhood obsession with war zones!)* Conte, on the other hand, is far more willing to locate his own participation in this pop-culture game somewhere in the realm of the silly. Nevertheless, he too is pulled in. Both men, in different ways, sought to change their lives in order to gain access to that ultimate dispenser of individuality, pop culture.

Ultimately, Conte's record breaking feat would be noted in newspapers across the continent from the *Albany Times Union* to the *Cleveland Plain Dealer* to the *Regina Leader Post*. "It's kind of a celebration of the ridiculous," he told me on the eve of the attempt. "If that has any redeeming value."

The Creeping Shrink: Pop Culture Everywhere

As John Conte and Ken Hechtman show us, the ridiculous is now everywhere. It has moved into our houses in the form of television sets, DVDs, stereos, laptops, and every other form of device that serves as a platform to some aspect of mass culture. The invasive creep of the culture of entertainment and constant stimulation—each incarnation preaching the pop *theme*—at once renders pop culture invisible and invincible, everywhere and nowhere. How much of your living space is specifically arranged to make it easy for you to interact with devices that allow you to engage with pop culture and compose your personal spectacle? It's not uncommon to see TV sets in the living room, bedroom, and kitchen. Laptops have wireless connections for games, downloading MP3s, and checking out websites devoted to your particular pop-culture kink. Stereos, VCRs, DVDs, Gameboys—much of our living space is arranged for pop culture consumption.

It wasn't always that way. I grew up pre-VCR, pre-cable, and presatellite; my parents grew up pre-TV; my grandparents grew up pre-radio; their grandparents grew up . . . and so on. In the United States, total recreational spending, adjusted for inflation, jumped from $91.3 billion in 1970 to $257.3 billion in 1990, an average annual gain of 9.1 percent that well outstrips population growth of 1 percent a year. So over twenty years, people went from spending roughly 5 percent of their total earnings on recreation to nearly 8 percent. Evidence suggests that this number is continuing to rise as more and more people invest in things like TiVo, satellite television, video games, high speed internet, and all manner of custom recreation technologies designed to give us what we want, when we want it.

At the same time, a 2003 survey found that 77 percent of Canadian citizens (whose spending on entertainment parallels spending in the US) see control over access to entertainment and information as the real benefit of new entertainment technologies. In other words, we are not so much paying for more entertainment as for the ability to choose, to participate—even in some marginal way—in our own cultural life. Why? Because pop looms large in our lives in a way that no previous culture, no previous era, could even imagine.

The message to turn your life into a success story is everywhere, beamed directly into our brains. The issue is not mind control (exactly). We want this stuff. We crave it. We seek it out. It feels good. Whether on film or TV or in song, the tale of the little guy making good is one that we simply can't get enough of. It appeals to all of us, rich or poor, success or failure, black or white, gay or straight. Who's going to argue against the little guy? Who's going to cheer for the corporations, the governments, or the Establishment when we can cheer for someone like ourselves, someone whose struggle is just and whose (fictional) struggle is invariably going to succeed? Do we cheer for the status quo that keeps us laboring over our daily business, or do we cheer for the surprise loner who surpasses the status quo and, best of all, *always wins*?

Once, film was the only peddler of the fantasy of transcendent reinvention. But now there are also pop songs, TV shows, video games, celebrity magazines. This material all promotes a whole new relationship to the self: a philosophy of "I'm Specialism," a belief that not only do we want to live in fancy houses and drive fancy cars like pop stars do, but we also desire their all-powerful sense of self, the validation they exude just by being who they are.

So urgent is society's need for a sustained connection between audiences and their dream-conveying pop stars that there is a trend in the media to demonstrate the ordinariness of celebs. The same month that *The Osbournes* went on the air (as a form of reality TV showcasing a heavy-metal star's dysfunctional family), *US Magazine* started a recurring photo feature called "Stars—They're Just Like Us." The feature shows celebrities doing ordinary things, like holding a plunger (former Spice Girl Geri Halliwell) and pumping gas (actress/Bond-girl Denise Richards). Such pictorials are now a regular occurrence in everything from glossy magazines to such tabloid TV shows as *Celebrity Justice,* which reports on the lawsuits, bar brawls, traffic tickets, and divorces of the Hollywood set.

Performers have also learned to star in vehicles that articulate their ordinariness. Jennifer Lopez felt it necessary to reassure her fan base that despite her immense fame and wealth, she remained "Jenny from the Block." She followed that hit song with a movie called *Maid in Manhattan,* in which she plays a poor servant girl discovered and elevated by the millionaire who comes to love her despite her low-class origins. India.Arie sings on her breakout album *Voyage to India* about the contrasts between her ordinary self and the usual sexy babes featured in videos. The gorgeous pop star tries to convince us she really isn't all that pretty but is simply a beneficiary of the pop theme. She's made it because she "kept it real," believed in herself, etc. And, since she isn't gorgeous and superficial, the implicit suggestion is: If she can do it, you can too!

Is it a coincidence that several people I met at the *Canadian Idol* tryouts were planning to sing the songs of Lopez and India.Arie? Celebrities are presented in what Michael Bracewell has called a "carefully edited form of stylized 'docu-drama'" that satisfies the public's need to see behind the scenes of fame and to be offered a "sniff of intimacy" with the stars. But India.Arie is stunningly attractive, despite her protests to the contrary. And for all Lopez's rhetoric, she is no longer a girl from the block whose existence promises similar opportunities to the poor and downtrodden. Whatever she once was, today she is a canny pop star trying to leverage the pop theme of ubiquitous specialness into continued love from a barrio demographic whose poor residents stand in stark contrast to Lopez's jet-set lifestyle.

"WHEN A SUBJECT APPEARS to be all around him," wrote American public relations specialist Philip Lesly in 1974, "a person tends to accept it and take it for granted. . . . It becomes part of the atmosphere in which he lives. He finds himself surrounded by it and absorbs the climate of the idea." Steeped in the "climate of the idea," more and more people want to make good on the pop promise that everyone can elevate themselves to new heights.

The message of pop compels us to be more ourselves, because we are intrinsically interesting, beautiful, worthy of attention and notice. But pop culture doesn't specify what about us is actually all that special. Nor does pop tell us how to garner notice upon successful completion of our reinvention. Like the semi-despairing John Conte, the compulsion to be noticed often translates into confusion and even a certain degree of sadness. Do we really want to quit our jobs, abandon our responsibilities, seize the day, break the record? Silly, of course we do. Who doesn't? But, all too often, seizing the day is not so easy. It's not clear what ambition we harbor, what world-changing activity we might embark on. Too often, we end up simply feeling depressed and devalued as we carry on through lives that have become all the more ordinary because glamorous pop stars are urging us to *just do it.*

Unable to realize either instant tycoon status or sudden pop-star recognition, many of us turn to fulfilling far more esoteric aspirations. If you don't succeed as a celeb in business or onstage, you can still reshape the narrative of your life and have some relationship to fame and specialness. We see this in the growing trend to participatory pop, from video game addiction to wrestling wannabes to Elvis impersonators. Is it a coincidence that more and more people are steeping themselves in pop culture as a way to give identity and order to their lives?

The stunning growth of spending on video games and entertainment on the Internet are both evidence of the way in which we are increasingly willing to spend money to find some way into the pop world. Price Waterhouse Coopers projects that revenues from video games in the United States, the second-largest market in the world, will grow from its 2004 high of $8.2 billion in revenues, to 15.1 billion in 2009. Meanwhile, a study of what American's bought online in 2004 concludes that "the biggest increases in 2004 came in spending for entertainment, which soared 90 percent to $413.5 million from $217.6 million in 2003."

Statistical evidence nicely merges nicely with the ancedotal. A website run by a Japanese software programmer is the home for those who want to post Björk songs they have personally remixed. There are more than ten thousand of them! "Digital technology, abetted by the Internet, is turning fans from passive acolytes to active participants in the artistic process," writes Matthew Mirapual in the *New York Times.* As the backyard wrestling enthusiasts demonstrate, this is undeniably true, and the number of people who are moving from passive to active expands daily.

Another *New York Times* trend piece discusses the phenomenon of ordinary people paying for the recording of their own CDs. The article appeared not in an arts section, but in a style section. The implication is that these young adults (in their twenties and thirties) are not creating culture so much as indulging in fad and fashion. The tone of the article is intrigued but dismissive—"the vanity CD has become the cultural equivalent of the novel in the dresser drawer, a talisman against the workaday pressures to abandon one's creative dreams." The piece quotes a studio owner who says: "It seems like everyone is doing it. The threshold of talent for making a CD is very low." This is one of the few articles to appear in a daily newspaper that actually discusses the lives of "real" (read: not already famous) people actually creating a cultural product, rather than just consuming it. Tellingly, the journalist can't decide if he should make fun of these people—who account for as much as 35 percent of the average recording studio's income—or sympathize with their desires. Nevertheless, we learn of a twenty-five-year-old teacher who has spent $10,000-plus on his CD, and a twenty-eight-year-old floor trader whose stage name is Storm and has just finished his indie rap masterpiece. As in backyard wrestling, we are tempted to wonder who these people are and why we should care about them. "American culture is centered around entertainment," the floor trader explains. "Making a CD is one of the easiest ways to become a part of that."

Is the pop theme really so pervasive? After all, most of us don't start backyard wrestling leagues, don't attempt world records, don't record rap CDs in our spare time. But, on the other hand, some of us do attempt these things, and certainly many more of us have sought to at least partly redefine our lives through participation in some aspect of pop culture. People try to access mass culture through many different pursuits: the writing and publishing of amateur periodicals in the form of zines and online blogs (amalgamations of diary entries and web links); the creation of pirate radio stations; the recording of indie amateur CDs; attending Lord of the Rings conventions and dressing up like Gollum and Gandalf. Still others become fans, compiling tribute websites and collections relating to the famous. Pick any human being who once held even a marginal degree of fame, and you are likely to find that some other human being in Manitoba, Maine, Monaco, or Munich has created a virtual world for that figure. Googling on, say, the fallen eighties teen star Corey Haim reveals hundreds of independently created websites discussing this largely uninteresting figure.

And yet there are those who will never feel that their need to be close to pop, to be part of pop, can be answered through the cool distance of the web. On the extreme edge, finding their way onto the stomping ground of the press-hungry serial killer, fans desperate to realize the promises of pop become stalkers, impersonators, even assassins, losing their grip on what is left of reality in order to assert themselves in a pop culture world where nobody dies or gets hurt, where everybody lives forever, happily ever after, on the big or small screen.

Though most of us don't personally know a celeb stalker, we certainly know of the other types: the just-a-bit-too-enthusiastic collector of memorabilia; the waiter who is really a director-writer perpetually adjusting his screenplay; the pop supplicant willing to spend long days polishing stacks of bottled water to be consumed by the performers after the show; the amateur critic, whose acerbic commentary on the latest efforts of Gus Van Sant, Pavement, and Lucinda Williams annoys friends long into the night; and, finally, the quiet fan, who sings along, watches all the awards shows, buys the records and videos and movies, cries on cue. Few of us lack opinions and thoughts and memories derived from pop culture. These days—and this holds true for the urban citizens of the majority of countries in the world—most of us are unlikely to ever meet another human being on the planet who has escaped pop culture's hold on the imagination.

Increasingly, the relationship is one of unrequited desire: We want in. The majority of us don't want to destroy the system, challenge the mass-market capitalism that degrades culture, and expose celebrity worship as a fraud. To the contrary—we uphold the system; we live for the system. The amount of energy many of us expend to get into the pop-culture system suggests just how much we love and want to be part of it. As Todd Gitlin writes in his book *Media Unlimited*:

Today, there are vast possibilities for micro-celebrity: the talk-show guest, the studio spectator, the website proprietor, the volunteer during the public television fund drive, the amateur performer selling downloads or CDs over the Internet. . . . the lottery winner, the eyewitness to the shooting, the neighbor on camera after the kidnapping next door, the character wading into the margins of "real life," saying, "Look at me, I'm here too!"

In a *New York Times* article on B-movie actors, wannabe starlets illustrate the way pop compelled them in the same relentless pursuit of fame. "I graduated fifth in my high school class," said Jenny McShane, whose work includes such straight-to-video classics as *Shark Attack 3: Megalodon*. "I was National Honor Society. I know I have the intelligence to do whatever job I have to. . . . I want to do this till the very end. I want to be like Katharine Hepburn."

"I'll do whatever it takes," says Tarri Markel, another thirty-something actor who so far has specialized in playing vermin and serial-killer bait in movies like *Rats* and *Death Train*. "A break could come tomorrow or six months from now or six years from now . . . I don't have a time limit."

And so a good number of us record our demos, market ourselves, network, retain the services of an agent, line up for *Idol*—do whatever we need to do to break in. We fill out our applications and—inevitably—all but 99.9 percent of us are told to forget it. Does this dissuade us? Clearly not, if the six thousand people in the Toronto gravel field are any indication. Why the enthusiasm, the desperation? After all, the best most of these people could expect might be a kind word, a polite dismissal. Nevertheless, it's a chance to be part of it, the system, the pop dream.

As the enthusiasm for *Idol* auditions demonstrates, when we are provided a forum to access pop culture, we throng to it like ants to sugar. When Amazon.com ran a contest to see who could post the most book reviews, the winner clocked in with a staggering 2,164 write-ups. The runner-up wasn't even close, at 1,464, but made up for it by offering his own website, Review Don Mitchell's Reviews, which leveraged his Amazon.com profile by offering visitors prizes if they contributed critiques of his reviews to his site.

Meanwhile, millions of people are flocking to parallel-world online video games that allow them to live out their fantasy of special twenty-four hours a day. There are more than 100 million people around the world who pay a monthly subscription to play games like Warcraft, Magic Land and Second Life in which you can be anything from a mobster to a wizard to a seductive elf princess. A staggering $3.6 billion is spent on subscriptions every year. But the best evidence that this phenomenon is more than just casual distraction is the emergence of an entire parallel economy in which players exchange real money for virtual status like gold stockpiles, powerful spells, and, in some cases, even entire islands and personas. There are over 100 thousand young Chinese men indirectly employed by the Western specialites who not only want to play a game and distract themselves from their everyday lives, but also want to realize the pop dream of an all-powerful instant celebrity status they will never find in real life. Alas, who has the hundreds and thousands of hours you'd have to put in to achieve power and status in these massive multiplayer games? The 100 thousand Chinese employed in the task of killing monsters to build up gold stockpiles that can then be sold to American and Japanese gamers, the thousands of Ebay postings selling fantasy real estate, weapons and characters for real money, all tell us that many of the people who turn to these games are there to realize a pop dream of special that real life can never deliver. Online, all-powerful characters that can make you feel like someone really special are just a credit card purchase away.

THE UBIQUITY OF POP announces itself in weird ways. Psychologists at the University of Leicester have identified a mental disorder they are calling celebrity worship syndrome (CWS). Their study claims that one in three in the United Kingdom suffer from some derivation of the disease. Explains Dr. John Maltby, who reported on the study in the *Journal of Nervous and Mental Disease,* "Our findings suggest the possibility that many people do not engage in celebrity worship for mere entertainment. Rather, there appears to be a clear clinical component to attitudes and behaviors associated with celebrity worshipping." In other words, celebrity worship has moved beyond just another wacky thing the kids do and entered the realm of identifiable mental diseases. The doctor and his colleagues have even classified three levels of celebrity worship. At its least troublesome, there are those who simply like to casually follow the careers and lives of certain celebrities. At the mid-range of the affliction are those who believe that they have "an intense personal-type relationship with their idol." Finally, there are what Maltby calls the "hardcore CWS sufferers," who "believe their celebrity knows them and are prepared to lie or even die for their hero." Their celebrity worship is "borderline pathological." Maltby suggests that CWS is emerging as traditional relationships with family and people in the community are on the wane.

Rising out of the ashes of true mentorship and human connection is the pop-instilled desire to have relationships with celebrities. Alas, mighty few of us can actually have meaningful interactive relationships with celebrities. But our need to do so is embedded in a pop-culture system that asks us to get to know our performers, watch their movies, listen to their songs (ostensibly about their most intimate crises), read their biographies and tell-all interviews, but never actually assume that we have any right to communicate with these people except as passive, supplicating, paying fans. Well, according to Maltby, this tension, coupled with the decreased power of the traditional institutions that once infused our lives with meaning, is beginning to manifest itself in emotional crisis and mental disorder.

Getting pop culturites to believe that celebrity fascination is actually a mental-health problem may prove difficult. While searching the web for info about celebrity worship syndrome, I came across a fan site for pop star Kylie Minogue. Noting that Minogue was one of the celebs cited in newspaper articles on CWS, the site's creator put in a link to the story with the headline "Kylie is Worshipped." *See,* you can almost hear this Kylie fan thinking, *I'm not the only one.*

The identification of celebrity worship syndrome is an indication of the extent to which pop is changing our relationship to everyday life. The *Houston Chronicle* reports a new trend in which millions of Americans are spending lots of money having gold caps and rims put over their teeth in imitation of hip-hop and rap artists. This look is known affectionately as being *grilled out*. Alan Wolfe, when doing interviews with Greensboro, North Carolina university students for his book *Moral Freedom*, reports: "A surprising number of the students we interviewed, when asked what vice meant to them, immediately thought of the television show *Miami Vice*." In Russia, people were indignant that their president, Vladimir Putin, resembles Dobby, an elf from the movie *Harry Potter and the Chamber of Secrets*. According to Russia's *Novaya Gazeta* newspaper, at some point a major Moscow law firm was even preparing a lawsuit against Warner Brothers, claiming that they had no right to base their character's look on the Russian president. These are strange—but telling—examples of the way pop lodges in our consciousness.

In *The Ingenuity Gap,* Thomas Homer-Dixon describes the poverty of an Indian city. Frustrated, he points out that many of the people who could barely feed themselves owned televisions, which they took great pride in. He might not have understood this need, but anyone who has grown up with the box as a third parent knows that television infuses us with a certain value, a kind of individual cachet. When you are watching TV, it is as if the entertainment is just for you. You become special, targeted, a person. TV is a way to escape the burden of—say—poverty. Not necessarily because its entertainment value is so great, but because it (1) regularly features the lives of ostensibly normal people, (2) offers the illusion of choice, (3) is "free" and constant, meaning that you can never be denied—you are entertained when you say you are ready to be entertained, and (4) permits you a connection to the world of celebrities, products, and the good life, no matter how poor or distanced from the nexus of power you may be.

Pop culture, and especially its gift of "free TV," gives us access to a world we will otherwise never know. From the Amazon rain forest to the operating room to Michael Jackson's mansion to the mysterious life of a Mafia drug lord, we can enter into places far more exciting and seemingly real than our own everyday existence. At the same time, this process instills in us the desire to find similar intensity and excitement in our own lives. We don't just watch the movie, listen to the song, and play the video game, we try to replicate the scenario in our daily lives. Consumer-culture critic Juliet Schor has discovered in her research that the more time a person spends watching TV, the more money that person spends.

The ubiquity of the pop theme means we can never get far enough from it to make an honest assessment about our own expectations. Even educators lose their perspective when it comes to pop success. At the first blush of Avril Lavigne's fame as a teen pop star, her former principal was getting as many as twenty Avril-related calls a day from around the world. Rather than taking the opportunity to, maybe, gently question Lavigne's decision to drop out of high school at sixteen, the principal chose instead to dutifully read from a prepared text: "I am thrilled for her success," says principal Kerry Stewart of suburban Ottawa's Napanee District Secondary School. "We think she's an excellent role model for students who have lofty dreams."

In the case of pop stardom's lofty dreams, the mundane world of education steps aside. Such is the power and allure of pop culture in our lives, and so deep runs the myth that anyone can attain stardom. The result is a world filled with pop-culture supplicants, enthusiasts, and obsessives. The fantasy of the ordinary person turned international success has become a universal fantasy, encoded in the unconscious. This is the new conformity, which the sociologist Ulrich Beck calls "a compulsion, albeit a paradoxical one, to create, to stage manage, not only one's own biography but the bonds and networks surrounding it."

Mule Skinner Blues

Pop culture's just-do-it individuality has penetrated even the most downtrodden lives. Consider the people we meet in the documentary *Mule Skinner Blues* (2001). The film chronicles the denizens of a Mayport, Florida, trailer park. There's Beanie Andrew, a sixty-six-year-old alcoholic whose dream had always been to make a horror film in which he emerges from the primordial Southern swamp in a gorilla suit. There's rock 'n' roller Steve Walker, also a heavy substance abuser, whose band plays local bars. There's the seventy-something country yodeller Miss Jeannie, and the middle-aged janitor Larry Parrot, who methodically composes unpublished horror stories on an ancient manual typewriter. Is Mayport, perhaps, a hotbed for aspiring entertainers? Hardly. It's a hick town that the filmmakers stumbled upon pretty much by accident. Not unlike the better-known *American Movie*—in which filmmakers document the efforts of an impoverished film buff trying to shoot an indie horror feature—again there's the sense that *Mule Skinner Blues* could have been anywhere in the Western world, could have featured any number of lonely outsiders clinging to the dream despite all evidence that pop stardom simply could not be any further away.

The filmmakers behind *Mule Skinner Blues,* Stephen Earnhart and Victoria Ford, think it is more than just coincidence that all the people in their documentary are obsessed with earning pop recognition.

"It's a by-product of our society," Earnhart says without hesitation. "The clichéd fifteen minutes of fame, wanting to be in the movies, to be a celebrity. They see the lifestyles on TV. I don't know why, but everybody is obsessed with it."

"It's even more so for someone that's been down and out," adds Ford. "It's a recognition of their existence, a validation—I'm worth something."

Do the filmmakers feel they are personally perpetuating the dream of stardom and celebrity?

"This is our predicament as an art form," answers Earnhart. "These are our myths, the myth of celebrity and success, they are stories being told to our unconscious. It's hard to separate them from our mass culture. If a guy grew up in the woods, would he have those stories?"

Mule Skinner Blues chronicles the lives of a motley crew of pop dreamers, but finds its locus when the filmmakers actually help

Andrew make his movie, providing equipment and expertise to shoot a Larry Parrot–devised screenplay in which Andrew and Walker play leading roles. So *Mule Skinner,* at least partly, chronicles the usual triumphant ascendancy of the individual, clinging to his or her dreams and having them come true.

"It's part of the human spirit," notes Earnhart. "To create hope. To not have it would be to kill some sort of primal instinct. If Steve Walker wasn't playing guitar he would be dead with alcoholism. You can be critical of the dream, but you can't be critical of what the dream means. To give that up is to create the walking dead."

"I think part of the appeal of the film," adds Ford, "is that they are regular people out there expressing desires that people have across the board. So in that sense the film is more about desire and will than it is about outcome."

In other words, *Mule Skinner* avoids the cliché of the I'm-Special theme largely because it is an investigation of what the theme means, rather than a narrative simply reiterating the invariably positive outcome of what happens when you pursue your dreams. The most telling scene in the movie is in an interview with Miss Jeannie, who has spent her whole life as a singer-songwriter. At one point, she takes a plaque off her mantel and shows it to the camera. She notes that it is nothing more than a certificate of appreciation. That's it, she says; after fifty years of singing, that's all she has to show for her career. It's a scene that demonstrates how the pop promise not only raises up, but also devalues. Is that really all Miss Jeannie has to show for it? Didn't she give pleasure, enter the lives of people in her community in a way that is as important and powerful as entrance into the high-powered entertainment industry? Clearly, to Miss Jeannie and to all the characters in *Mule Skinner Blues,* those things don't mean squat. It's being on TV that matters. What matters is, to paraphrase Victoria Ford, having one's existence recognized by the pop-culture forces that shape our world.

In the end, by helping Andrew and his crew make their lame horror movie, *Mule Skinner* cannot avoid the pop theme of transcendent ordinariness. Says Earnhart: "We wanted to show people with this movie that you can just go out and do it, that was our philosophy, that we're all in the same boat, we all have this burning desire to create." All well and good, but *can* you just go out and do it? Without a New York film crew, Andrew's film would never have been made and Miss Jeannie would never have shot her video, another project the filmmakers assisted with and included in the *Mule Skinner* release.

How many Larry Parrots are out there, banging out horror story after horror story? How many Steve Walkers are trolling the small-town taverns, hard-rock crooners with tattoos and long stringy hair who dream of screaming arenas and MTV heavy rotation? In *Mule Skinner Blues,* talented filmmakers put forth a positive message of indie creativity and hoped that their honesty and low-budget aesthetic would prevent the film from becoming just another articulation of the you-can-do-it-too pop fantasy. Alas, I'm not sure it is possible to demonstrate the existence of the pop fantasy without, in some way, choosing sides. Stephen Earnhart agrees that the fantasy is all-pervasive, but goes ahead and makes the fantasy, in some small way, come true for the hapless inhabitants of one little nook, in one little cranny of the world. But what about the rest of us? Where's our New York film crew? Are you for the fantasy or against it? Or does it even matter? Like an oil slick, the pop promise spreads and sticks to everything and everyone.

Simmel: Outside Looking In

Despite having ample real-world evidence of the fact that pop and its message of individual redemption and reinvention clearly influence our lives, I wanted a theoretical framework to hang these ideas on. Someone must have an abstract philosophical approach to the pop world that might explain how the mass production of stories could have become such a beckoning, unattainable, contradictory, and often alienating presence. I found what I was looking for in the ideas of Georg Simmel, a German philosopher who wrote in the early part of the twentieth century.

Simmel lived in a time when mass-culture production—with its attendant ramping up of propaganda and entertainment—was just developing. Caught between the rapidly developing world of mass culture and the rarefied high-art world, Simmel saw the culture of his time as an entity standing outside the human beings who produced and perpetuated it. That is, he was one of the first to see that a culture industry was developing, one which could manufacture cultural product by rote pattern and format.

Simmel argued that culture was becoming not a direct, integral manifestation of the human spirit, but rather something more distant and, at times, even threatening. Culture was separating from humanity. The singing of songs, telling of stories, and playing of instruments was falling into the hands of experts and technocrats. Simmel wrote of a situation in which creative life was "constantly producing something that is not life, that somehow destroys life, that opposes life with its own valid claims. Life cannot express itself except in forms which have their own independent existence and significance. This paradox is the real, ubiquitous tragedy of culture." For Simmel, cultural manifestations that spring from individual psyches come to stand outside us as independent of individual human existence and act as a cultivating or even colonizing force. Life is, ultimately, in danger of being subsumed by the demands of a culture existing on a parallel plane to life and opposing life with its own "valid claims."

This idea of life and culture standing outside each other and interacting with and against each other helps explain the way pop culture stands outside the life of, say, John Conte, allowing him to see how ridiculous his involvement in the record-breaking piano event and documentary are, even as he cannot resist participating. Conte, infected by a pop culture churned out on an assembly line, ends up pursuing a world record he doesn't want in order to make a documentary nobody really cares about.

In conjuring up a culture that "opposes life," Simmel provides the framework to understand how it is that pop culture begins as something that is so closely aligned to the interests of individual human life, and ends as an entity that stands outside us with a life of its own. Simmel articulates a pop culture that stands outside us and infects us; an entity that, in Simmel's harsh words, actually "destroys life." Simmel writes of the "paradox": the essential tension between our own desire to create and be noticed because of our creation, and the creation itself, an entity that stands so much outside us that it becomes separate, alienating, colonizing—the omnipresent fantasy infiltrating our conscious and unconscious thoughts. "It seems to be in the nature of inner life," Simmel warns, "that it can only ever be expressed in forms which have their own laws, purpose and stability arising from a degree of autonomy independent of the spiritual dynamics which created them."

This brilliant theorist, emerging at a time of rapid cultural change that was affecting everything from political systems to religious institutions and even the sanctity of marriage, connects the development of this new kind of separate autonomous culture to the emerging "world of things." That is his term for the mass-produced world that he sees as being far more capable than our solitary selves of containing the glut of ideas and entertainments that, on an individual level, Simmel predicts will lead to "fragmentation" and a "state of simultaneous dissatisfaction and over-satiation."

What Simmel sensed "in theory" in the early twentieth century can now be observed in our everyday lives. John Conte represents this culturally induced fragmentation, as does Ken Hechtman, Miss Jeannie, and the Idolites. All are dissatisfied with what they have accomplished, and yet none live in poverty or desperation; in fact, their needs—emotional and physical—are more than met. Today, as Simmel predicted, Western society is fragmented, over-satiated, and dissatisfied. Our things, particularly pop culture, keep getting more alluring and evocative. Our expectations are raised, but the world we live in—the world we made!—is unable to fulfill what our own pop culture promises us. Bloated on promise, starving for opportunity, a good chunk of us search for a way into the pop world through mind-altering drugs (prescription and otherwise), TV tryouts, liposuction, ill-thought-out trips to combat zones, and ever-more-virulent outbreaks of starvation-inducing eating disorders. Our culture has become separate from us. In the struggle to renew our claim to our own fantasies, we seem to be moving further and further away from ourselves.

Chasing Fame at the Hard Rock Academy

How will the new generations access the fantasy they have been promised their entire lives? Instead of starting funds for their university education, we might soon be contributing to their tuition at places like the Hard Rock Academy. Striving for fame by acquainting oneself with its rituals and practices is what the Hard Rock Academy is all about. It is, in a way, the literal embodiment of Simmel's depiction of a culture that is us but also stands outside us, alienating and beckoning at the same time. The academy is affiliated with the Hard Rock Cafe chain, and its flyer shows a museum wall featuring a Madonna dress, a Lenny Kravitz guitar, *NSYNC's shirts and, smack in the middle, a big SPACE AVAILABLE sign. "Find out what it takes to fill this space," urges the flyer.

Hard Rock Academy is based in Florida, home to Don Wood, a local businessman and one of the academy's founders. Wood describes the academy as a "boot camp where would-be performers can see where they stand." Teenagers gather for a week or two to work on their singing, dancing, and general look. They get to record a CD single. When they're not playing pop star, they're touring the Hard Rock Cafe's memorabilia collection or taking a limo ride to their very own wrap-up party. "It's an opportunity to see what the music business is all about," Wood enthuses. "How to create an image, how to market, what goes on behind the scenes."

Wood explains that most kids—and their parents—don't have a clue how to develop talent and, even worse, don't understand that connections are far more important than talent. "People don't really get discovered because of their talent," he says. "There are lots of talented people in the world; some make it, some don't." The academy will help kids understand what they have to do to make it in today's cutthroat music industry. "What we really want to tell them is: Work hard, and you have to work smart. If you really want to make it, here's stuff you should know before you spend fifty thousand dollars of your parents' money making a CD no one cares about."

Anyone can enroll in the Hard Rock Academy. You don't audition to get in—you just pay the hefty fee. You train with the coaches and choreographers of the stars and, according to Wood, you leave with greater confidence, believing in your ability to go all the way. "A young guy came here who had never sung or danced in his life, and he left believing that he could do those things. . . . We don't promise fame, we promise the experience. What we're trying to do is give them an appreciation of what it is to be a star."

Appreciation of what it is to be a star as opposed to actually telling the kids at any point that they will never be stars. There's a fine point here, a kind of transmogrification in which "the experience" implicitly suggests future fame. After all, the flyers explicitly allude to future stardom, and the fancy booklet on the academy repeatedly references the celebrity bands and industry experts the kids who attend will work with. When I met with Don, the academy was just getting underway and had so far played host to only one group of kids. Nevertheless, Don insists that staff will keep an eye out for talent and use their connections to further the careers of worthy attendees. "Record companies and management companies are already asking to see the talent that comes through our program," he says. "So there will be lots of opportunities."

The Hard Rock Academy promises potential fame, but of course really just offers a prepackaged taste of that fame, with its cutesy limo ride, its recording session, and proximity to celebrity paraphernalia. The academy promotions never mention the *unlikelihood* of getting discovered, though there are plenty of allusions to the potential fame waiting in the wings to sweep teens away. This is, essentially, a new-conformity factory, where our need to get noticed can be married to the for-profit systems of lifestyle capitalism. At once a taste of what stardom might be like and a serious attempt to connect you to the business of pop, the academy does it all and leaves you wanting one single thing: *more.*

Wood, it seems, truly believes that a two-week stint at the Hard Rock Academy can prepare a teenager for stardom, and that his academy might actually discover the next teen starlet. At the same time, he knows perfectly well that the majority who attend will be talentless, will never be discovered, and will leave with expectations that will never be realized. The Hard Rock Academy offers an *Idol-*like tryout atmosphere in which everyone makes the cut. Who will discourage the youngsters of today from pursuing their pop dream? Not Don Wood; not their parents, who gladly pay to have their kids attend the Hard Rock Academy; not the society we live in, which accords pop success the greatest respect. In Don Wood's mind, there is a way things get done: training, a long-term plan, a unique product you hone to perfection then unleash on the market with the help of carefully cultivated contacts. Yet in every way, his vision is the antithesis of what pop and the Hard Rock brand promises, which is doing it on your own: kids jamming in a basement, struggle then triumph, but most of all, originality and genuine talent.

Like so many of us, and in accordance with Georg Simmel's thinking, Wood seems caught between the reality and the fantasy. Or am I giving him too much credit? Is he a partial believer in the rock 'n' roll dream, or a canny businessman angling for a new way to insert money-making into the pop-culture methodology that relentlessly peddles the you-can-do-it-too mantra? The Hard Rock Academy is merely one entity in a long line of institutions that have sought, since the arrival of pop culture and its legions of experts, to trade on our desire to be more than what we are. From poetry anthology scams (your work of genius automatically included with purchase of the book) to film academies to modelling schools, preying on the naive and hopeful has always been part of the pop legacy. But something like the Hard Rock Academy not only trades on our emotional connection to pop, but also pretends to offer its young clients genuine spontaneity and a real sense of what it takes to be a star. Don Wood recognizes an economic opportunity born from the rise of the new conformity. But he's also someone who really does want people to understand what it takes to launch a pop act in North America. Unfortunately, his academy cannot both critique the music industry and be part of it. Here, again, we see how pop culture usurps humanity, by promising more—far more—than it can ever deliver. Ultimately, the Hard Rock Academy will be another portal, purveyor of the perpetually unfulfilled promise, the lie of pop we all want to believe.

LATE IN THE AFTERNOON, I take a break from my computer and pull my guitar out. I unearth the ragged notebooks in which I've scribbled attempts at songs over the years. I select one and tentatively start singing and playing. Though I am alone, I am not playing for myself. Not really. Instead, I imagine an audience. Adoring fans. Record contracts complete with studio musicians and technicians who can give my nasal croon an Al Green suavity, and my choppy guitar playing a punk edge. Soon the words come fast and furious. I belt them out. I hit the strings as hard and as fast as I can. The cattle pens of *Canadian Idol* supplicants, the John Contes, Ken Hechtmans, and Hard Rock Academies all leave my mind. Tomorrow and yesterday disappear. I am nowhere and everywhere. Alone with my fantasy.

In a few minutes, the song will end.

I close my eyes.

Until then, I'm a star.

4

CROWD CONTROL

CONFORMITY VERSUS THE POP PROMISE

ONSCREEN, in a darkened high school auditorium, pop stars speak soberly about their adolescent problems. "Geek, loser, insecure," they dutifully assure the watching assembly of teenagers. Clips from their videos punctuate ten-second sound bites. The beautiful host nods sensitively.

Parkdale Collegiate is an inner-city school in a down-and-out Toronto neighborhood. The students come from myriad races and ethnicities, largely united by their families' lower income bracket and their experiences as recent immigrants. They know full well the struggle to overcome the past and aspire to a better future.

One freezing February morning I wander over to take in a presentation by self-styled teen therapist Karyn Gordon in the school's auditorium. This thin, blue-eyed blonde in her mid-twenties gives regular talks to teens across North America on the subject of bolstering their self-esteem. I want to see what she tells these kids, how she navigates between the reality of their situation and the pop promise that swirls around the youth of today like sharks around chum: You can do it, be anything you want; work hard enough and you'll achieve your dreams!

The auditorium is full, with about two hundred students in

attendance. Teachers flank the room, leaning against the back walls and keeping an eye out for boisterous behavior. The two young women sitting a row ahead tell me that they have no idea what the presentation is about. They chuckle, happy to get out of class. It takes quite a while to get the students quiet, particularly a gaggle dressed in the latest hip-hop styles who laugh loudly throughout the introductions. Finally, the pixie-like Gordon takes the stage. She launches into a description of her TV show *Spill Your Guts*, a low-budget affair that ran for a few seasons on cable. The premise of the show was that Gordon talked to pop stars about the problems they experienced as adolescents. Lights dim; murmurs rise from the students in general, exclamations from the loudest cluster.

The ensuing highlights from the show are sponsored by Pepsi, Pizza Pizza, and Doritos, with attendant onscreen logos. Cut to an assemblage of videos by already slightly out-of-date pop stars. The students groan when an unpopular band comes on the screen and whoop when a band they like makes an appearance. Don't confuse this with excitement. This is their Pavlovian response to pop which, even in the context of a poor video projection in a school auditorium, predictably arouses the senses. The show soon falls into a pattern: clips from videos followed by fifteen-second snippet interviews with pop stars who all report that their greatest problem in high school was a lack of confidence. Their confessions sound as forced as their lyrics. "I felt really insecure," one says. Another, in designer sunglasses and a perfectly crafted stubble shadow, reports: "I was a geek." A beautiful singer tells Gordon that she had an eating disorder, bulimia. But, she says, "finding the band and the music" made that problem go away.

With a final groan-eliciting montage of Gordon posing with various celebs, the video ends and Gordon returns to give a brief lecture about how important self-esteem is to success. She tells us that "how we feel affects almost every single decision we make during the day." Then she calls up four students from the audience to participate in a skit. They are arranged on four chairs and introduced as siblings aged twelve to twenty-five. The "twenty-five-year-old" says that the rest of his family are losers. The "fourteen-year-old" and the "fifteen-year-old" say they ignore what their older brother says about them. The girl acting as the twelve-year-old says that she's a loser and feels like a failure because she doesn't have a boyfriend. The "twenty-five-year-old" announces that he has many girlfriends, tons of girls.

The skit ends. Gordon explains how the oldest brother is a bully masking his low self-esteem and insecurity with bravado and insults, the middle pair can ignore him because they are well-adjusted with high self-esteem, and the youngest kid has low self-esteem so she wants a boyfriend to validate her existence, which is bad. Gordon keeps referring to the kids in the middle who, apparently, have the right attitude because they "strive for excellence but don't beat themselves up if they don't get it."

Gordon gives more examples from her private therapy practice of kids whose lives are negatively impacted by low self-esteem. She speaks of a teen who wants to go to college and become an artist, even though he is failing high school. She tells us that he is afraid of trying, because he is afraid he won't succeed. With that revelation in hand, the boy, apparently, goes on to pursue his dream. Gordon tells us that she also suffered, as an adolescent, from an unidentified learning disability. She overcame it by promising to always believe in her abilities and try hard regardless. Now she has her own TV show and she's working on her doctoral degree in "marriage and family therapy."

Gordon lists the three essentials for positive self-esteem: (1) Stop blaming others for your problems; (2) start setting realistic goals; and (3) start seeking positive influences. It isn't easy, she warns her restless audience, but "it is possible!"

Perfunctory applause and Gordon, who has had to stop the presentation several times to wait for quiet to be restored in the auditorium, proclaims that Parkdale Collegiate has been a great audience. Actually, it's been a restless, inattentive audience. But saying so might hurt feelings and lead to life-long disappointment. Gordon announces that any student who comes to the front of the stage and gives her feedback on the talk will get a free Pizza Pizza coupon.

It's All Your Fault: Meet the Self-Help Industry

Karyn Gordon is part of a huge therapy industry that, as the authors of the sociological study *Habits of the Heart* put it, "takes the functional organization of industrial society for granted, as the unproblematical context of life." In this model, which presents increased self-esteem as the solution to a host of individual difficulties, the goal is to, again as the *Habits* authors write, "achieve some combination of occupation and lifestyle that is economically possible and psychologically tolerable." In other words, in preaching the self-esteem you-can-do-anything pop myth, most therapists—be they popular speakers and TV personalities (think Dr. Phil and Oprah) or accredited professionals—aim to create good little individualists who at once believe they can do anything, but don't actually upset the ratio of one superstar to every million people by successfully managing to *do* anything.

In the new conformity we take the system for granted and do not seriously oppose it. Instead, we believe wholeheartedly that it may be possible to enter the system, and that all our energies should be directed toward figuring out what the system wants so that we can fulfill that need. Karyn Gordon and other therapists assist us in reinventing ourselves for this purpose. They do so by peddling self-esteem as the source and cure for any failures we may experience in the course of attaining special status. These therapists are essentially pop culture's missionaries, trying to convert us to the ideals of self-reliance, reinvention, individuality. This mantra inevitably puts the burden on our shoulders: your problems, your self, your needs. What can *you* do to make your life better? The focus is turned away from the system and how it works, and aimed back at the individual: Oh, you aren't the movie star you wanted to be? Well, honey, you just didn't try hard enough. You aren't the young rebel who bucks the system and earns a pay raise and a big corner office? Well—your self-esteem quotient is low, others can sense the limitations of your aura, your image needs an update.

At Parkdale Collegiate, where the kids face the pressures of poverty, racism, and cultural confusion, should *all* the disappointments in their lives be attributed to low self-esteem? Self-esteem, it is suggested, is about what *you* have or have not managed to accomplish. The implication is, of course, that what you need is a new attitude, a new image, a new interior look. Like Charmaine Semon advising her corporate bigwigs, the answer is to adjust your values and expectations to the way of the world; it's all just a matter of looking at things the right way.

The self-esteem industry places the emphasis on you, your desires, needs, expectations, sacrifices, willingness to work hard. This not only encourages us to consider ourselves capable of changing and taking control of our lives, but discourages any examination of the overall system in which we live our lives. By failing to present anything even remotely like a realistic picture of the chances of pop success, self-esteem mythology teaches us to internalize failures and limitations, and conditions us to accept lives of disappointment and regret. When we believe in the self-esteem mantra, we believe that we are always the source of our failures. Though our lives are steeped in a pop-culture promise that can rarely be realized, we feel our inability to become whatever we've set our sights on as *our fault, our failure.*

AN ALIEN VISITOR surveying our culture might well conclude that it is lack of self-esteem that plagues North Americans more than any other problem—more than cancer and heart disease, more than severe inequities in the distribution of wealth and resources, more than disillusionment with God and government. After all, none of those other issues generates even a quarter of the cultural paraphernalia devoted to good old self-esteem. Marianne Williamson, the New Age guru who famously was consulted by the Clintons, sold two million copies of her book *A Return to Love.* Her argument basically was that individuals have the power to cure themselves of what ails them by accepting their ability to really and truly love. Typing *self-esteem* into Amazon yields a staggering four hundred titles. Which to choose? There are self-esteem niches to cover every conceivable scenario, each one with a catchy moniker and lavish subtitle: *Heart at Work: Stories and Strategies for Building Self-Esteem and Reawakening the Soul at Work; The New Hide or Seek: Building Self-Esteem in Your Child; Higher Powered: A Ninety Day Guide to Serenity & Self-Esteem; The How to Book of Teen Self Discovery: Helping Teens Find Balance, Security & Esteem; Building Your Mate's Self-Esteem;* and my personal favorite, *Life's Too Short: Pull the Plug on Self-Defeating Behavior & Turn on the Power of Self-Esteem.*

The therapists/authors of these myriad titles herd us into the middle, teach us how to survive the many disappointments of postmodern life through a trick of perspective. "The solution to modern angst," writes James Twitchell in his *Living It Up,* "to filling up the self, happens both at the psychologist's office and down at the mall. In the office you are offered a choice of therapeutic personalities, and at the store you are offered an equally varied choice of adaptive lifestyles."

If we look closely at how Karyn Gordon and her colleagues function, we see a powerful demonstration of pop and its self-esteem mythology working together to limit options and keep us conforming to the parameters of faux individuality.

Gordon assures kids that they can achieve anything in real life. But the way Gordon articulates her promise sets her apart from real life—a glitzy fast-moving TV show, a glitzy fast-moving website, a book filled with cutesy scenarios from her life and private practice. In her presentation, Gordon talks of reasonable goals, yet her TV show features only pop stars—not bank tellers, teachers, garbage collectors, or even ballet dancers. Is pop stardom a reasonable goal? Certainly the video implies that it is: Once you overcome your self-esteem deficit, you can do or be anything you want. But Gordon's reliance on pop-culture figures puts her in the mass-culture world, elevates her to pop icon—she becomes the Dr. Phil of teen Toronto. Gordon's own life embodies the pop theme: She has overcome adversity (her learning disorder) to achieve presence in mass culture (in other words, stardom a.k.a. individuality). So if you have self-esteem, you too will have your own book, TV show, and speaking gigs. You will be super-special, an entertainment vector complete with name, niche, style, and corporate sponsor.

In her teen self-help book, *Analyse Yourself,* proudly adorned with the Pepsi and Pizza Pizza logos, Gordon writes about a client named Jessica: "The time I spent with Jessica focused on her uniqueness. What could she offer as a friend to people?. . . Jessica and I worked on discovering what made her special."

What we need to achieve better lives is to rewrite our narrative so that we feel special. Never mind a social milieu where having the wrong friends is tantamount to being excommunicated from teen society. Karyn Gordon tells us to pursue excellence but also be reasonable: If we don't succeed, that's okay too. Can one truly pursue excellence and accept merely average? Gordon's skit literally puts the well-adjusted in the middle: in the middle chairs, in the middle of the make-believe family. The middle succeeds. Don't be angry. Don't be sad. Don't be emotional. The middle kids are well-adjusted. They don't need boyfriends or girlfriends. They don't listen to their angry older brother. Well-adjusted in our society means atomized, solitary, on your own, and able to handle the burden of being on your own. This is the ideal of the new-conformist society steeped in pop: solitary figures who know how to project security and confidence through appropriate articulations of the self-esteem philosophy. The middle makes for an ideal citizen consumer. He is passive, focused on the self, willing to work hard to buy the stuff that will make him stand out. The bully is angry. The loser is angry. Either might make waves, disagree with the assertion that they are the source of their own problems. The middle goes to work, buys items exuding "I'm Specialness" and, if things aren't going his way, blames himself and turns inward to therapy, image adjustment, altar consultation, yoga, and/or creative-writing classes.

More and more people are turned on to the power of self-esteem, yet few seem to be happier for it. Rates of depression, stress, anxiety and suicide continue to climb. In 1999, suicide became the 8th leading cause of death for Americans. It is estimated that 90 percent of suicides suffered from a mental illness—usually depression. A 2003 study in the *Journal of the American Medical Association* found that 16 percent of Americans—some 35 million people—will suffer from depression severe enough to require medical treatment. The Western world is plagued by depression: there was a 95 percent jump in the number of prescriptions written for antidepressants from 1988 to 2002 in Canada while the World Health Organization cites depression as the leading cause of disability in developed nations and predicts it will be the second leading cause of disability worldwide by 2020.

The number of people who report contentment and happiness is shrinking, and the teenagers at Parkdale Collegiate can see for themselves that self-esteem alone does not make you cool at school or lift you out of poverty. Yet a belief in self-esteem, even when couched in the myth of stardom, is hardly to be dismissed out of hand. After all, it's a start, a possibility, a potent if naive hope: Hey, if I change myself, the world will change too. So it is that the Parkdale students seem at once to intuitively grasp what Gordon says while remaining apathetic in response to the self-esteem pep rally. The teens struggle to parse the mixed messages of Gordon's self-esteem presentation. After showing them the pop-star video and telling them how she transformed from a devastated teen with a learning disability into a veritable franchise of teen counselling, Gordon tells students to set "reasonable" goals. Do they hear the word *reasonable* amid the barrage of celeb video clips? The teens seem almost trained to respond to pop: Their response to it is automatic—eyes light up, ears perk, heart beats harder; here comes the excitement; here comes something that makes life worth living. Just as they are drawn to free pizza, the teens cannot walk away from the pop promise: Self-esteem plus reinvented narrative equals celebrity-type specialness.

The System: Exclusion, Accidental and Otherwise

The media/pop-culture industry has become an intensely homogenized profit-obsessed hydra with multiple heads. Movies are the best example. Despite increased access to movie and video cameras, despite innumerable film schools, and despite a small art-film subculture, as a society we are seeing more and more of the same films on our screens. In the United States, some 37,500 cinema screens feature about 500 movies a year: 500 movies a year for a population of 300 million people. The average cost of making and marketing each movie is around *$89 million*. No wonder the cinemas are saturated with the same products. To make that kind of money back, every cent has to be squeezed out of the entertainment. No movie studio can afford to have a single screen showing a local talent's indie feature. The technique now is to release a movie on as many screens as possible. That way, even if it's a stinker, the movie-going audience has no choice but to stumble into the product. The first weekend or two can make a movie—why wait for reviews and word of mouth to dissuade the entertainment-hungry populace?

With total saturation of the American market and cross-ownership of the cinemas and the film distributors, Hollywood has a stranglehold on the film business. The few notable exceptions seem to have the effect of galvanizing indie filmmakers to try even harder to make a Hollywood-like movie that could break through; so it is that an entire world of independent film and video production is practically erased from view. Even movies that are acclaimed at prestigious film festivals like Cannes and the Toronto International Film Festival and written up in major publications around the world are shown briefly in one or two small theaters in a handful of cities before disappearing. How many of us saw the stunning *Atanarjuat: The Fast Runner,* the world's first feature-length film shot in the Inuit language? How long did Denys Arcand's Cannes-winning *The Barbarian Invasions* play in your hometown? The fact that it was relatively difficult to see these globally acclaimed films gives you some idea of what a first-time independent filmmaker faces when trying to get a movie seen.

Hollywood has a stranglehold on the movie biz, but the rising cost to maintain it means that even the few risky, interesting films it once occasionally sanctioned have an even harder time gaining screen time.

Summer 2003 brought us sixteen sequels, prequels, or franchise installments, double the number that appeared in 2002. I don't know about you, but I *treasure* my memories of summer greats *Legally Blonde 2* and *Scary Movie 4*. Summer 2005 wasn't much better: Critics fell all over themselves panning the big-screen version of *The Dukes of Hazzard* but that didn't stop the movie from opening on thousands of screens and taking top spot as that weekend's box office money-maker.

Having successfully used the techniques of saturation, monopoly, and celebrity-building to conquer its own country, the American film industry set its sights on the rest of the world. The neighbors to the north quickly gave in—Canadian movie screens show 95 percent American movies emerging from the Hollywood system. The once-proud European film industry has been humbled. Now more than 80 percent of the films shown in Europe are American. Not even countries officially hostile to the U.S. film industry can escape its grasp. Notes Benjamin Barber in his *Jihad vs. McWorld*: "China and Cuba . . . unable to import American trash . . . produce trash of their own that imitates the very American obsession with sex, violence, and soap opera, which their own propaganda condemns and their censorship is designed to exclude."

The monopoly on distribution and marketing severely limits the number of individuals who can actually play a meaningful role in the predominant culture. You can make all the films you want, write all the articles or stories, sing all the songs. What you can't do is access stores, cable TV, newspapers and magazines, radio stations, cinemas, and so on. Because only five hundred films are going to make it to movie theaters and video stores each year, we can pretty much forget about our own movie getting a viewing. "The form of the system . . . facilitates the view that the opinions of ordinary people count," writes Patrick Colm Hogan in *The Culture of Conformism,* "even though the system in fact allows virtually no room for those opinions, no scope for their articulation, no possibility for their implementation."

The United States' culture industries set the agenda in America and increasingly, the world. If you want to truly understand how our options to be true cultural creators are diminishing even as the self-esteem industry and the pop promise of potential stardom are ramping up the *you-can-do-anything-too!* rhetoric, you have to look at just how little access "ordinary" everyday people have to the media. In radio, the Clear Channel corporation owns a staggering twelve hundred radio stations in the United States, an estimated 60 percent of the rock/pop market. Constantly looking to expand, the company got permission to start a new radio station in the crowded Washington, D.C. market in 2001. The corporation started Hot 99.5, which, in the words of the *Washington Post,* was "almost an exact replica of rival Z104." Following the methods of the movie studios, Clear Channel also owns the booking rights to large numbers of stadiums and clubs across the United States. In other words, they control the airwaves as well as the live-music scene, working together to make sure the performers they choose will attract an audience, if for no other reason than total saturation. Clear Channel and its dwindling number of competitors offer different versions of the same thing. In the shadow of near-total consolidation of the radio airwaves, you can flip through the dial and find the same songs—the new country hits, the pop hits, the hip hop hits, the oldies hits—on every channel. Variation is nonexistent, uniformity is total. New artists are made or discarded not in studios, or in moments of songwriting inspiration, or even in the mercurial world of public opinion. Rather, artist reputations are decided via Clear Channel's "call out" scheme, in which, after a song has been played 150 to 200 times, listeners are phoned at random and played ten seconds of the song. If enough people say they've heard the song before and like it, Clear Channel adds it to their playlist. In fact, getting a song added to the playlist of a Top Forty–type station costs big money—a *New York Times* article on the U.S. record biz noted that the cost of getting a single on Top Forty radio is anywhere between $250,000 and $1 million. "Homogenizing playlists and a corporate culture in which dirty tricks are a way of life," writes a

Salon commentator, "Welcome to the world of Clear Channel— radio's big bully."

Industry and government continue to work well together in their efforts to stamp out pirate radio stations. The U.S. Federal Communications Commission (FCC) is known for going after pirate radio stations, confiscating equipment, issuing fines, threatening jail. After a protest against radio monopolies at a radio industry meeting in San Francisco in 2000, the FCC began shutting down micropower broadcasters, including legendary Springfield, Illinois, station Human Rights Radio, which had been operating for thirteen years. Why? What harm are they doing, other than giving individuals and communities more voices, more chances to hear themselves? That should be a good thing, right? Critics pointed out the hypocrisy of massive deregulation in the television and radio industries while the FCC still maintained the power to issue licenses and dole out frequencies to the highest bidder, and in 2000 the FCC reinstated the Low Power FM Radio program it had cancelled in 1978. Three thousand four hundred stations applied, so many that the commission has now indefinitely closed the window on further Low Power radio station applications while it ever so slowly wades through the thousand-plus hopefuls. So far, only a small fraction of the stations have been approved, which is better than none, but pretty frustating for those wanting a legal local nonprofit radio station in their community. As the advocates behind the Prometheus Radio Project wrote in a recent submission to Congress, at this point in time "not even the President of the United States knows when" the next "filing window will be open."

The magazine industry has also undergone a massive consolidation, with fewer titles owned by fewer companies. Newsstands are increasingly unwilling to stock anything that isn't a proven seller. Again, it is distribution and access to the market that creates an ever-more-controlled industry. In 1995, 320 wholesalers distributed magazines in the United States; by 2002 just four companies controlled 90 percent of the marketplace. As a *New York Times* article said, "The fallout has meant that magazines that do not sell enough copies or are not part of a bigger company can lose access to consumers."

New magazines cannot find a readership because they are refused entry to the newsstands by those who control distribution. Because they are not on the newsstand and cannot reach large numbers of people, these magazines cannot attract the advertising agencies that will place ads in their pages. Ad agencies want big magazines with huge proven readerships. They want clout for their clients, the ability to dictate placement and content. Today, four huge advertising agencies control half of the industry's business in the United States. Again, the *New York Times* explains: "By deciding when and where to spend their clients' ad budgets, they can indirectly set network television schedules and starve magazines to death or help them flourish."

Only a handful of the most popular magazine, book, and music titles are to be found in the most popular and fastest-growing type of stores—big discount chain stores like Wal-Mart and Kmart, as well as stores like Costco. They are, themselves, an aspect of increasing conformity and uniformity imposed on the cultural landscape, particularly in the way they put smaller, more diverse stores out of business and suck the life out of urban neighborhoods and malls alike. These stores try to encapsulate what they call "family values" and, in so doing, further limit consumers' options to find diverse cultural products. For instance, Wal-Mart has banned guy-oriented magazines like *Maxim* and *Stuff*. It won't carry the music of Eminem. It won't sell Kurt Cobain's diaries. It banned a Sheryl Crow album featuring a song that criticized the chain for selling guns. Big deal, you say. Those who want that stuff will just shop elsewhere. But, really, these are just the brand-name examples we *will* be able to find elsewhere. What cultural products have these "family-friendly" outlets silently squashed that no one will ever know about? Wal-Mart has the power, quite simply, to turn something into a hit or relegate it to the obscure. In the United States, discount chain stores account for more than 50 percent of a bestselling album, 40 percent of a bestselling book, and more than 60 percent of a bestselling DVD. Wal-Mart has clout. It uses that clout to, as one commentator put it, bend "popular culture toward the tastes of their relatively traditionalist customers."

By now I'm pretty sure you are getting the picture: More chains put independent stores out of business, creating fewer outlets for corporations to sell their products (indie culture, of course, is as far away from being sold in Wal-Mart as you are, right now, from walking on the surface of the planet Mars). Those fewer outlets have so much power that, if they don't like something, it is probably going to disappear. In fact, it might not even get made. So, further exclusion, consolidation, homogenization is the result. Everyone works together to make sure that only a handful of corporate-approved pop-culture products reach consumers. There's no conspiracy here. Like the executives at Clear Channel and the movie studios, the standard defense of the box stores is that customers get what they ask for. Representatives of these chains told a *New York Times* reporter that "they worry only about their customers, not their impact on the culture." But we should worry about their impact because giant retail outlets are part of a monoculture that, when joined with film, the pop-music industry, and consolidated blocks of newspapers, TV stations, and ad agencies, replaces real variation with an endless treadmill of similar products, each one claiming to be more exciting than the last.

THE SYSTEMATIC SUPPRESSION of independent cultural pursuits and products extends beyond North America. As multinational U.S.-style entertainment aggressively spreads across the globe, much of the atomization and confusion of the affluent new-conformity society is taking hold in countries where it was once believed that cultural differences created too vast a gap for pop's sensibilities to translate.

Antje, a young woman working for music company BMG Germany as a product and marketing manager based in Munich, says that Germany is largely devoid of its own homegrown music industry. Despite fanatical fans who will do almost anything to come in contact with their fave American bands, there is little or no pop music actually created by Germans. Antje notes that the Top Ten is all American—and, at the time I was talking to her, it included the Rolling Stones, the Red Hot Chili Peppers, Bruce Springsteen, Elvis Presley, and an American boy band called Natural. Why aren't there any, for instance, German homegrown boy bands?

"A boy band singing in German would sound ridiculous," she notes without the slightest hint of irony. "We drink Coke, we love McDonald's. We always look to the States, especially the kids and especially for music."

They come from abroad and conquer. Antje tells me that many American bands, particularly boy bands, have bigger fan clubs in Germany than in North America. Natural, for instance, has a German fan club of more than a thousand paying fans. "They don't understand the lyrics completely but they know how to pronounce the words. They just want to have a little piece of that country [the United States]."

In other countries too, mass culture in the form of bands and brands has come to be synonymous with a life of laissez-faire individuality. *The Globe and Mail* reports that Christmas is "taking off" all over the world, even in countries with no Christian tradition. Writes Jan Wong:

> Christmas isn't a bunch of meaningless symbols to the rest of the world. The symbolism couldn't be clearer: Success, upward mobility and the freedom to shop till you drop. That may be why the rest of the world, especially the Third World, is embracing Christmas.

It is pop culture, of course, that spreads the Christmas message through ads, Christmas songs, and those annual Christmas movies.

Global cultural conformity is spreading something else: a very particular idea of beauty. Many countries are redefining their archetypes under the influence of pop. In Thailand, "the round face, arched eyebrows and small mouth of the classical Thai look have given way in popularity to the . . . features of the West." A poll found that seven of the nine people considered Thailand's sexiest men and women were of mixed blood, and sported dominant Western features.

China is quickly adopting a Western-style idealization of fame. "In China," says Zhang Yimou, China's best-known movie director, "we now have 20-something young girls who have become famous overnight. The power of those role models is boundless." Indeed, newsstands bulge with celebrity gossip mags snapped up by young—usually poor—teenage girls. When Yimou held a star search contest for the leading role in his next film, a staggering one hundred thousand hopefuls turned up for the audition. But, notes Miro Cernetig of *The Globe and Mail,* "In China, just as in Hollywood, the star machine mostly churns out broken dreams." Cernetig talked to one of the hopefuls, a nineteen-year-old who had been eating just one meal a day to save money to get to Beijing for the audition. Upon arrival she discovered that her application had been rejected, and she never even got to try out for the part.

While most people in the world can hold out little hope of becoming a Hollywood movie star (or the equivalent in their own country), almost everybody can at least sample the wares of the American dream. In China, as in Russia and other nations that were once hostile to the West, the allure of the Big Mac is strong. McDonald's reigns supreme in Beijing, as does an array of copycat Western-style fast-food burger joints. You can even order a decaf latte at the downtown Starbucks. The food, which appeals to young students, is increasingly separated from the ideology of nationalism. "I am for China in all matters," explains twenty-two-year-old Chen Hongcheng, a Beijing student. "That doesn't mean it is wrong to eat a hamburger or drink Coca-Cola."

Hamburgers, Cokes, frothy coffees, boy bands. The appeal is not so much a sense of being close to the United States, but, rather, being able to sample the specialness that the United States purportedly embodies. Of course, as me-first consumer culture spreads, entire landscapes are transformed to look like everywhere else. In Russia, suburban-style condos are being erected to meet the needs of the newly minted middle class. A new Russian term has been coined to describe these structures: *town khaus.* Says a St. Petersburg architect, "These condo residents want their house to be their castle so they can retreat away from the rest of the world." Sound familiar?

Global monoculture spreads, changing not just what we eat and how we look, but also how we *think.* The high-tech city of Bangalore is one of the bastions of the middle class in India. Since it's also the bar capital of India, multinational booze companies are anxious to make inroads against India's indigenous alcohol producers. Foreign companies take over popular bars and sponsor fashion shows and events "with names like Bacardi Jailhouse Night, Bacardi Pajanner Party, Smirnoff Arabian Nights, Jack Daniels Future Fridays," the *New York Times* reported. Thirty-three-year-old software developer Umesh Malhotra was quoted as saying: "I go for foreign alcohol because it is better tasting and has brand value. We have evenings where we drink nothing but the best quality imported alcohol. It's an aspirational thing, and splurging makes sense."

American-based multinational companies face competition in the peddling of individualistic-seeming pop and leisure cultural products in other countries. The Canadian television network CityTV has a global division that sells not just its generically titled shows—Fashion TV, MovieTV, etc.—but the entire concept of an interactive semilocal TV network. Franchisees pay royalty fees for using City trademarks like Speaker's Corner, as well as research, training techniques, and business plans. There have been buyers in Colombia, Argentina, Finland, Spain, the United States, and even China. The El Tiempo building, headquarters of CityTV Colombia, apparently looks exactly like the network's Toronto headquarters. Soon another look-alike headquarters will be up and running in Shanghai. "I would never have thought in our wildest dreams we would have a chance to break China," said Kevin Byles, vice-president and general manager of CHUM Television International. "Just like you walk in off Queen and John [in downtown Toronto], you're going to see a CityTV environment or a MuchMusic environment." CityTV's business model offers short bursts of intensely local news—fires, murders, sports stars—with long stretches of generic entertainment featuring Hollywood movies, pop stars, fashion shows, and reality TV. CityTV is a great example of the pop paradox: a wrapping of locality and individuality, but the box is filled with cheap, generic gifts. CityTV founder Moses Znaimer chalks up interest in the CityTV model as a response to globalized culture. "It's precisely because you have global economics that people feel a very passionate need for local culture—something that distinguishes, something that makes them special." Of course, it is only the feeling of special that is being offered—a fleeting sense of being noticed, appearing in the background when CityTV airs one of its "live, everywhere" promo spots or the opportunity to call in and ask an expert a question, so long as you don't stay on the line for more than fifteen seconds. CityTV does not really offer communities and individuals a chance to participate in the channel's programming—it only seems to. A local TV producer notes that global sales for generic TV shows like the Canadian-made *La Femme Nikita* are actually declining, because the trend today is to export the idea or formula for a show and then have the show produced indigenously. City TV is at the forefront of that trend, exporting a formula that encapsulates a kind of pretend-inclusiveness better than any other network in the world.

As pop culture and its products spread, the addictive promise of the new conformity spreads with it. But local culture withers. Options shrink. "The world looks more homogenous because it is more homogenous," writes O.B. Hardison in *Disappearing Through the Skylight*. "Children who grow up in this world therefore experience it as a sameness rather than a diversity, and because their identities are shaped by this sameness, their sense of differences among cultures and individuals diminishes."

Peddling Pretend Participation

There is no widespread backlash against monotone entertainment. We have become used to the seemingly infinite variety of entertainment products that make up the cultural conformity dominating our world. We even seem to appreciate it and expect it. When we travel, many of us want things to appear as they are at home. When we turn on the TV, we generally want to know, instantly, what genre we're working in, what predictable plot line we are going to be following, what channel shows Fox. When we listen to the radio, we usually want to tune into the exact style we like and to be able to hear songs that are familiar to us. Pop culture's conformity, in fact, provides us with a unifying principle, a comforting space into which we can retreat, its expectations and offerings seemingly no more complicated than a mother's hug. Pop's assurance that you can do it is as comforting as Dad's presence at the Little League game. The cultural industries extend their dominance over the mental landscape, changing our expectations and lives without our noticing or objecting.

The length of a *Time* cover story has dropped from 4,500 words to 2,800 words over the past twenty or so years, Thomas Homer-Dixon reports in *The Ingenuity Gap*. Similarly, a *New York Times* story has shrunk by 20 percent and the length of a *Scientific American* article has declined by 40 percent. Homer-Dixon is horrified to report that the average news sound bite has slipped from a 1965 high of forty-two seconds to a present-day low of eight seconds. But the outraged Homer-Dixon misses the obvious fact: We *prefer* shorter sound bites. Forty-two seconds is a long time. We want more entertainment better and faster. Shorter sound-bite bursts of entertainment seem to give us more. And the more there is, the more we think there might be a place for us in that speedy world. The faster our pop culture and media are, the more we feel included and inclusive, part of the barrage, immersed in it as a participant. Which is why, for instance, spectators are increasingly willing to forgive fakery in the name of entertainment—the 3,500 fans who petitioned Britney Spears not to lip-synch on her 2004 Onyx Hotel Tour were "shouted down by peers from around the world who not only don't mind a little gimmickry, they prefer it." Noted one high school senior who paid $91 and drove six hours to see Spears perform: "I'd rather she not ruin my favorite song and just put on a good show." It seems that laying bare the underpinnings of cultural power does little to dissuade us from giving corporate entertainers our money. We know the news is superfluous, that concerts and televised performances are faked, and that behind Disney's family-friendly image is a merciless entertainment giant. But we don't really care—so long as we get to hear, in person, that favorite song. Disney offers us a way inside: You saw the movie, you bought the plush toy, now attend the concert or ride the ride and hug the character. Disney extends the experience, makes us feel as if we are participating in the I'm-Special universe we are perpetually promised and permanently excluded from. Tell us about Disney's tentacle-like reach and its hold over an entire world's imagination and we might very well respond negatively. But planeloads of us will still go to Disney World and hug Mickey Mouse.

Society's ever-more-powerful need to be seen and heard through mass culture means that we can accept any degradation of our culture, so long as it continues to promise us access. We will accept any lowering of standards, any perversion of information into entertainment, any invasion of our private mental space, so long as it seems that pop culture is on the verge of giving us what we have been promised: recognition in the media world.

MASS CULTURE CONTINUES to evolve and meet our desire to be in the picture by, as we've seen, speeding up the tempo and finding ways to give us more of what keeps us obsessed: more flashes of our own faces, more promises of more to come. The trend is toward inclusivity and interactivity, buzzwords that can be defined as methods by which individuals are invited to have predetermined interactions with their entertainment. Video games are the fastest-growing entertainment sector and it is no surprise that entertainment overall is seeking to imitate the video-game aesthetic. Video games immerse the player in an environment that subscribes to the pop culture/self-esteem mythology while perpetuating the illusion that we are players in the system who control our own destiny and our own fun. A great example of this is the revamp of the popular computer game The Sims. In The Sims 2, you can tailor your characters to look like celebrities and there is a feature to shoot home movies of your Sims as they go about the business of being your virtual family.

In the future, we'll see more schemes like the one developed for MuchMusic USA. This now defunct digital cable channel offered interactivity through the use of a system called IMX (interactive music exchange). Viewers logged on to a website and started an account where they "bought" and "sold" pop stars. As a *New York Times* reporter explains:

> Pop star popularity is traded like virtual stock, with an artist's shares going up or down in value as his or her popularity index—determined by the "buy" and "sell" orders of the IMX players—crests and wanes. Online, there's an interface that lets users monitor both their own accounts and the general shape of the market; on air, a ticker bearing information like "NORAH 146.78 +5.67" scrolls at the bottom of the screen as the hosts chat and banter.

Contestants get one million IMX dollars when they sign up, and the IMX money is redeemable for prizes in the form of Sony Playstations and CDs. In addition, players determine which videos get played: The more expensive an artist's stock, the more their videos get played. "This generation of viewers wants to be involved, and they need a reason to be involved," says Marc Juris, president of MuchMusic USA.

MuchMusic USA is no more, but the ideas behind the scheme have become HSX.com (Hollywood Stock Exchange). Here players "invest" in actors, TV shows and movies and are rewarded with prizes as their choices become popular and a celebrity or show's stock value rises. (Last I checked, Carmen Electra's stock was down.)

Schemes and contests abound, but they are always carefully controlled to ensure the predominance of mainstream mass-market product. Lucasfilm ran a contest to find the best indie films related to *Star Wars*. For devoted fans of the movie series, this was to be a defining moment: The winning film would be chosen by George Lucas himself. However, the majority were excluded from the competition when Lucasfilm decided to limit the contest to spoofs and documentaries. Those who paid tribute to *Star Wars* with short dramatic films that acted as subplots were cast aside, for "copyright reasons." Said a Lucasfilm vice-president of marketing:

> We love our fans. We want them to have fun. But if in fact somebody is using our characters to create a story unto itself, that's not in the spirit of what we think fandom is about. Fandom is about celebrating the story the way it is.

The fact that there are thousands of fans who love *Star Wars* so much they feel the urge to add new twists to its plot lines is the new conformity in all its glory. The infamous "Phantom Edit," an unauthorized version of Lucas's film *Star Wars: Episode I—The Phantom Menace,* cuts out the much-maligned Jar Jar Binks character and various plot redundancies. Twenty minutes shorter and, according to many fan comments on the web, superior to the Lucas version, the Phantom Edit crystallized what many of us knew all along: The amateur fans may be just as talented as the directors. The Phantom Edit led to several other anonymous edits of the film being circulated around the globe via the internet and even handed out at conventions by rabid fans, until Lucasfilm issued a news-release threat about copyright infringement. The furor died down, but the message was clear: A series of movies can relentlessly preach individuality, rebellion, and taking on seemingly impossible odds to its millions of ardent fans, but applying those lessons to make your own movies (or versions) is definitely not what fandom is about.

The *Star Wars* fans are part of a growing movement of those creating what has been dubbed *fan fiction*. In this genre, fans pay tribute to their favorite books, movies, and TV shows by writing new stories or episodes—in which familiar characters appear in new scenarios—and posting them on fan websites. These "based on the characters of" projects are admitted derivatives, pale imitations of the expert original, and on that basis they cannot be judged for either their originality or their blockbuster appeal. They are one of the few outlets for the hordes who are saturated with the pop dream but unable to find a way to be part of the fantasy. While Harry Potter fans sit through the agony of waiting for another novel, they turn to the next best thing—creating their own fictions, which they swap via Harry Potter websites. There are, literally, thousands of Harry Potter stories to be found on the web—indeed, fan fiction amounts to probably the fastest-growing literary tradition in the world. Many of these writers would never think of composing an original screenplay or tale, but they don't hesitate to dive into fan fiction. In this small safe terrain they can inject their personality into mass culture without having to fear rejection. Nothing is at stake. There is no one to tell them their creation has failed. And so, in their own small way, they are free to feel special.

The website iwannabefamous.com invites people to submit photos and statements regarding their desire for fame. Sixteen-year-old Rachel writes:

> I want the thrill the happiness and the fun like I see in movies . . . I want to give people the joy of seeing me in movies like my movie heroes did with me!!! I figured out that I am tired of just dreaming about doing something, I am sick of a looking for a "regular" job, I know that nothing but acting interests me, I feel life slipping by, and that "something is missing" feeling begins to dominate me all day and night.

Rachel reminds us that we are not talking in the abstract here, but about real individuals with an overwhelming longing for a fame they believe is their birthright. Rachel's yearning, combined with the explosion of fan fiction stories and films, reveals how pop culture works: Mass media exclude not only alternative opinions and ideas, but also the majority who harbor *no* alternative ideas. People like Rachel who want to sing pop songs, make movies, and star in TV shows aren't shut out because of their politics or originality. It is simply that the pop system, for all its you-can-do-it-too promises, depends on shutting us out. To create celebrity and sell the most of one thing to as many people as possible, the system must be exclusionary. Big money is made when a billion people all go to the same movie. This is far more likely to occur when those billion people have only five hundred movies a year to choose from. The tight control over access to creative product stifles dissent—aesthetic and political—along with the bulk of our generally mainstream aspirations.

As we've seen, movies and video games relentlessly preach self-esteem and individualistic rebellion against the system. As more and more of us seek special status and want to become like the rebels on TV, our closed entertainment system has to manufacture more and more scenarios that will make us feel like the rebels so many of us think we want to be.

A game released in North America in 2002, called .hack, puts us in a digital environment owned by CC, an evil tech firm. When a friend in this virtual environment, called *The World,* is mysteriously attacked and lapses into a coma, it is up to you to figure out what happened and how to stop the bad corporation. The game, developed for PlayStation 2, was created by CyberConnect2, a.k.a. CC. In 2002, it was already a popular televised cartoon in Japan, along with a comic book and a straight-to-video animated series. Another wildly popular pop-culture entertainment product peddling pseudo-rebellion is *The Matrix,* in which we are asked to identify with our hero Keanu Reeves, a.k.a. The One. With its what-if-we-are-all-just-puppets-in-some-evil-corporate-plot plot, the movie epitomized the appetite for pretend rebellion in which highly stylized rebels take on a world governed by clones in black suits (a.k.a. Corporate Ken drones) manufacturing a false reality in order to oppress us. This, I guess, is what our bad-boy computer programmers and scriptwriters pass off as defiance of the system. In our fantasy play, we defy the interlocking evil fantasy world. In real life, we pay the corporation to give us the feeling of defying their—our—world.

Ersatz rebellion mixes with passive entertainment and ends up occupying the space where real active voice and dissent once had a chance to make a difference. We see this in the passive-aggressive posturing of an ever-fluctuating crop of pop culture icons.

Consider the stance of famous snowboarder Danny Kass: He consistently dissed the 2002 Winter Olympics, in which he was expected to win a gold medal for the United States, as irrelevant and uncool. Wrote a commentator: "His rebel persona has made him the biggest act on the circuit . . . he can hardly afford to be any other way." And yet Kass is an entrepreneur with various successful product lines to his credit. His seeming disaffection, coupled with his vigorous product line, has helped inspire an entire subculture who believe that all organized competition is lame. Instead, as a journalist reporting on the scene noted, boarders "build a following with fifteen-second clips of wild stunts, like riding on the roof of a house or jumping giant cliffs in the back country."

Naturally, all of this filters through the net. It commands intense interest, provides the illusion of radicalism and dissent, an entire world of hip-hop-listening, extreme-sports-watching, perpetual teenagers who believe in nothing other than their own incarnation of rebel I'm-Special self-esteem attitude. In the new conformity of extremity, every seemingly spontaneous action is recorded and broadcast as evidence of one's devotion to rebellion and special. The HBO series *Project Greenlight* featured movie stars Matt Damon and Ben Affleck searching for a first-time outsider director whose film they and Miramax would then produce. The winner of the contest is decided after he makes an impassioned speech about the evils of the studio system he is competing to join. Notes columnist A.O. Scott: "What was striking about the 10 finalists . . . was how conventional their ambitions were, and how the contest sold careerism as a form of rebellion . . . everyone is fighting the system, which is how the system works."

The Search for a Way In

Star Ray TV, Canada's first and only "low-power" TV station, was the brainchild of Jan Pachul. Located in a rundown strip mall in east-end Toronto, the TV station was run on abandoned UHF channels (remember the upper dial you desperately spun in the hopes of turning grey static shadow into *Batman* or *Rocket Robin Hood?*). Pachul's idea was to serve Toronto's Beaches and surrounding community, and to try out an entirely new model of localized television. "You need a community station that can compete in the market and at the same time communicate alternative viewpoints," Pachul explains. It was under that premise that Star Ray in 2000 received an experimental license from the Department of Canadian Heritage to broadcast. Not long afterwards, however, the Canadian Radio and Telecommunications Commission (CRTC), which is responsible for issuing licenses across the country, turned down a request for the license to be renewed. After negative interventions by, among others, the Canadian Association of Broadcasters, Rogers Cable, CTV, and CHUM/CityTV, the CRTC ruled that Star Ray was, in fact, in violation of the low-power television policy. Star Ray kept broadcasting anyway, and the CRTC threatened Pachul with a $20 thousand-a-day fine. At that point, Pachul demanded to see the low-power broadcasting regulations he was violating. The CRTC did not have a lower-power television broadcasting policy. The commission backed off.

But Pachul couldn't keep Star Ray TV on the air. He soon ran out of steam and cash. In a cluttered office illuminated by a single lamp, he spews conspiracy theories and vague programming ideas. He cites his planned monster-movie daily "Creature Feature" as an example of innovative television, and badmouths the "assholes" in Ottawa. Pachul started Star Ray because he had worked his whole life in various aspects of the TV industry and, after contemplating the offerings of Canadian television, became convinced he "could do a better job." He drags a hand through his unkempt hair. "I didn't want to be an activist," he says. "I just wanted to run a TV station."

Pachul couldn't think of a single reason why he shouldn't have his own TV station. Pop-culture aspirants aren't activists and radicals, but people who just want in (think backyard wrestlers, Elvis impersonators). Pachul has no particular vision, no real connection to the community. Just an abiding sense that he should have his own goddamn TV station if he bloody well feels like it. His stubbornness took him all the way to a partial victory over the CRTC, which decided to back off and let him self-destruct rather than risk looking ridiculous for suppressing a channel with a reach of thousands and a viewership of, maybe, hundreds, under the guise of a non-existent policy. Some of the biggest companies in Canada lined up to speak against Pachul. What were they afraid of?

The fate of Napster and other related online technologies suggests an answer. That file-sharing software allowed millions of people around the world—most of them young—to exchange music on their computers. Started by nineteen-year-old Shawn Fanning in 1999, it was perhaps the most successful example of independent cultural dispersion since the rise of the independent press in the sixties. At its height, 60 million or so users were joyously downloading free music. Like the mimeographed or photocopied newsletter, it was simple, brilliant, and provided people what they most wanted—a modicum of control. There are good arguments to be made about lost royalties and copyright infringement, but it's interesting to note that those who protested were already fabulously rich and the indie bands who had the most to lose were extremely sanguine about Napster. They believed, correctly, that they would reap the rewards of people being able to download their songs anywhere in the world (at a time when selection at the local chain music store is tightly controlled) through future fan interest in albums, tours, etc. Napster was shut down, and now exists as a members-only site where you pay to download corporate-owned pop songs. Other file-sharing sites/software like Bit-Torrent are being aggressively pursued out of existence. The siege continues as the combined forces of industry and government go all out to attack large-scale trading of music and movies on the internet. Already, high school students, internet service providers and even universities have been slapped with large lawsuits for "stealing" music. As a result, many young people have absorbed and believed the hype that file trading is stealing and will lead to the death of the music and film industries. This is total nonsense for so many reasons, but the more serious issue is the effective suppression of *the idea* that people might trade songs, movies, and stories rather then sell them like so many cans of beans. Keep that concept under wraps, and you're also keeping a good many people from figuring out just how much independent cultural activity exists, and how much better most of it is compared to the corporate pap.

The real question of online interactivity remains: What if there were no more systems of control, no more monopolies over what gets into the music stores and what gets played on the radio? What if you could hear anything you wanted anytime, and buy or download anything you wanted online, anytime, directly from the source? What if anybody could start his or her own television channel?

All the cultural industries depend on a closed system. But, because music-making is such an elemental activity, and because it is easier to trade and copy, the music industry is having a much more difficult time suppressing independent activity. As the backyard wrestlers show us, in the near future creating your own TV shows will also feel like an unconscious elemental activity to coming generations of wired I'm Specialites. They will want, demand, and perhaps ultimately create parallel television worlds that will, like Napster momentarily threatened to do, cut corporations out of the business and make indie culture accessible and accountable in a whole new way.

PACHUL, the filmmakers behind *Fast Runner,* and your average *Idol* applicant have all been trying to work at least partly inside the system—seeking licenses, distribution, approval, permission. They all sought to become that much-vaunted exception to the rule that fuels I'm-Special fantasies. They went as far as they could. And then, for the most part, they were rebuffed.

There is, of course, a world of underground and independent culture where creators do not seek permission to pursue their cultural endeavors. And yet this world too is not immune from the enticements of the pop dream. In the realm of independent culture, the underground and the mainstream are increasingly blurred; mass culture and the new conformity of individuality it preaches infect our best intentions. That explains the recent trend in indie culture to parallel or mimic mainstream notions of celebrity, turning indie into amateur.

Found is a zine that consists entirely of notes, diaries, and photos found by strangers and submitted to the periodical. It sounds obscure, but its creator, Davy Rothbart, managed to parlay the concept into a book published by a big American press and appearances on *The David Letterman Show*. Before he achieved that level of notoriety I caught up with Rothbart on an indie North American *Found* tour. Onstage, the charismatic redhead pulled a crumpled sheet of paper from a large stack. He read a rant that ended, "Why would I take your stuff, when I can get my own? Love, Mom." He selected a communiqué from a jilted lover concluding, "Mario I hate you— You're a fucking liar—p.s. page me later?"

Rothbart is part of an ongoing movement to turn ordinary people into celebrities. The notes he reprints in his *Found* zine are each given a title and thus an identity. Through this process, the anonymous writers are elevated to, within the *Found* world, fame status. "The more you get into these found notes, the more you start quoting them like you would quote a movie," explains Rothbart, who tells us how several of his friends have turned "found moment" punchlines into personal epigraphs.

Another indie periodical, *K Composite*, is a zine-turned-glossy-magazine that features ordinary people in full-color photo spreads complete with celebrity interviews. The latest issue features several personalities, including Brooke Anne Skinner, a twenty-one-year-old who was born in Iowa City, has brown-green eyes, and clocks in at 50 kilograms and 165 centimeters. (This surely must be the only U.S. mag to go metric.) There are multiple portraits of Skinner, from soulful to sultry. The reader learns her thoughts on wearing hats, getting massages, and her job as an up-and-comer at an ad agency.

Then there are PeopleCards, "the official people trading card," each pack containing "7 real people, 1 real artcard, 0 celebrities." There are 120 cards in the first edition of the set, and they feature such real-life individuals as Kathy Ann Pernatt, a.k.a. Looney Tunes, whose motto is "Honesty is the best policy." On the front of the card, Kathy floats in a swimming pool. On the back, we learn that the cheeseburger is her favorite food, orange her favorite color, and her hometown is Chaffee, New York. The PeopleCards manifesto, found on their website, states: "Celebration of individuals in society should focus on real people as often as possible, rather than relying on a handful of predetermined celebrities."

In the paradoxical world of the new conformity, the urge to turn the ordinary into the celebrity has become a motif in independent culture, as if the tidal wave of fame might be somehow averted by a trickling stream going the other way. Even here, in the furthest reaches of independent culture, we can see how projects like Rothbart's are still wrestling with the notion of celebrity and finding a way into mass culture.

Toronto-based indie speakers' series Trampoline Hall has hit upon a popular formula for its monthly gatherings. People are selected (sometimes it seems at random) to speak as if they were experts on subjects that, quite often, they know little or nothing about. The subsequent lectures are often fascinating, mainly because we are not used to seeing speakers take the podium who (1) aren't necessarily comfortable with public speaking, and (2) don't always have that much of interest to say. Inevitably, we in the audience end up thinking: Hey, wait a minute, I could do that. Which is, of course, at least part of the point of the whole exercise.

In the absence of context, the magazine, the cards, the diary, and the found notes are remarkably compelling reading, leaping off the page in a way that prepackaged corporate-encouraged celeb tidbits never can or will. The beauty of this kind of work is its accessibility. "These found notes give us an instant," explains Rothbart, "a sudden and powerful look into people. These are real . . . people laugh but we're not mocking them, we are recognizing ourselves, the pitiful love notes we might have written."

But as the crowd giggles and Rothbart delves into yet another sad, deluded, dysfunctional life that might just as well belong to the guy sitting next to me, I start to wonder about all of this. I mean, what is it exactly: Entertainment? Social criticism? Is it really outside mainstream values, a challenge to the celeb system, or merely a footnote, a way for a bunch of indie-type hipsters to feel as if they are outside the mainstream even as they follow, basically, its forms and values? "I think people are entertained by the notes," Rothbart says. "I don't know. People respond to them because they feel real and true."

THE FEELING OF "TRUE," of finding a way to make prefabricated feel real, is increasingly the business of a rapidly merging amateurunderground-independent culture. Nowhere is this more evident than in the world of karaoke, a worldwide I'm-Special trend that fuses pop's most saccharine and invasive tendencies with the desire of real individuals in real communities to have real participatory outlets for the expression of undeniably real emotions.

"I don't want to spend every night sitting in front of a TV set," says Pat, forty, a Rogers Cable employee waiting for his chance to sing at Nite-Caps, a small pub on Toronto's Dupont Street. "I've been singing since forever. Everybody sings, every child sings."

In Montreal's Club Date, an area hot spot offering karaoke practically every night of the week, Micheline, a pharmacist from the city of Longueuil, explains that singing karaoke is a way to let loose and relax from the pressures of the everyday. Onstage, a nondescript guy in jeans plows methodically through a Talking Heads song. Soon, two women in short skirts laugh their way through a melodramatic tune by Quebec sensation La Chicane, crooning an aging hit called "Juste pour Voir le Monde," about being addicted to singing. At the table next to Micheline is Nathalie, who works in a food shop and has been singing karaoke for ten years. She says that Club Date is the best venue because "no one hassles you." Middle-aged, almost painfully normal-looking, she reiterates what many at these clubs say: She sings karaoke for the no-hassle fun.

Karaoke was developed in Japan as a way for salary men to blow off steam in a culture that struggles with its conformist facade. In a world where people have fewer and fewer avenues in which to publicly express feeling, karaoke might seem to be a temporary remedy for alienation. In the Sofia Coppola film *Lost in Translation,* Bill Murray's fading moviestar character half-jokingly, half-soulfully croons his way through Bryan Ferry's "More than This." Surrounded by newfound Japanese friends and a young woman pal whose friendship he knows can only be brief, Murray's character shows karaoke's ability to encapsulate longing and emptiness while passing itself off as meaningless good times. Even the translation of the Japanese word—"kara" comes from *karappo*, meaning empty, and "oke" is the abbreviation of *okesutura*, or orchestra—suggests a vacuum waiting to be filled.

Dropping in at the XO Karaoke Bar in Toronto, one finds tiny lounges just big enough for groups of five or six to gather on a couch in front of a television screen. Inside one of these rooms are four ESL students—three Japanese women and one Chinese man. They are belting out a line about how they can be "your hero, baby," from Enrique Iglesias's "Hero." In the small room, the mike and amplifier seem unnecessary. Nevertheless, the microphone is passed around with the respect one would give to a talisman or sacred object. The students move on to the Ace of Base tune "All That She Wants." Sheepishly, one of them sings a Japanese love song, accompanied by its own cheesy romantic video. Afterwards, she apologizes to me and her friends for singing a song in Japanese. "It's a break," she says. "I'm always trying to speak English, so it's so stressful. I just do a song or two to relax, it is a reminder of home."

Like a postcard from home, it's a pretty generic reminder. The Japanese song could be any cheesy North American tune. Though exact translation is elusive, the raindrops and soulful grimaces onscreen leave no question about the content. The global pop-music industry has colonized karaoke, replacing varied song lists with rock classics and whatever insta-tunes are currently topping the charts. Even the Asian songs offered at XO are, more often than not, remakes of Western pop-music hits. Clearly the fans care deeply about their karaoke. But when talking to them about why they want to sing karaoke, one often encounters blank stares and muttered, sheepish accounts of how much fun it is, and how it acts as stress relief. It's as if they suspect that deep down their pastime—and, in some cases, obsession—is a paltry substitute for the real thing.

Others admit that karaoke acts as a kind of stand-in for lost opportunity. At Club Date, Kathy, a Montreal homemaker with two kids, reveals that she once thought about pursuing a career in music. "But now I'm too old," she says.

Similarly, Annie at Nite-Caps in Toronto, a once-a-week regular with a big show-tune voice and a fondness for Barbra Streisand songs, admits that, despite her current occupation as a medical secretary, she often thinks of pursuing singing more seriously. At the very least, she says, "I would like to take singing lessons. It would be a nice hobby to have."

Back in the XO booth, one of the Japanese ESL students explains that she played piano for fourteen years and contemplated a career in music. "But I wasn't good enough," she says. "I couldn't compose. So I had to give it up."

But at Nite-Caps, cable installer Pat has no delusions. "This is not existence, this is survival. If this didn't exist there would be an uprising, a rebellion. They have to create something to get you away from your problems. Even if it's only for two or three minutes." Pat looks wistfully around the seedy barroom. "I think about writing my own songs. I've thought about it a million times," he says. "But I'm forty years old, c'mon, let's get real. Sixty thousand fans aren't going to come watch me."

AMERICAN PHILOSOPHER John Dewey wrote that "Communication can alone create a great community." Few in the Western world today would describe their surroundings as a community, let alone a great community. We are connected—yes. Joined together by the glow of the TV screen, the blare of the car-radio stereo, the brush of arms as strangers sit next to each other in the crowded movie theater. We are also connected by the self-esteem movement's message, dispensed on daytime TV, taught in schools, embedded in every pop entertainment, that if you believe in yourself, you can accomplish anything. Ironically, what we seem to most want is to replicate our celebrities. This we cannot have.

We have virtually no access to the mass media, and when we try to circumvent it with schemes as varied as Napster and PeopleCards, we are undermined (or find ourselves already colonized) by the system. Davy Rothbart and Jan Pachul demonstrate that some people don't give up. Force-fed the fattening syrup of self-esteem, we are nevertheless starving, hungry to graze amid the pastures of fame. To give up would be to admit that the pop dream that is so much a part of our lives is a lie. For an ever-growing number of people, life has come to mean achieving the pop dream. In the schools, they call it self-esteem; in leftist cliques, they call it hedonism; and in New Age circles, they call it personal spirituality. What it amounts to is the new conformity——the search for a way in.

Ultimately, we end up extending our lust for the real thing. Rather than debunking the celebrity myth, indie projects and the amateur universe of karaoke simply add another layer to the celeb game, another component in the overall project of devaluing normal life. Trying to explain the appeal of found notes, Rothbart says that "there's universal experiences, feelings, emotions, and so you sense the commonality . . . at the same time each person's stories have a little twist that makes their story individual." The global experiment that is pop culture can be described similarly. Pop, too, taps into the well of communal experience while promising every person the right to add his or her own flavor to the water.

Compelling as they are, karaoke, the found notes, Trampoline Hall, the PeopleCards, and *K Composite* do not offer real glimpses into the human soul. Nevertheless, they show another side of the fandom/pop-culture nexus: its good side. Too small to be shut down or repressed, projects like these give us new ways to understand the pop experience as fleeting, memorable yet forgettable, unifying, and accessible to all. They may not represent genuine dissent, but they do show the way we can create smaller systems of inclusion that, if nothing else, open ourselves to the unexpected quirks and quarks of other like-minded, similarly colonized people around the world. However, the most important question remains unanswered: Can homogenized pop culture ever reflect our inherent need to be recognized as particular individuals from particular communities?

PART THREE

THE PARADOX OF INDIVIDUALITY

3

5

"WHO ELSE IS ME?"

FINDING OUR OWN SPECIAL ROLES

L OU PEARLMAN SITS, Buddha-like, behind a messy desk. Young men in their twenties wander in and out, sprawl on his leather couches, talk shit. This is the scene at Orlando, Florida-based Trans Continental, an outwardly shabby suburban industrial park office that, for a time, was the world center of bubblegum pop. Lou Pearlman didn't just manage but actually fabricated out of thin air three of the bestselling bands of all time. As creator of the boy bands The Backstreet Boys, *NSYNC, and LFO, Pearlman sold a combined 41 million records and radically altered the landscape of pop culture.

It all started when Pearlman was running a plane-leasing company and found himself renting a jet to the members of the boy band New Kids on the Block. How can these kids afford to rent a plane, Pearlman wondered. The rest, as they say, is history.

Pearlman's latest act is that American band with the giant German following, Natural.

"We're putting the *band* back in boy band," he says. At a time when the bad-kid image of Eminem, Pink, and Avril Lavigne dominates (and even young girl idol Hilary Duff is seeking a sexier image) this new act is Pearlman's attempt to engineer another hit without abandoning his trademark formula of five clean-cut boys singing about love.

"The bottom line is that the guys can sing," Pearlman tells me. "We cultivate them, but we don't give them their vocal cords. They weren't manufactured, they really sing. Natural came to me, they played their own instruments."

Despite the new twist—the band actually plays instruments!—Pearlman is sticking with his tried-and-tested formula of different boy archetypes making up each group. In other words, each carefully constructed band has a jock, a clean-cut type, a bad boy, a Latin lover . . . "I invented the concept," he announces. "The concept is that the girls don't want the same person, they want different people in the band. You have to see what the fans are looking for, build and create that."

Pearlman didn't invent the concept of forming groups of boys into potent pop juggernauts—there were canny managers behind the Monkees and the Sex Pistols. Most notably, original manager Andrew Loog Oldham lays claim to creating the Rolling Stones' enduring image, their look and sound. The members of that iconic boy band are still going strong at age sixty, but Oldham's ability to see rock 'n' roll in terms of an ongoing performance, script and all, falls slightly short of what goes on at Pearlman's Trans Continental office. Pearlman's twist is the total co-opting of personality. He delves into the psyches of his young performers, seeking to define personality and micro-manage behavior.

According to Pearlman, the pubescent girls he intends Natural to attract are looking for bland but nevertheless discernable personalities. Pearlman's genius is not rooted in music but in the idea of actually predetermining the roles within the band. Each boy gets his personality handed to him on a silver platter. A Trans Continental hairdresser once explained to a reporter how talent was developed at the Orlando nerve center: "Lou would say, 'This is the heart throb; this is the Latin guy,' and we'd create that with the hair. Then there's the innocent guy, who we give a softer look to, more combed down." Pearlman found his model challenged by a new breed of teen idols that may be no less contrived, but, like a Tommy Hilfiger shirt minus the logo, do a better job of conveying the appearance of nonconformity. "That's a fad," Pearlman snaps at the mention of Eminem, white rapper from the wrong side of the tracks. He explains that the boy band will be in style "as long as God keeps making little girls." He also talks about a few new ventures prompted by the thousands of unsolicited demo tapes he gets every year from teens begging to be morphed by him into the next great supergroup. One such venture is the launch of a product called "Making A Hit," which he describes as "a home recording unit with mike and video instructions on how to make your own demo." Another plan involves a website hosting service that wannabe pop stars can inhabit "for a one-time fee. We modify it, maintain it, add the photos you want, various snippets from songs." According to Pearlman, his website has the edge over do-it-yourself sites because "Professionals visit it, talent agencies."

Does Pearlman feel any responsibility for the millions of teens he hopes to encourage to "make a hit" with his new product and service? Like Don Wood from the Hard Rock Academy, he insists that failure is irrelevant. He argues that teens will take the experience of "making a hit" and apply it to some other aspect of their lives. What other aspect of life replaces the über-dream of total celebrity, total individuality? What substitute is there for a limo ride and the Hard Rock stage?

Never mind. Lou is anxious to get to the Natural photo shoot happening down the hall. Natural is leaving tomorrow for a tour of Germany. "Number two in Germany right now," Pearlman brags. "Their album broke big there first, just like *NSYNC."

In a large studio, a photographer is adjusting fans, trying to get just the right breeze on a member of the band. The young man at the center of attention is shirtless. A fog machine belches menacing atmosphere, meant to swirl around him. He is supposed to be the bad boy. Pearlman immediately sees a scratch on his stomach and yells for makeup. While we wait for makeup, Pearlman adjusts the boy's pants to cover his underwear. "You can't sell the Calvin Klein

logo," he says. The boys' girlfriends and families look on, mill about
the sidelines. Finally, makeup is dabbed. Meanwhile, Pearlman tells
the photographer that the lighting is wrong. "You can't see the cuts
in his stomach," he points out, indicating the shadow falling over the
boy's abdominal muscles. Another member of the band is trying to
convince a matronly handler that he has time to run to McDonald's.
The members of Natural are old enough to be superstars, but not
old enough to have a glass of wine in the state of Florida. "I tell
them," Pearlman revealed earlier, "when you go platinum, then you
can get tattoos. Until then . . ." The lights are readjusted, fans are
reoriented, and the girls retreat back to the sidelines. Pearlman sur-
veys the scene, grabs some tissue, and blots at the Natural kid's
stomach. Then he too retreats. While the photographer fires away,
Lou loudly explains the concept to the rest of the band. "They see
you onstage, then they see the poster after the show and they buy
it immediately." The boys of Natural nod. "Tighten up!" Lou yells at
the kid on the podium. "Tighten up!"

TO WATCH NATURAL in rehearsal is to be confronted with the paradox the band represents. These young men grew up in a theme-
park world and can do nothing more than articulate its assertion of
clichéd adventure. They want to be "real," but they have no sense of
what real experience might feel like. Like the many who have
grown up or are now growing up cradled by pop culture and prefab
fun, they are part of a world where real is relative, where everything is performance. Natural is polished, choreographed, stylized.
Tightened up. Listening to these boys sing is like watching the
crowds move through nearby Disneyland. There are plenty of sen-
timental guitar and keyboard solos, lots of four- and five-part harmonies. I lose track of how many songs use the words *oh baby*. Like
the group's name, the lyrics are unintentionally funny: One chorus
involves the band crooning about being "too human being human."
The room tenses noticeably when the band starts into its hit single
"Put Your Arms Around Me." "Top Ten in the U.S. and number one
in Lebanon and the Philippines," one of the Natural boys proudly

tells us, his audience of adoring family and friends. The song is, of course, insipid. I can imagine the twelve-year-olds swooning. By fourteen, they'll be embarrassed. "Put your arms around me," the boys churn soulfully.

While Natural plays, I notice how each young man is different but the same, not unlike Florida's theme-park rides, not unlike the band's tunes—every one saturated with lush harmonies and calculated to instill maximum levels of unrequited desire in the audience. When I talk to the boys of Natural, they give me pat responses. They love Lou. They love their band. They're just regular guys. Not yet in their twenties, they are already their own best public relations machine, spouting what they know they are supposed to say, their words a perfect match for their charming smiles and spiky hairdos.

In the quest for celebrity (and the automatic "individuality" it confers like a Get out of Jail Free card), the boys seem devoid of genuine personality. Pearlman has it all mapped out for them. Do what I say, be who I want you to be, and you will attain fame. The boys are willing. They strain their muscles and have their scratches obscured by makeup. So far it's working. They are already being mobbed by teenage German fräuleins. One member of the band tells me about the overseas craziness of their last European tour: girls staked out their limo, slept on the street in front of their villa, climbed the fence, and snuck into their living room. Such stories are part of the legend in the making. The boys of Natural recite their numbers like a mantra. Top Ten in the United States, number one in the Philippines, big—very, very big—in Deutschland.

A Certain Way of Life: Some Theories on the Nature of Individuality

Natural represents a natural endpoint for the phenomenon of conformist individuality. In order to attain ultimate individuality, the band members must dispense with . . . individuality. They must play a role. The role is that of normal-plus, the normal of special. Such is the paradoxical effect of the new conformity on our conception of individuality. Each step of Natural's journey on the road to fame is carefully monitored, noted, and adjusted according to a prearranged plan. Individuality becomes a goal to be framed by rules and regulations and measured in predetermined plans and models. The paradox of "natural" is the paradox of having to follow a communal and well-travelled path in order to arrive at individuality.

States social scholar Ulrich Beck:

> In modern life, the individual is confronted on many levels with the following challenge: You may and you must lead your own independent life, outside the old bonds of family, tribe, religion, origin and class; and you must do this within the new guidelines and rules which the state, the job market, the bureaucracy, lay down.

The Princeton professor of psychology Hadley Cantril noted as early as 1941 that almost every individual was born into a highly organized society. "Almost all the experiences which constitute his life are likely to be prescribed roughly for him by the particular culture within which his life happens to be lived." Cantril softened the blow, and ceded that some small changes to the way society operates were still possible:

> To be sure, the individual will develop the capacity to select alternate courses of action. He may also set about changing some characteristics of his culture which are by no means to his liking. But still this selection and this desire to alter certain practices are themselves bounded and determined by the original conditions imposed by a certain way of life.

What are the conditions imposed on us, what is the "certain way of life" that constitutes our particular existence in postmodern capitalist society? De Tocqueville's 1835 travelogue/social study *Democracy in America* points us in the right direction. The author's primary observation concerned the way the political and economic system of the United States was creating a new kind of individuality. As he saw it, freedom American style was forcing everyone into their shells, with their social framework reduced to immediate family and friends, and their only interest personal success. De Tocqueville wrote of an "innumerable multitude of men all equal and alike, incessantly endeavoring to procure the petty and paltry pleasures with which they glut their lives. Each of them, living apart, is as a stranger to the fate of all the rest."

De Tocqueville's description of early North American society is as accurate today as it was then. We members of the affluent West are relatively indifferent to anything other than ourselves and those closest to us. Most of us ignore social issues, the plight of strangers, the workings of government, the degradation of the environment. Voting rates in elections are declining precipitously. After several decades of supposedly mounting concern regarding the environment and climate change, the most popular vehicle in North America in 2003 was . . . the gas-guzzling, smog-spewing SUV.

In an intensely segmented, defined, and organized society, individuality has come to have an increasingly narrow application— what's in it for me? Notes conservative pundit Wendy Shalit about our anything-goes age: "Today we may all be independent, but are we really free in a society where we can only commit to ourselves?"

If we depend on anything, it is the largely bureaucratic structure that shapes our increasingly atomized, solitary lives. So it is that the appearance of independence is underscored by a vast world of regulation and restriction. "We might have lost the imagination of alternatives, but we scarcely worry because we are more than compensated in the here and now," Keith Tester argues in his book *Moral Culture*. "We lose the freedom to be different, but gain the freedom to lose ourselves in the pleasure of the world of commodities, domesticated arts and entertaining spectacles." True feeling, true discovery, is replaced with pretend excitement in the form of mass culture. Our inherent need to explore and adventure, to partially separate ourselves from the group, today emerges in the form of pop-culture ambition. Millions buy into the Hard Rock Academy, take home Lou Pearlman's Making A Hit kit, and find their dreams converted into prepackaged pop songs. On TV is Natural—boldly going where many have gone, and many more wish to go.

Trapped? Power and Foucault

The shared anxieties of thinkers as diverse as Beck, Shalit, and Tester are fairly common. In a regimented, isolating world set up largely to ease the way for individual striving, we are free, primarily, to be all alone. The result is the paradox: intense individuality fenced in by intense regulation that breeds intense conformism— in the form of pseudo-individuality.

The French philosopher Michel Foucault articulates the great philosophy of postmodern life. He is concerned, primarily, with power. Foucault's genius is to show us how power is concentrated within the diversity of systems, rather than located in a single king, court, army, or pope. The quasi-democratic capitalist states we live in cannot be changed by electing a new prime minister or blowing up the stock exchange. For Foucault, power is embodied in the systems themselves, each institution capable of regenerating elsewhere, should it be cut off. "Power and knowledge directly imply one another," writes Foucault. "There is no power relation without the correlative constitution of a field of knowledge, nor any knowledge that does not presuppose and constitute at the same time power relations." For Foucault, far from embodying freedom and individuality, the postmodern state embodies unrestricted power. It's a power that is particularly insidious: It is outside of the control of any single leader or individual; it is also made up not of obvious and often grotesque exertions of power and control such as public executions, but of bureaucracy and procedure—tiny invisible assertions of control perhaps best represented by the supermax out-of-sight solitary-confinement prison system found today in the United States.

In his classic Discipline and Punish, Foucault describes the individual as being "already the effect of a subjection much more profound than himself." He adds:

> A "soul" inhabits him and brings him to existence, which is itself a factor in the mastery that power exercises over the body. The soul is the effect and instrument of a political anatomy; the soul is the prison of the body.

For Foucault, the soul is created by the confluence of power and knowledge—religious institutions, governments, ideologies. As a result, the soul is corrupted, trapped in its time, an "instrument of a political anatomy." In the pop lexicon, we understand the reverse to be true. Everything from religion to mass culture will tell you that the body may be enslaved in the gulag, the concentration camp, the assembly line, or the faceless cubicle, but the soul inevitably sets the body free. Foucault sees an opposite reality. We are free to alter our surface personality and our surface circumstances. We can surgically improve our looks, we can—as rapper Eminem supposedly did—exchange a life on the wrong side of the tracks with pop fame and riches. But because our souls are subjected and bound to the systems we live in, any surface change we perform is always within the confines of intense bureaucracy and regulation. What we can't do is truly articulate a freedom devoid of the constraints of society. What we can't do is evoke an individuality that has not already been implanted in us by a combination of state-sanctioned regulation and the wish-fulfillment fantasies of our pop culture.

Ideas such as the freedom of the soul and the individualist rebel are, essentially, built into the system. There is no clear way to move outside the system, because everything we know *is* the system. Essayist Tim Parks puts the paradox this way:

> The vociferous declaration of dissatisfaction together with the tacit acceptance of authority is the conjuring trick of contemporary conformity; this explains how people can crowd into a cinema to see an anti-establishment movie (but every movie is anti-establishment) and *all* agree with it.

AT A FESTIVAL of underground culture and publishing I helped to organize, I included on our festival survey this question: "In what way do you consider yourself to be an individual?" The answers were as clear as they were ambivalent. Martin asks: "Who else is me?" Debbie writes: "Because I care what people think of me but I do what I want anyway." Smart-ass Daniel says: "By proxy." Cheryl: "My ever changing sexual identity and hair style." Sara: "I (mostly) go my own way." While this is hardly a conclusive sampling of the population of North America, I think the answers connote the kind of confusion around individuality that the new conformity represents. What is the right answer? There isn't a right answer. So how do we know we are really and truly us? The survey answers reflect our ongoing tension and ambivalence regarding the nature of contemporary individuality. *"Who else is me?"*

"Every individual is partly someone else," wrote Freud, "there is always something else in an individual besides himself." Early French psychologist Pierre Janet went even further, arguing: "The persons we live among give us a certain social function and force us to fulfill it. They attribute a particular character to us and often educate us in order that we preserve this character." Put Freud and Janet together and you have a good idea of how the individual has been colonized. Today the "something else" inside us is the pop dream. Could this explain why so many of us seem to have someone else's generic ambition gnawing a hole in our cerebellum from the inside out? So it is that we love and hate our celebrities, collect the details of their lives the way an entomologist watches a rare species of butterfly. But, increasingly, we seem to want to pin our celebrities to the specimen tray, more than we want to observe them in the wild. We want to rip off their wings and glue them to our own backs.

What we inherit and absorb from our society isn't necessarily up to us. Georg Simmel, writing in post-First World War, pre-Nazi Germany at a time of great cultural foment, seemingly could not decide if society was a colonizing force challenging our primal individuality, or vice versa. For instance, he notes that fashion combines "the attraction of differentiation and change with that of similarity and conformity." Score one for oppressive mass-culture society and the beginnings of Natural and the new conformity. But he concludes that the struggle between content and form, between personhood and prepackaged individuality as sold by an industry like fashion will ultimately be won by the individual: "Life refuses to be governed by anything subordinate to itself, but it also refuses to be governed at all."

Were Simmel around today, he might not be quite so optimistic. Add a dash of genocidal history and Foucault to Simmel's thinking and the conclusion is different. Life cannot triumph over mass culture (form) as expressed in the world we live in; it can only be subservient to it. The boys of Natural disappear into their own prefab myth.

The Gullible Crowd

In the twenty-first century, the individual seems doomed to a quest for an individuality that itself is more a product of the power relations of an essentially conformist and elaborately micromanaged society than an authentic expression of true human need. This is our world: focus groups, elaborate surveillance gear, a single televised sporting event beamed simultaneously into a billion homes. We are alone and on our own as never before. But we are also intimately part of the collective. Every aspect of our life is watched over, chronicled, legislated, recorded, and turned into a massive database on the likes, needs, habits, desires, and activities of millennial *Homo sapiens*. How did we get ourselves into this paradoxical state?

Two nineteenth-century French thinkers help us find the source for at least some of the confusion around what an individual is or should be today. First came Gustave Le Bon, who believed that the 18th-century Enlightenment and its political reforms—liberty, fraternity, and equality for all—had separated the mass from its natural tendency to be ruled by what he called the "intellectual aristocracy." In his 1895 text *The Crowd,* Le Bon began a new field of study: how to psychologically control large groups of people. Le Bon characterized the masses as an intrinsically dangerous, unpredictable, and irrational rabble. But he also suggested that because of and despite their volatility, crowds could be manipulated. "Whatever be the ideas suggested to crowds," noted Le Bon, "they can only exercise effective influence on condition that they assume a very absolute, uncompromising, shape." Le Bon, father of mass psychology and patron saint of propaganda, had a clarion call that would come to affect future billions: *Dumb it down!*

Le Bon's theories found plenty of attention, not to mention sympathetic followers. Foremost among them was Gabriel Tarde, who compared the crowd's actions to an epileptic fit. Tarde's early writings were on criminology. He worked as a judge and headed an office that compiled statistics on crime for the ministry of justice. There he observed that most criminals he encountered were just copycats lacking innovation. Tarde believed society to be "a group of beings who are apt to imitate one another." He pictured the masses sleepwalking through life, noting that "society is imitation and imitation is a kind of somnambulism."

Similarly, in the second half of the 1800s, the first French media critics, figures like Legrand du Saulle and Despine, warned against the "moral contagion" in which the press publicizes crimes and sensational stories that are immediately imitated. Despine actually went so far as to formulate a maxim that essentially said the masses are susceptible to sentiment—they will copy whatever they are shown or told. The famed Romanian-born social psychologist Serge Moscovici, who has spent the past thirty years looking at the implications of collective decision, deftly and disdainfully sums up the model of mass irrationality that the crowd psychology of the nineteenth century constructed:

> Conformity is the distinctive quality of mass man. He conforms because he is suggestible. Once suggestible, he submits to ideas and emotions of which he was unaware, rising up from the depths of his psyche. Half asleep, he plunges into the mysterious world of dreams, which he takes for reality. He copies automatically, obeys somnabulistically, and together with the rest, flows with the human tide.

Tarde took the cliché of the suggestible crowd and began to extend ideas around how the crowd could be manipulated. His familiarity with statistics and bureaucracy led him to believe that one might extrapolate from statistics to arrive at facts that can be used to characterize and thus influence a specific group. This methodology can be seen as the beginning of marketing, the start of precision propaganda. Le Bon and Tarde's reduction of the crowd to a purposeless impressionable beast that wants only to be fed—and will eat anything—created the fundamentals of mass-culture manipulation. Le Bon and Tarde encouraged the rulers and taste-defining tycoons of industry to ignore what the people in the crowd might actually want by pronouncing that crowds are by nature crazy and hysterical. It followed that the crowd was open to manipulation for the crowd's own good. The crowd, faceless and sometimes dangerous, must be picked apart, studied, made to obey.

Tarde also developed a model by which to extend this conception of the crowd into everyday life. Tarde articulated a mass described as a "spiritual collectivity, a dispersion of individuals who are physically separated and whose cohesion is entirely mental." *Mental cohesion*—sounds pleasant, doesn't it? Riffing off the Romantic notion of each person being accorded a separate place by the Industrial Revolution—which, indeed, gave each person a solitary (if not so special) job to perform—Tarde noted how the morning papers set the agenda for the day's conversation, and wrote of the "increasing similarity of simultaneous conversations in an ever more vast geographic domain." In the same era, the American playwright Oswald W. Firkins, writing in the *Atlantic Monthly*, compared people being packed in "solid and uniform rows for the enjoyment of a common experience" to the "simultaneous perusal of the newspapers and the magazine." Eureka! The sheep can be sheared even as they graze. "We sit in a crowd," Firkins wrote, "even by our own firesides."

When Georg Simmel ruminated on the meaning of individuality, he identified two modern conceptions of what an individual is. He noted that the Enlightenment "sought individuality in the form of freedom, the lack of every kind of restraint of personal powers, regardless whether this restraint came from estates or from the church, whether it was political or economic." In this kind of individualism, "even national integration recedes behind the idea of 'mankind.' The particularistic rights of status groups and of circles are deplaced in principle by the rights of the individual, and these, quite significantly, are called 'human rights.'" But by the increasingly industrialized nineteenth century, a different and contradictory conception of individuality emerges out of what Simmel identifies as Romanticism and its "practical expression in the ascendancy of the division of labor." This conception of individualism believes that there is a unique place for each person, and that the goal of the individual is to assume a position "he and no one else can fill." In this kind of individualization, "the personal and social, the psychological and metaphysical meaning of human existence is realized in this immutability of being, this intensified differentiation of performance."

From the Renaissance and the Enlightenment emerges this idea of human rights, of a humankind in which each person deserves to be free and uplifted. But in the Romantic period that coincided with the arrival of the Industrial Revolution, we get the idea of specialization—that each person has a unique destiny, a place where he or she fits like a cog into the great machine of life. This second conception of individuality allowed for the engine of commerce, with its standardization and rote roles, to advance into society without challenging the Enlightenment ideal of individual human dignity, which was now enshrined in society. Starting largely in the nineteenth century, entire disparate branches of human thought—from economics to demographics to psychology—sought to reconcile the differing conceptions of the noble individual and the conformist individual—special, but nevertheless part of the crowd.

Tarde and his ilk sought, then, a reconciliation of the two great notions of modern individuality under democratic capitalism: You are at once permanently a member of the crowd, and permanently your own special individual. You have both the inalienable sacred rights of personhood, and the special place where you belong in the vast ant colony of human life. The individual, at that point, became both part of the mass, dangerous and deluded and in need of guidance, and standard-bearer of a new world where each and every one of us deserves equal treatment and is equally capable of logic and rational thought.

The mass-media system integrates newspapers, magazines, radio, and television into everyday life and comes complete with slogans, jingles, and memorable pop moments, each one seemingly spontaneous and individually empowering but actually carefully researched and derived from an ever-growing body of knowledge on the manipulation of crowds. Disdain for the masses à la Le Bon and Tarde was transferred into the contemporary program of manipulation, hype, and public relations. The science of keeping us alone in the gullible crowd began to make impressive leaps forward.

Edward Bernays, in his 1947 essay "The Engineering of Consent," embodied the lessons of Le Bon and Tarde when he argued that advertising could transcend mere shilling for products and actually set the agenda for society. "The engineer of consent must create the news," wrote Bernays. "To be successful, the themes must appeal to the motives of the public. Motives are the activation of both conscious and subconscious pressures created by the force of desires." And so our motives are activated, our desires stimulated in the form of James Bond movies, the apartments of our television "friends," reality-TV instant millionaire shows, constant celebrity updates and, of course, an endless accompaniment of ads that no longer talk about a product but instead talk about us—how special we are, how we deserve the best, how we should "just do it."

Today, advertising, the media, and pop entertainment are all intertwined, interchangeable. We are appealed to in the same moment as individuals and troop members. My wife comes home with a kit of lotions, a present from a friend. Each comes adorned with its own philosophy, because the lotion company is called *philosophy*. The "philosophy" of exfoliating foot cream reads (devoid of capitalization) as follows:

> let's review your only true assets. you own your values, your integrity, your thoughts, your words, your actions and therefore, your destiny. questions: are you proud of what you own? what is your true net worth to the world and the people around you? are you really rich or do you just have money?

Never in my life did I imagine exfoliating foot cream to be imbued with that kind of profundity. Never in my life could I imagine a bigger load of bullshit squeezed into such a thin little tube. Foucault tells us and Natural shows us that the foot cream's devotion to the soul is a sham: We own and control what happens with our houses, our cars, and our feet soothed by expensive foot cream. The one thing that we don't own, that we don't possess, that can't be charged on MasterCard and protected through hiring private security, are our values, thoughts, and integrity. These are assets compromised and invaded by the paradoxical creation of a herd-like individuality that is today exemplified by the success of lotions adorned with moral maxims.

6

THE SEARCH FOR HOME
COMMUNITY REINVENTED

Neo-Traditional Community

TORONTO, SUMMER 2002. Half a million young Catholics and their chaperones from around the world are in Canada's biggest city for a week of events dubbed World Youth Day (WYD). The counter-attraction, Alternative World Youth Day, draws about twenty people. But I'm not surprised. Young Catholics aren't in Toronto to have their faith questioned and challenged. They are here to remind themselves that they are not alone, to reaffirm centuries-old traditions with like-minded souls from around the world. They want to see their spiritual leader, the Pope.

At Alternative World Youth Day, young Catholics don't want to see the Pope. They want to confront him. The four young people in their twenties on the panel discussion I am attending at the downtown Church of the Holy Trinity blame their religious leaders for a host of worldwide problems: the spread of AIDS, poverty, sexual abuse of choirboys, vilification of homosexuals. "The religious hierarchy has remained the same," says Maria of Mexico. "The mentality and ideology on reproduction has not changed since the Middle Ages." Tobias from Germany offers up a manifesto on how the

Church should change; he advocates increased honesty, communi-cation, and democracy.

Fifteen minutes or so into the alternative talk, a gaggle of eight World Youth Day attendees quietly file in and take seats. They are American teenagers wearing tank tops, shorts, stars-and-stripes bandanas. Are they doubters, concerned about the direction of the Church? The manifestos from impassioned panelists continue, but I am distracted by the glowing tans of these new additions to the scant audience. The girls have "save the babies" etched in pen in their arms. The boys have "JPII" scrawled in marker down the sides of their legs. Something tells me that these particular audience members are not here to open their minds to dialogue.

"You see all these pilgrims," Tobias is saying. "They have the same shirt, the same badge, and it looks like the 1930s. And I'm from that country and I don't want to say it, but they are cheering for some-thing they don't know, they don't understand."

The pilgrims, blond and blue-eyed, are all dressed pretty much the same: Nikes, Gap shorts, T-shirts, baseball caps. They hold onto their red-and-beige WYD bags for dear life as they listen in disbe-lief, their expressions contorted between disgust and confusion. The Canadian delegate outlines the problems she has with the Church's stand on abortion. The WYD blonds murmur intensely. I can see agony and anger on their smooth faces.

Finally, the earnest speeches end and the panel invites questions. A prim woman in her fifties stands up. The WYD kids stop whisper-ing. I realize that she is the group's chaperone. She says that she's from Arizona and that where she comes from it's clear that abor-tion does much more harm than good and that the babies need to be saved. Her group bursts into applause.

Tobias says he totally disagrees. He says that the World Youth Day organizers should have put condoms in the bags of all the partici-pants. The Arizona kids twist on their seats, visibly antagonized. Constance, her tan body bursting out of a tank top and white shorts, leaps up to take the microphone. "Why do you call your-selves Catholics? Why don't you just become Protestants?" She doesn't wait for the answer. "You're missing the point," she screeches into the microphone. "Don't you understand? Abortion is murder!" With that, the group jumps up en masse and storms out of the talk. "Save the babies!" they yell as they go. "We're going to hear the Pope!"

I chase the group outside, where they gather in the sun, their faces flushed with indignant triumph.

Why did you come here today? I ask them.

A tanned blond girl answers fervently: "We came because we want to know what they're saying so we can pray for them and to see how many people are actually here."

"I came to see what they're talking about, not to shout them down," explains another girl in the group. "But we care about what we believe, we're trying to help, see what their opinion is. We're going to say what we think. We aren't brainwashed, we volunteer. We're not being forced, we're all confirmed, we're doing this on our own."

But don't the critics have a point, I ask them. Doesn't the Church need to reconsider its positions on sexual matters, particularly with the recent scandals about Catholic priests molesting children?

"The Church makes mistakes," a young man blurts out. "No"— he corrects himself—"the Church doesn't make mistakes. We're all sinners, we're not perfect, we can't expect anyone to be perfect like God."

Their chaperone announces that it's time for her group of young Arizona Catholics to move on. The sun glints off their shaded glasses, casts halos over blond heads. They stride off in unison. In a few hours, the Pope will be leading a mass just for these young people. Watching them, I can't help but feel jealous. They believe in something. It's more than many of us can say.

The Neo-Traditionalist Movement

In these days of pop-saturated self-obsession, there are still those who find succor and meaning in tradition. Though fewer and fewer in number, those who seek out tradition in the new world order of individualist conformity adopt the code with an intensity and fervor that seems jarring. Who are these people and where do they emerge from? Very often, they dress like us, they look like us, they seem to have all the same influences as us. But are they not instilled, as most of their peers are, with the triumphant greatness of the individual as preached through a million pop-culture products? They follow a leader, a code, a god, and they give their lives meaning not by seeking to attain control of their narrative and reshaping it as pop fodder, but through the opposite: by relinquishing it.

The neo-traditionalist movement is relatively difficult to document. It can manifest itself in phenomena as stark as a secular lefty suddenly joining a restrictive sect, and as vague as the movement toward "family values." In fact, as a *Harper's* commentator writes, "A lot of the action that is interpreted by the mainstream media as a return to faith has been a clamorous shift from the lame liberal theologies to the more righteous infuriated evangelisms." In other words, much of the neo-traditional movement is made up of those who have watched their religions transformed into social clubs and ended up seeking out more radical ideologies that could protect them from the relativisms of the new conformity.

They may be difficult to categorize, they may represent a relatively small percentage of the population when compared with their now conventional I'm-Special peers, but the neo-traditionalists have a big impact on society. In the U.S., slowly but surely the neo-tradionalists have managed to influence who gets elected, what gets taught in schools, what gets sold in stores, and what rights people are going to have in order to make decisions about their own bodies and lives. The new traditionalists represent a wider movement that encompasses the many of us who can't help but feel the vacuity of our times; neo-traditionalism thrives on the collective post-millennial sense that something is missing in contemporary technological society—some purpose and connection that our ancestors seemed to have, but we most obviously lack.

Returning to the Past

Perhaps the most noted and extreme neo-traditionalist of recent times is John Walker Lindh, who left a permissive California upbringing and his dreams of being a rapper to become first a fundamentalist Muslim studying with a mullah in Pakistan, and then a Taliban freedom fighter battling the Americans in Afghanistan. "In the U.S. I feel alone," Lindh said by way of explaining his career choice as a Muslim warrior in Pakistan and Afghanistan. "Here I feel comfortable and at home."

How does a twenty-year-old from California who should have been dropping E and swaying to the beat in a pair of baggy pants end up obsessed with an Islam he calls home? Lindh's longing for the simple, unthinking strictures of old-style conformity is acute, palpable, desperate. His explanation for leaving the United States and adopting a fundamentalist religion is heartbreaking, a damning condemnation of pseudo-individualist society: He felt alone. Lindh was said to have slept on a rope bed in his teacher's study, which had no hot water and where there was no electricity after 10 P.M. According to one report: "He peppered the mufti with questions about the devout life: 'Should I recite verses in a soft voice or a loud one? While I am worshipping, how should I hold my hands?'" In giving up his individuality to accept the seemingly medieval conventions of orthodoxy, he is an enigma to the North American mainstream. As *Newsweek* incredulously puts it: "Most teenagers, when they rebel, say they want more freedom. John Walker Lindh rebelled against freedom."

It's worth noting that Lindh started on his journey to Islam by pretending to be African-American, communicating in inner-city vernacular on internet chat groups. A schoolmate described him as being "really into hip-hop music . . . one of those guys who acted like a gangster, like a black tough guy." Lindh was turning away from himself, from the complexities of moving from a churchgoing Virginia family (like me, he came of age in the conservative suburbs of Washington, D.C.) to a nondenominational liberal California teenhood with little or nothing to tell him about who or what he was or should be. In another day and age, Lindh might have been able to find the guidance he needed in the repressive rules of American family and religious life. But Lindh couldn't hack the age of individuality. His personal choice was to reject the bewildering array of personal choices ushered in by modernity and well represented in middle-class California. Like pop-star-turned-Muslim Cat Stevens, Lindh exchanged West Coast good times for Islamic orthodoxy. In a quest to rebel against the nothingness of all-encompassing freedom, Lindh joined Islam, found brotherhood in the Taliban, and banished individualism's most common by-product—loneliness. Like many of those who exercise their freedom by abandoning it, he paid a terrible price. John Walker Lindh, charged with conspiring to murder Americans and assist foreign terrorist organizations, accepted a plea bargain and is now serving a twenty-year sentence in a U.S. jail. But he also sent a message: In an age when individuals are expected to make their own meaning, people will do just that, often to extremes that expose the churning insecurities under the surface of a seemingly content society.

JOHN WALKER LINDH may seem like the freakish exception, but the move from unfettered liberal to claustrophobic fundamentalist is not as exceptional as it first seems. Since Lindh was accidentally discovered in the battlefields of Afghanistan, the phenomenon of the middle class neo-traditionalist living in the relative lap of luxury suddenly turning to radical ideology and eventually violence is becoming recognized. The September 11th hijackers were middle class or even, like the perpetually elusive Osama Bin Laden, from rich influential families. The suicide bombers who attacked the London public transit system in the summer of 2005 weren't outside radicals imported to wreak havoc – they were British citizens whose sudden radical turn to extreme faith perplexed their friends and surprised their families.

Despite the seeming novelty of Lindh's conversion, his actions have many precedents, though unless they lead to acts of destruction most such shifts go unnoticed in the public sphere. A dramatic conversion some may recall involves Shelly Pennefather, one of the world's greatest female basketball players. She set extraordinary records at Pennsylvania's Villanova University in the mid-eighties, leading the team to back-to-back championships. Then she headed to Japan, where she earned a six-figure salary as the star on the number-one women's professional team in that country. Abruptly, she gave away all her money and joined an order of cloistered nuns in Alexandria, Virginia. Not only did she enter a convent, but one of the most austere religious orders in the world. The Colettine Poor Clares "sleep no longer than four hours at a time, eat one full meal a day and don't use phones, TVs, radios or any publications except religious texts," says the *Atlanta Journal-Constitution*. "They sleep on a bed of straw; they're barefoot except for an hour each day, when they don sandals to walk into the courtyard, where they're allowed to converse with each other." Ironically, Shelly's sudden departure from secular life only makes the media want her more. Well over a decade after her entry into the cloister, her mother and six siblings are still turning down requests for interviews, including ESPN's desire to do a twenty-minute feature on Shelly as part of their 2003 Women's Final Four broadcast.

Most conversions are far less radical. A friend of mine went from non-practicing Jew living in a co-ed dorm at an East Coast liberal arts college to living in Israel and studying full-time at an Orthodox yeshiva. And yet he returns home to the suburbs of Washington, D.C. frequently, has not rejected his non-religious family, and is also pursuing a career as a writer of secular fiction. His shift mirrors my own brother's adoption of Orthodox Jewish conventions: Today he keeps kosher, spends long hours in synagogue, doesn't drive or turn on lights or watch TV from sundown Friday to sundown Saturday, and occasionally tries to get me and my parents to do likewise. But he also works as a lawyer, loves the Food Network, and subscribes to *People* magazine.

The shift to neo-traditionalism is borne out in many different ways. For instance, it has been noted that after decades of trying to fit in, Muslims in many Western countries are returning to a fundamentalist version of their faith. These are the children of immigrant parents whose main goal was to assimilate. Fauzaya Talhaoui was once the only Muslim woman member of the Belgian parliament. Of her generation turning to Islam, she says: "They took the view—if you want to treat us differently, we will act differently." In other words, if the Western Muslims find they cannot get full status as secular citizens, if they find they cannot compete in the I'm-Special sweepstakes, why not carve out a religious enclave? In doing so, they lay claim not to the Western-infused individuality that puts them at a disadvantage, but to its seeming opposite: restrictive commonality.

The neo-traditionalists are not only embracing old faiths, but in some cases adopting new extremes of orthodoxy. The London bombings in the summer of 2005 and the 2004 stabbing of Amsterdam filmmaker Theo van Gogh are examples of Western-raised Muslims being led by radical neo-traditionalism to take extreme action in the name of supposedly defending their new-found religious convictions. "I did it out of conviction," said van Gogh's 27-year-old killer. "If I ever get free, I would do it again."

Devotees to versions of radical Islam are not the only ones to commit radical acts out of neo-traditional conviction. Though the overall number of practicing Catholics is dwindling dramatically, in January 1999 the Vatican revised the Catholic rite of exorcism for the first time since 1614. There are now ten full-time exorcists in the Roman Catholic Church; a decade ago, there was one. The Archdiocese of Chicago appointed a full-time exorcist in 1999 for the first time in its 160-year history. Outside the Catholic Church, Denver-based Rev. Bob Larson, whose Bob Larson Ministries runs the proselytizing Do What Jesus Did "teams" in cities around the world, lays claim to an expertise in the occult and oversees forty "exorcism teams" across the United States. There have been at least two cases where intense belief in spirit possession has led to the ultimate suppression of individuality: death. In Sayville, New York, a mother suffocated her seventeen-year-old daughter while performing an exorcism. In Pawtucket, Rhode Island, a man jammed two eight-inch steel crosses down his mother-in-law's throat during an exorcism. Seemingly isolated and strange moments reverberate out into the world. A tiny but meaningful cultural trend like the rise in exorcisms suggests a world of neo-traditionalists seeking to subsume a bewildering array of choices in the rituals of yesteryear. It also suggests how neo-traditionalism fits into the I'm-Special social shift. Michael Cuneo argues in his book *American Exorcism:*

> The practice of exorcism in contemporary America is remarkably well suited to the therapeutic ethos of the prevailing culture. No less than any of the countless New Age nostrums or twelve-step recovery routines on the current scene, exorcism ministries offer their clients endless possibilities for personal transformation—the promise of a thousand rebirths. . . . Exorcism is oddly at home in the shopping mall culture, purchase of happiness culture, of turn-of-the-century America.

Being possessed by an other-worldly demon is a guarantee that you'll be noticed.

Neo-Tradition Lite

Neo-traditionalism provides the ability to receive greater recognition in a smaller, delineated social grouping, thus solving, for some, the main problem of individualist conformity: how to be special. In answering this dilemma, neo-traditionalism also provides the ability to subsume one's identity and recognizability into the assigned role of the group, thus being able to at least appear to escape the pressures and paradoxes of the I'm-Special world we live in. The neo-traditionalists, from the liberal downshifters we will shortly encounter to the radically conservative born-again Christians we've already met, seem to solve two problems of conformist individuality: first, they are explicitly recognized within the small group, which alleviates their need to start their own TV channel just so people will notice they are alive; second, this sense of stable recognition provides them with automatic meaning, so they don't have to constantly reinvent the rules and traditions of their lives and endlessly search for an elusive individuality that may well be unattainable.

The neo-traditional movement is tiny compared with the all encompassing, I'm-Special societal shift. Nonetheless, it is extremely influential. In our confusing, constantly shifting age, more and more of us long for the traditions of a supposedly simpler time. Though we may not join fundamentalist religions, trade in our cars for horses and buggies, or set off to foreign lands to fight against the liberal values of the imperial West, we cannot help but occasionally think that times were better when our values and our lifestyles were protected by restrictive codes governing behavior. One might label this kind of thinking *neo-traditionalism lite*. Not quite a movement, and evidenced by a grab bag of different societal trends, neo-trad lite is that unsettling yearning for past simplicity many experience when confronted by the vagaries and complexities of the new conformity. Here, the small town looms large as the bastion of a simpler, better time when values were shared and people worked together to uphold the sanctity of family and community. In this mythical small town, no one was out of place, no one was taking Prozac, everyone had a role and a purpose. In neo-trad lite, the small-town model provides a fictional relief from freedom through effortless recognition. It's hardly surprising that the simple life of the small town looms so large in our imagination. Ulrich Beck and Zygmunt Bauman argue that a free society is a daunting prospect. Writes Bauman:

> The more freedom we have, the more troublesome and threatening it seems. I believe that people today are not so much concerned with the need to belong to a community as with the liberation from the compulsion of constantly having to choose and decide.

Similarly, Beck writes: "Where freedom becomes a cage, many choose the freedom of a cage (new or old religious movements, fundamentalism, drugs, or violence)." The neo-traditionalists— from downshifter to right-to-lifer—seek an escape from a society that compels loneliness by placing the highest values on individual achievement. Middle-class joiners also seek to be born again into yesterday, stripped of their fears and uncertainties, protected from the ravages and confusions of the shape-shifting present.

Though found all over the Western world, the rise of neo-trad lite is most easily seen in the United States. This makes perfect sense: The country that pioneered I'm Specialism would, naturally, harbor the strongest desire to escape the pressures of constantly creating individuality. If we look at a new generation of young people in the United States currently emerging into their own, we find that an America relentlessly dedicated to the myth of rugged individuality leads the way toward an emerging neo-conservative outlook. A poll of American college freshmen showed that, in 2002, 54 percent of some two hundred thousand freshmen agreed abortion should be legal, down a substantial amount from the 67 percent who agreed with legal abortion in the early nineties. Another poll done in 2003 found that 75 percent of American undergraduates said they trusted the military "to do the right thing" either "all the time" or "most of the time." Participation in conservative groups on U.S. campuses is at an all-time high. A reporter visiting the founders of one such group at Pennsylvania's Bucknell University discovers that the young conservatives believe they are fighting for their "individuality" and "freedom" on campuses supposedly awash with political correctness and knee-jerk liberalism.

Another example of neo-traditionalism lite is President George W. Bush's desire to amend the sacrosanct U.S. Constitution to state that marriage can take place only between a man and a woman. In a country where, it often seems, anything and everything is permissible, suddenly the issue of gay marriage is galvanizing a population that, according to an ABC poll, agrees with Bush that gay marriage should be banned. But remember, this is neo-trad lite. Fifty-five percent of Americans polled said they want to see gay marriage be illegal, but only 38 percent said they want the constitution amended. In other words, they want liberating individuality and Judeo-Christian conservative values too. Though few in the United States take radical action to prevent gay marriage from becoming law, societal trends suggest that the neo-traditionalists are the radical embodiment of a much larger group of people who possess, though rarely act on, neo-traditionalist tendencies.

At least part of the attraction of neo-traditionalism is what author Juliet Schor calls *downshifting,* the trend whereby people abandon highstress lifestyles in favor of lives centered on family and community. Writes Schor: "Downshifting is happening because millions of Americans are recognizing that, in fact, their lives are no longer in synch with their values . . . the money and the consumption-identity line has started to seem meaningless." Though she puts a progressive liberal spin on it, downshifting can often be the secular equivalent of, say, joining a fundamentalist religion. In both cases, the emphasis is on the return to so-called traditional values.

Examples of downshifting could be seen in the wake of the dot-com bubble burst, wherein would-be millionaires sought simpler lives and the satisfaction of making something people might actually want. One newspaper article on post-dot-com careers cites a Columbia University MBA holder who decided to open a hot-dog stand in Brooklyn. The fellow apparently got his inspiration from a documentary on the history of the hot dog and was moved to try to recreate the heyday of the sausage in a bun, but with upper-middle-class twists such as organic meats, freshly baked buns, and fancy mustards. Similarly, the article introduces a thirty-one-year-old Wharton Business School graduate who took his post-dot-com career in the direction of crepes. He opened a stand and has since expanded. He now calls himself the "West Coast Crepe King."

Downshifting can also involve physical relocation. Deblekha Guin, for example, was once just another one of those work-obsessed city types. Battered down by stress and obligation—more so than an obsession with money—she decided to take a temporary time out, a momentary downshift. "In Vancouver," she tells me, "I was working so hard that I got shingles. I needed to get a grip." Guin ended up arranging to take a temporary time out on a small island.

By the time I meet Guin, it is clear that she is permanently ensconced on her chosen rural outpost. It's winter, foggy, and perpetually drizzling, but Guin's simple loft-style house is warm and cozy. The wood-burning stove crackles, and the kettle is boiling.

"I never expected to stay," the energetic and articulate thirtysomething tells me. "But as soon as I moved here, I knew it was the smartest thing I'd ever done." Guin lucked out by finding that rarity in rural and small communities: employment. When I spoke to her she was working with an outfit that gives poor urban youths from British Columbia's big cities a rural respite. They come to retreat and work on making short videos in which they have a rare opportunity to articulate what and how they feel. (The program itself is a testament to the new conformity—increasingly, the best thing we can give the disadvantaged is an opportunity to hear themselves speak through, and in, the language of pop.)

But it wasn't really the employment opportunity that kept Guin on her island. It was the sense of belonging. "Every time I go shopping I bump into people I like," she explains to me. "I don't want to engage in a romantic cliché, but here I feel something, I feel part of something." Guin cites the "little banal things" that make up a sense of community and purpose. "If I had a cold someone would take care of me," she notes. She says that even the strangest and most socially awkward people find a place on the island. "They all have a place here, even the most wacked-out individuals, all sorts of people that would be just nowhere in an urban environment. There's this guy named Bear and they sent the police over, they wanted to institutionalize him, but the community protected him, no one would say where he was. There are people who can't leave because they have a place here, they have a place even if it's just a rut. It would be really hard to go back to being anonymous. I would feel invisible."

Invisibility is banished when you live in a community where everybody knows everybody. In the larger anonymous society of big cities and suburbs, as Ulrich Beck notes, "one has to do something, to make an active effort. One has to win, know how to assert oneself in the competition for limited resources—and not only once, but day after day." Beck speaks of the disappearance of "traditional society and its preconditions" in the absence of "the preordained, unquestioned, often enforced ties of earlier times." Without such ties, you are constantly forced to articulate your individuality and existence—you must manufacture ties. The pressure of needing to constantly justify and give notice of your existence is ameliorated by living in a (comparatively) closed society. Guin enjoys not just the quiet of the giant cedars and the many hidden beaches, but the instant recognizability of yesteryear's small town. The clock is turned back. The nobody can be somebody just by existing. The roles—town drunk, town loon, town rabble-rouser, town gossip, town genius—provide identities that would otherwise have to be carefully maintained and retooled and projected. Perhaps this is why small towns always seem so sleepy and nonchalant. They are protected from the perpetual necessity of narrative reinvention.

Many of us seek, either consciously or unconsciously, to replicate this idea of the small town. We yearn, as Benjamin Barber puts it, "for the collective intimacy of the tribe and the gang, yet groove on the anonymity and solitude of cyberspace." Guin tells me that she does not wish to totally abandon the city. She considers herself to be half in the rural sleepy island world and, at least mentally, half in the hyperactive city mindset. On the island, with its many highly intelligent, world-weary, liberal-minded residents, she gets the best of both worlds: small-town recognition without small-town provincialism. A downshifting liberal with an underlying longing for a tradition that will not limit her individuality, Guin embodies an increasingly common mindset. What separates her from most of us is that she has actually acted on her longings and found that rare place where she can remain a part of the greater, pop-infused society while being effortlessly recognized as a member of a tiny and exclusive community.

Most people are unable to relocate out of the influence of fast-paced and largely anonymous urban centers. As a result, many try to capture the sense of downshifting in other ways. The broader neo-traditionalist-lite trend reveals itself in movements like Slow Food—an international group that preaches slow cooking, traditional ingredients and customs, and nostalgia for a past of village farms and ancestral banquets.

Slow Food started in Italy in 1986 and has spread across Europe and into North America. Allen Katz, New York Slow Food Convivium leader, explains that Slow Food has 7,500 U.S. members and is steadily growing. Katz describes Slow Food as "an eco-gastronomic movement." He plays down the idea that the movement is for the rich and idle who have the time to research the way things were done in the old days and have the money to buy pricey organic and near-extinct ingredients. "It's all about a new experience, tasting, travelling, hearing from cultural and historical experts," Katz says. But Katz also talks extensively about saving indigenous crops from the single-crop focus of modern agribusiness, and he talks about local farms and family operations. He talks about a fund to help new immigrant farmers set up their operations because, he notes, it is only the immigrant farmers who still have enough knowledge of the old ways to replicate the successful farming techniques of a time before fertilizer and pesticide. "There is a nostalgic element to it," he grudgingly admits.

Discontented former members of the dot-com crowd who are desperately casting about for an identity that comes close to the values of a mom-and-pop business of a simpler time mirror society's desire for real substance and meaning in a technology-driven chimera. "We hunger after the old lifestyle but we can't have it," a museum curator in Canyon, Texas, tells author Robert Kaplan, and adds:

> So we fake it for a while. . . . What do you think country-western music is all about? You hear it everywhere, on every channel in the Panhandle, because we need it now more than ever—to convince ourselves that we're still cowboys.

Attempts to convince ourselves that we are what we might once have been go way beyond the North American West. In September of 2002, for instance, a quarter of a million people converged on London for a rally "in support of fox hunting and against the erosion of rural life." Notes *Sunday Times* critic Stephen Armstrong: "Ask any British soldier going off to war what he's fighting for and he'll tell you it's the country village." *Independent* columnist Miles Kingston says: "A strong conviction in the British psyche is, 'One day, I'll get back to the country.'" Canadians and Americans also love to wax eloquent on the small town, the land, the pastoral and rural. From Stephen Leacock to Norman Rockwell, a near-desperate nostalgia has been ever-present in our lives since the rise of the Industrial Revolution. The social psychologist Serge Moscovici calls this nostalgia "an echo in the memories of the people." He writes of human nature not being fully served by individual desire nor the groups and societies people join freely for their private interests. Fully realizing individual potential, Moscovici argues, is possible only in a mass, "understood as a nation, a political party, a tribe . . . and so on." Without cohesive nations and tribes that we can become fully attached to, we become creatures of longing and dissatisfaction. Moscovici writes that, today, our lives are "dictated by memories of things past rather than by the perception of things present."

This dogged reliance on remembrance emerges in the form of a muted desire to return to the past where we lived in restrictive but predictable collectives of interlocking hierarchies of class, religion, and community. From Ronald Reagan to Margaret Thatcher and back to George W. Bush, we have often elected those who promised a return to a former, superior moral order. Reagan, who best symbolizes this movement, was elected because of his traditionalist aura. He continues to embody it through today's somewhat bizarre yearning for a supposedly idyllic Reagan era. As Stuart Ewen writes in his history of public relations, "he embraced Hollywood's conception of righteousness and heroism." Since Reagan, North Americans have endured everyone from Bush-Quayle to Bush-Cheney and the reign of Governor Arnie. We continue to endure a seeming eternity of rhetoric from right-wing politicians who cater to the tension between our desire for order and tradition and our desire to do whatever we feel like. They do this by deliberately combining libertarian, anti-government rhetoric with a call for a return to the old ways.

Also catering to this unspoken need for order and tradition lost are an endless profusion of neo-traditionalist critics who defy demographics by emerging from all age groups, classes, races, and categories. One of them is Wendy Shalit, whose book *A Return to Modesty* I've quoted a few times in this work. Shalit could have been a contemporary of my high school pal who went from non-practising Jew to orthodoxy. They are of the same generation; they were both raised in liberal Jewish families and attended ultra-liberal East Coast colleges. Shalit is typical in giving voice to a kind of wishy-washy yearning for a predetermined moral order without actually articulating how we might get there and what we might have to sacrifice to attain the comfort that comes with collective moral purpose. She writes:

> Our choices are always "given" to us in some sense, and as long as they are going to be given, why not have them given to us by God, by traditions that hold warehouses of stored wisdom, rather than by Gallup polls?

She conveniently neglects to pose the obvious question: Whose God shall give us our choices?

It is the nature of neo-traditionalist-lite yearning for the past to ignore the reasons why we jettisoned theocratic society in the first place. Today, desperate for a center in a system of faceless, seemingly unrelated power nodes, people look longingly back at what they think were the simpler times of yesteryear. And so we relentlessly search for something meaningful and seek to flee the ravages of globalism and conformist individualism through the reclaiming of so-called past ways.

MY BROTHER LIVES in a suburb made up of people with the same faith as him, socializes exclusively with them, and sends his kids to a private school where they learn to blindly conform to the beliefs of his sect. My high school friend lives in a yeshiva in Israel. Pennefather is in a cloister. Lindh is in jail as an enemy of the state, though if it wasn't for the terrorist attack on the World Trade Center and the subsequent invasion of Afghanistan, he would probably still be at his mufti's feet, contemplating the Koran.

In each case, those making the radical shift to neo-conservatism seem to be seeking not just a set of alternative values but a buffer zone between themselves and contemporary society. However dropping out of I'm-Special society in favor of restrictive fundamentalism does not necessarily mean that the escapers have not been affected by the new conformity; in many cases, the resurgence of traditionalist lifestyles suggests just how powerful the I'm-Special impetus is.

It works like this: Lost and bewildered, unable to find a place in this new, perpetually shifting world, the neo-traditionalists seem to turn away from individuality. They do so by adopting the codes and principles of a smaller group with a clearly defined hierarchy and set of rules. They seek to have their lives ordered. This is not to say that they wish to give up *all* choice and free will (though often that is what gradually happens). Rather, in moving away from the anything-goes demands of an individualistic society, they are seeking to deliberately subsume themselves in something bigger than themselves.

How does all this fit into the new conformity? Once again, the paradox prevails. By choosing to join the group, neo-traditionalists these days are very often acting on their pop-inspired need for differentiated individuality, the "I'm Special" need for recognition and notice. In assigning one's self to a smaller, clearly defined community, one has a better chance for recognition than in broader society where, despite the pop theme of individuality, we have largely become nothing more than statistics and potential consumers. Those who deliberately isolate themselves from the whole create a smaller community in which they can be noticed. In an age where everybody's search to articulate individuality seems the same, neo-traditionalists find a way they can stand out—by all being the same. In the neo-traditional cloister, society's urgent demand that you become somebody is answered—the joiner exchanges the trappings of individualist identity for the trappings of communal identity. And yet, within this communal identity, the joiner can expect to assume a unique, unquestioned, perpetual identity as a member, if not exactly as an individual.

In a 1994 critique of postmodernity, Queen's University sociologist David Lyon writes:

> The greater the ephemerality, the more pressing the need to discover or manufacture some kind of eternal truth that might lie therein. . . . The revival of interest in basic institutions (such as family and community), and the search for historical roots are all signs of a search for more secure moorings and longer-lasting values in a shifting world.

The prophet of systemic individualization, Ulrich Beck, is quick to note that this search does not suggest an opposing force balancing out the urges of the new conformity. On the contrary. He writes: "The upsurge of local nationalities and the new emphasis on local identity should be seen as unmistakable consequences of globalization, and not, as they may first appear, as a phenomenon that contradicts it." Given a role and history, blessed by the religious leader, perhaps even assigned a spouse, the joiner is sheltered from the vagaries of our fluctuating make-it-up-as-you-go-along world. The urge to return to the old ways, the old tribes and localities, is the urge to protect oneself in an era when everything and everyone is up for grabs. The joiner finds momentary or even lifelong peace and comfort. Safely ensconced, this individual is buffered from society, becomes permanently somebody.

Pop-Culture Communities

Alternative World Youth Day organizer Milton Chan is a Catholic dissenter. Standing on the steps of the church and watching the Arizona kids retreat into the sunset, he shakes his head, clearly disappointed at the way the abortion discussion ended inside. "There is brainwashing," he says. "You're brainwashed by your surroundings. There are cultish tendencies. What is more important, the Pope or Jesus? What about the sanctity of life?" Chan is a Torontonian in his early twenties. He seems an excellent candidate to answer the question blurted out by the neo-conformist Catholics confronting their critics: Why don't you become Protestants? Why indeed? Why *were* the dissenters still Catholics? If they hated the Church's policies so much, why didn't they just convert to some other religion or renounce organized faith altogether?

"I can't abandon him [Jesus]," Chan says. "Every one of us who believes, they will have to sit with the boss upstairs who will want to know what have you done when you saw injustice. This religion didn't look like this five hundred years ago, it was open to discussion in the past. What happened?" Chan was raised Catholic and says that he first sensed there was a problem with the religion when, in ninth grade, he saw people picketing an abortion clinic and screaming "Go home!" at young women trying to enter. "Love God and respect the people around you," he explains, trying to describe his version of what Catholicism should be. "Everything else stems from those principles. We have to seek renewal. We can't repress that."

Like Chan, Janice Sevre-Duszynska, an American of Polish descent originally from Milwaukee, is a Catholic activist who refuses to abandon what she believes is *her* religion. Sevre-Duszynska has come to take part in Alternative World Youth Day in the hopes of furthering her agenda of getting the Catholic Church to accept women into the priesthood. Now in her forties, she has spent the better part of her adult life working on this struggle and forming communities with like-minded individuals. "I grew up Catholic," she says. "I wanted to be a priest. I worked in the church as a kid. Every Saturday for seven years I cleaned the sanctuary. I wanted to be an altar boy." Sevre-Duszynska describes how she interrupted an ordination in Lexington, Kentucky, where she now lives. "I'd already written to the bishop, the rector of the cathedral, and the man being ordained about my intentions. I threw off my coat, went up to the podium, and spoke to the bishop. I prostrated myself, lay down there, and he said, 'Get back to your seat, you're interrupting the service.'" Sevre-Duszynska has unfurled banners in Rome and gotten herself arrested for the cause. Again, we are reminded of the question the World Youth Day teens shouted at the alternative panel: Why not quit the Catholic Church and join a religion that welcomes women into the priesthood? "I'm steeped in my religion, why should I have to change my religion?" Sevre-Duszynska demands. "My aunt and uncle ran the parish the entire time I was in grade school. Church is part of my daily life, my grandmother, my mother, father, aunts and uncles, my extended family. I want to be a priest, extend the sacraments. The young people need more ritual and meaning in their lives. Church needs expansion to include more respect for the earth and the daily events of our lives. I'm not going away," she says. "That's what they would like to me to do."

OBSESSIVES OR PIONEERS? Janice Sevre-Duszynska and Milton Chan are probably a bit of both. Born and raised Catholics, they seek to change the religion to suit their interpretation and personal conviction. They are inventing new traditions and rules, ones that will better suit their own agendas. We've seen this before at Temple Kol Emeth, with the difference being that here, the supplicants are not met halfway by the accommodating religion. Here, the supplicants are rebuffed. As a result, the would-be joiners are forced to invent new kinds of communities that they can be part of. Communities connected by, in many cases, a single thread such as a unified desire to see women become ordained Catholic priests.

What would happen if the Catholic Church did give in to their demands? Would Chan and Sevre-Duszynska then lose interest in the organized religion they profess to love? Embraced by the mainstream, their sense of outsider identity would certainly disappear. Though their honest belief in God would remain, they might very well find themselves needing something else to reaffirm the rebel stance that has dominated so much of their lives. Dr. Marc

Galanter, a psychiatry professor at the New York University School of Medicine, has noted that the anti-cult movement itself functions like a cult, with "those who were de-programmed" exhibiting a "much more negative attitude toward the sect" than those who simply left the cult of their own accord. Galanter points out that the deprogrammed cult members generally become involved in the deprogramming movement and end up the most "articulate and active critics of sects such as the Moonies and the Hare Krishnas, in contrast to the majority of ex-members who had left on their own initiative." Galanter seems bemused when he notes that the deprogrammed members' "animosity toward the new religious movements in general parallelled the intensity of feeling found in the sects they opposed." This revelation has clear implications for the phenomenon of neo-traditionalist communities: The anti-cultists form, in a way, their own community devoted to being anti-cult. It's a cult against cults that may be no less enticing than the original neo-traditional community they now gather together to oppose.

EVEN AS COMMUNITY seems to be shattering and crumbling, it also reconstitutes. The communities that Milton Chan and Janice Sevre-Duszynska have established—communities united in both their faith and opposition to the institution of the Catholic Church—represent an attack on traditional community, but also a kind of resurgence. In the minority, community reasserts itself in the form of restrictive sects, cults, and fundamentalist religions providing buffer zones and replications of the small town that contemporary middle-of-the-road religion cannot. But the wider majority of seekers are entering groups that more closely resemble the communities of Chan and Sevre-Duszynska, only minus the connection to faith. In the same way that anti-cult gatherings can form cult-like communities, thousands of communities now find their impetus not from geography, religion, nationality, or even financial opportunity, but from a shared fascination or hobby. A new world of pop-culture communities has sprung up to provide stability, meaning, and overt channels to access the new-conformity I'm-special mantra.

In the often-cited book *Bowling Alone,* Professor Robert Putnam charts what he considers to be the decline in American social life. He writes:

> Surveys show sharp declines in many measures of collective political participation, including attending a rally or speech (down 36 percent between 1973 and 1993), attending a town meeting on town or school affairs (off 39 percent), or working for a political party (off 56 percent).

Putnam also finds statistics to support a decline in attendance or participation at churches, sports clubs, professional associations, literary discussion groups, unions, and almost any other kind of "official" social structure. Predictably, and in the spirit of critics who espouse a return to the traditional values such as Neil Postman, David Frum, and Neil Gabler, Putnam blames television for this decline. (For these types of critics, TV almost always functions as an easy culprit, responsible for the collapse of all morality.)

Certainly no one could deny the shift in our cultural mores— the political rally, the sermon, the union are all in decline as community traditions (though I'm not sure about the book club). At any rate, Putnam's argument is not entirely dissimilar to mine: We are moving away from structured social groupings and toward a society of individuals. Putnam is also unquestionably correct in placing television at the heart of this nexus. But from this point on our opinions diverge. What Putnam fails to recognize is that even as traditional types of communities decline, other variations on the community come to the forefront. TV creates community, even as it eradicates it.

There is a whole world out there that Putnam refuses to explore. The pop culture he reviles has spawned a parallel universe of social structures and communities he ignores or condemns because they don't come out of glee clubs, bowling leagues, and associations of women voters. In the dim light of the flickering screen, we can see new communities forming, drifting away, and forming again. Like backyard-wrestling leagues, these are unquantifiable communities in which people paradoxically and necessarily come together to highlight their—you guessed it—individuality.

Community without Pity

Cohn Moser grew a community out of a Chia Pet.

"Using a webcam I actually grew a Chia Pet [pottery planter]—as seen in *TV Guide*—online," this twenty-six-year-old Edmonton internet aficionado explains. "People loved it. They came every day."

Moser used the results of his 1999 experiment in the "different ways there are to get people to go to a website" to start the meeting hub edmsingles.com, which has several thousand regular visitors. On his own site—chiaweb.net—he has stopped growing Chia Pets in favor of positioning webcams inside and outside his house, allowing sightseers to check out the view as they please.

At one point, 3,500 people a day visited the site, dropping in for a peek into a stranger's living room. Moser says he's made "many friends" from these visitors, and even more from interactions on edmsingles, where he chats with old pals but also tries to "meet three strangers every day."

Moser is hardly alone in his pursuit of virtual connection. There are thousands of webcams pointed at people's private spaces, and probably three times that many blog sites where total strangers enter into the minutiae and lives of random people they've never met. Online diaries, blogs, and other similar variations on the theme of online confession and personal opinion have gone, like backyard wrestling, from being a faddish craze to a seemingly permanent part of life. They are our new anti-community communities, testament to the power of pop, the rise of the individual, and the strange belief that every time you pick your nose, someone else should know about it. Sites such as pitas.com, diaryland.com, angelfire.com, and opendiary.com offer thousands of daily detailed confessions. Nycbloggers.com collects the ramblings of more than 2,100 bloggers who live in New York City. While it's impossible to get a complete, accurate account, most observers agree that there are roughly 6 to 10 million blogs active in the United States. The diaries range from the harrowing (confessionals of a girl struggling with an eating disorder) to the cliquish (self-referential remarks mostly addressed to people we don't know and never will) to the amusingly mundane (the vast majority fall into this category). Here's a snippet from a week in the life of Ericka Bailie; I've never met her and yet know, from reading her diary, that she is a Minneapolis hipster with a decent taste in movies and a penchant for navel-gazing:

[Sunday, August 20, 2000] [10:40 P.M.]

> we saw *cecil b. demented* at the uptown today. we sat in the balcony, in the first row so we could put our feet up, and talked about glasses before the previews came up. brian needs glasses but has been hesitant because he thinks he'd look "geeky." he looks good in my glasses even (old lady cat-eye with rhinestones) & i know he'd look good in the glasses i'd like to see him in. all day brian kept mentioning how "mod" i looked today & how much he liked it. now i have to make a conscious effort to dress more mod? oh the pressure.

Pundits whine about the death of letter writing and the demise of reading, but no one ever cites the rise of these diary sites and blogs as evidence to the contrary. Why put your life on the internet for public consumption? "About once a week someone responds to what I've written," explains an blog enthusiast named Angela. "Positive feedback spurs me on to write more; it's a huge motivational factor and actually makes me feel more free to express myself in any way I choose." Trish Allen, an eighteen-year-old blogger from Kentucky, is more succinct: "I love to be the center of attention." A thirty-one-year-old art dealer and restaurant-critic blogger notes that those in the bloggite posse start to look at life differently than non-bloggers. "We're professional reviewers," he said. "I don't just go to a restaurant anymore. I go with a critical eye."

As the would-be food critic suggests, there's also an air of exclusivity to the blogger phenomenon. Indeed, popular sites like

LiveJournal, Friendster, MySpace, YouTube, Linkedin and Facebook.com not only let you blog, share files and present your personal profile, but also measure your popularity by indicating how many people have linked to your page or have agreed to be your "friendster." On Friendster, you are marooned on a solitary social island until others on the network confirm that you are, indeed, their friend and agree to link with you. This link instantly connects you to everyone who has linked to them, and everyone who has linked to them, and so on until you have met thousands of online friends, joined together in semi-community and attracted, at least in part, to the notion of semi-exclusivity. (That exclusivity is enhanced by the Friendster feature encouraging friends and ex-partners to add "testimonials" regarding the worthiness of a fellow Friendster to that member's profile.)

Blogs, backyard wrestling, and Elvis impersonators all point to our desire to be noted (or at least footnoted) in the electronic mass community. In a culture where it is common to obsess over other people's problems as a kind of entertainment—from the travails of the stars as chronicled in *People* and *StarWeekly* to the agonies of boy-toy doctors on the boob tube—it really isn't that much of a stretch for someone to decide, "Well, my problems can be entertaining too." And though there's a problem of access to the airwaves of radio and television, no one has yet figured out how to keep us from chipping away at the entertainment monoculture via the net. And so Ericka and Angela and thousands of others form de facto communities in which they read and comment on each other's lives. Their participation reaffirms their sense of self in a mass-culture era, but at the same time it embeds them more deeply into the pop-culture world of the new conformity, a world where it seems natural that we should know more about disembodied strangers discussing their boyfriends' fashion hangups than we do about our neighbors or our co-workers in the next cubicle. As Georg Simmel once noted: "Differentiation and individualization loosen the bond of the individual with those who are most near in order to weave in its place a new one . . . with those who are more distant."

The new pop-culture communities arise in a multitude of incarnations as reaction to the demands of an I'm-Special world. As with the neo-traditional communities, there is a mix of limited, organized actual gatherings (think of Kris Verri's triumphant comeback against Mask Guy in Chapter 1), and much broader participation in the form of mental, cybernetic affiliation. People are anxious to be noticed for who and what they are. We have communities arising that anyone can join, so long as they conform to the particular restrictions and enthusiasms—the mindset—of the group. Again, the created community serves no real purpose other than to provide individuals a place where they can be noticed, where the narrative of their lives can be manufactured and infused with meaning. Both pop-culture and neo-traditional communities offer assurance. Individuals receive an identity, the opportunity to perpetually reinvent (Cohn Moser meeting three new friends every day), and the comfort of knowing that they have a place in the world (no one can challenge, dilute, or replace Moser's webcam exhibitionism). Are these types of new communities so different? Both seek to give us back what we seem to have lost: a place in the world.

PEOPLE WHO LOVE a certain celebrity or pop phenomenon so much that they link up with like-minded others and spend their time and money pursuing this passion are a familiar pop-culture phenomenon. The mass-culture industry encourages these fans because they individually deepen the person-product bond and, if there are enough of them, they create new secondary markets for figurines, magazines, conventions, and so on. The best example are the Trekkies, with their *Star Trek* conventions, vast array of collectibles, and insatiable appetite for personal appearances by Sulu and Uhura. But fan clubs offer only a partial resolution to the urgent need for self-expression that the new conformity creates. They provide stability and recognition and purpose within the group—"Hey, it's John, the guy who dresses like a Klingon! How ya doing, guy? Haven't seen you since the Vulcan convention in San Francisco"—but they provide little in the way of a true creative outlet or assertion of control.

As a result, our enduring and widening obsession with pop culture is now yielding a strange fruit: thriving subcultures that span everything from the Backyard Wrestling Federation to tribute bands. These "communities" also include those who come together to create zines, novels, CDs, fan websites, blogs, webcam sites, and videos on an independent basis. Each permutation of independent activity transcends its singularity and, very often, its obvious amateur lameness, by conveying the heartfelt desire of the millions who long to be *known*.

We've already met many people whose lives revolve around pop-culture communities. From Harry Potter fan fiction writers and *Star Wars* amateur filmmakers to day-trader and wannabe rapper Storm, millions around the world have formulated their own truth, an answer to the lie of pop culture. In the same way that some retreat to the confines of the cult or the safety of a fundamentalist community in order to be noticed, many more find refuge in pop-culture communities where we find what we crave: community recognition, spiritual meaning, and the ability to reinvent ourselves.

TORONTO'S TARA ARIANO is the pioneer creator of an online pop community. Ariano oversees, with an American partner she met online, the extremely popular pop-culture critique sites Fametracker.com and TelevisionWithoutPity.com. Ariano started both sites in the late nineties. She has watched their profitability expand to the point where she could quit her job, and then shrink back down to the point where the most time-consuming and expensive of the sites, TelevisionWithoutPity, is now just breaking even without Ariano or her partner taking a salary. Ariano has thought of shutting down the site, but feels compelled to continue, partly because she's addicted to the net community she oversees, and also because of her sense of responsibility. "I do it out of obligation," she says.

Who does Ariano feel obligated to? In 2003, TelevisionWithout Pity.com was attracting three-quarters of a million visitors a day. Its forum, where visitors post their thoughts on their favorite TV shows, had thirty thousand registered users. They can read recap reviews of their favorite shows, incredibly elaborate overviews of what happened on, say, last week's episode of *Buffy the Vampire Slayer*. They can also vote on the episode, either contradicting or affirming the reviewer's position (the reviewers, Ariano says, are paid for their efforts even though she admits that there are thousands who would happily do the job for free). Visitors to TelevisionWithoutPity also have the opportunity to read and post to the forum, where the various episodes are debated, and arguments rage regarding such matters as who the best couple on *Buffy* is (was), and so on. To visit these forums and follow the discussions is to enter a world just as strange as *Buffy*'s enchanted town of Sunnydale, California. This is a parallel world where TV matters a whole lot to a whole lot of people. It is to these people, her network of TV-addicted users, that Ariano feels obligated. To shut down the site, she feels, would be cruel, sudden, painful. And obligation, it seems, is a two-way street: When the site threatened to close due to lack of funds, Ariano's viewers came together. They held garage sales and even bake sales to raise funds, and sent contributions by the thousands. The message was clear: They did not want to lose their site.

TelevisionWithoutPity has many of the hallmarks of a community: dedication, interdependence, reciprocation, people diligently following the rules so that everyone can get along together. Says Ariano: "They speak about the site as *We*. 'Are we going to be recapping *Mr. Personality*?'" While the community members function as a kind of neighborhood watch, Ariano and her partner work as the mayor, police force, and better business bureau, keeping the community safe for visitors and making sure everyone who visits finds what they are after. "We keep everyone in line. If they are on the boards [i.e., participating in a discussion group], they want to have a reasonably intelligent discussion—as intelligent as a discussion about *Charmed* can be," explains Ariano. Which is to say that they keep a tight rein on the forums, making sure discussions stay civil and focused and there aren't thousands of postings such as "Sarah Michelle Gellar is soooo hot!!!"

People come to the site to find like-minded individuals who can validate and listen to their opinions. In that sense, these pop communities are almost an improvement on traditional communities. "Online, you can choose the criteria of what it's about, what unites you," Ariano tells me. "In real life, you can't choose your friends and family. If you pledge allegiance to a certain show, you can define what makes up that community. If you feel very strongly about a show, you can find people who will agree with you. It's not that you are only interested in TV, but the net helps you find people with the same interests."

But, sometimes, shared passion for a particular pop-culture kink takes people into the realm of the obsessive and the bizarre. "Factions of fandom start to define people's identity," notes Ariano. "You can't make personal attacks on individuals on the board, but for some people the line is blurred. They feel that the Willow couple in *Buffy* is the best and [when] you say you don't think so, they complain that they have been personally attacked." Ariano says that the factions organize their friends to vote-multiply using different computers in their offices, so that the approval numbers stay high. "They take it really seriously," Ariano says. "They think it's a real vote, they think it actually means something."

Does Ariano consider TelevisionWithoutPity.com a community? "I usually think when users on boards talk about the 'community,' they have a very inaccurate view of what that means," she says. "I hope it's not the only community they are in. The closer they get, the more cliquey it gets. They sit around and tell each other they're great, their observations about the show are great." Ultimately, Ariano thinks people visit the site mainly to have their existence and their opinion validated. They are not as interested in other people as they are in reading their own posts and having their wit and knowledge admired. Not only that, but some of them seem terrified at the prospect of losing their forum, the only place—community or not—where their particular genius and knowledge is valued and recognized. "Some of them definitely replace real community with the site. Once a show goes off the air, we stop recapping and the forums go off the site. When that happened with *Buffy,* users started asking us several months before whether the forums would stay up. They didn't want the forum to go down, even though the show was going off the air," Ariano says. Then she adds, with remarkable frankness, "These people could stand to go outside and make some new friends." Will Ariano regret her role perpetuating a faux community offering I'm-Special recognition and existing almost purely out of the need for self-actualization?

"Am I their dealer? Am I their pimp? I'm sure that 99 percent of them are perfectly functioning normal members of actual communities . . . probably." Ariano laughs, and continues: "If I felt like I was taking away their time working for Amnesty International I would feel bad, but I don't feel that. It's a total drug-dealer argument: If it wasn't us, it would be someone else."

Still Alone

Television and other pop platforms allow disparate souls to form instant connections. Many of us turn to pop culture and its most successful conduit, television, as a kind of model to which we apply our ambitions (as inspired by TV) toward increased selfhood and individuality. We want to be somebody, recognized and noticed the same way our pop stars are recognized and fawned over. And yet we also seek meaning and vestiges of tradition, a connection to community and spirituality that belies the specious allure of fame. So it is that our connection with pop culture is often nostalgic. Fleeting as it is, pop can provide momentary bursts of synchronous empathy, cross-world ripples of self-same emotion that evoke the old cliché of Marshall McLuhan's global village. And yet, since pop culture must constantly change and refresh itself to conform to the demands of the I'm-Special marketplace, the connection is always momentary and tenuous. A favorite TV show is taken off the air, a favorite movie reduced to a TV rerun hacked and sliced to accommodate twenty minutes of commercials. The second, third, and fourth times are never like the first. So increasing numbers of us form pop communities to help reclaim the feeling, keep the dream alive, and the loneliness at bay by assuring us a place where we will always be understood, noticed, recognized. Where once an interest in Evel Knievel that lasted beyond boyhood would be considered embarrassing, today such an obsession provides a grown man with a fan base, an audience, an individuality, even a community.

Unfortunately, clustering around identity-creating communi-ties—whether pop or neo-traditional—does not solve the prob-lems posed by the demands of the new conformity. The bigger a community gets, the more accepted into the mainstream, the less likely it is that it will satisfy the individual's need to be proclaimed special through sheer association. We want to get further, deeper, faster into the pop culture that dominates our lives, and we're increasingly willing to abandon normal life to achieve what pop promises us. And yet, the more we join together in groups that help us clamor and claw at the gates, the more difficult it is to gain access.

For a time, communities based on shared interests, whether they were neo-traditional- or pop-culture-inspired, seemed like the solu-tion. Such communities combine the fervid intensity of the cult and the recognition implicit in small-town living with the potential for reinvention and achieving notability. But the new communities—both neo-traditional and pop—only partly remedy the isolation of individuals under the new conformity. Battling against the decen-tralized, self-perpetuating system that preaches individuality and depends on conformity, the new communities do the opposite: They preach conformity but depend on our desire for individuality. As a result, no invented community can ever fully embody or ful-fill what seems to be an inherent conflicting human need for both a particular unique identity and a sense of having a place in a soci-ety, a culture, a community that one will always be able to identify as home. Representing a new wave of community seekers, John Walker Lindh chose to do something about his inability to feel—or find—a home. The conventional reasoning was that by joining a fundamentalist Islamic group, Lindh rebelled against freedom. But this son of permissive Marin County–based parents didn't rebel against freedom. Just the opposite. In searching for a community that would give him a sense of self, Lindh embraced the freedom of nonconformity in the most radical way possible. By immersing himself in the antithesis of what we think of as freedom, he freed himself from the bondage of having to constantly be free. The measures to which Lindh had to go to find himself free of the loneliness of freedom are made all the more poignant when we consider where he has ended up.

In the age of I'm Special, John Walker Lindh sought a community that really would make him feel special. For a time, sitting at his mufti's feet, he must have thought that he had finally found an escape, a way to make peace with the ravages of individualism. But he ended up exactly where he most feared: alone in the heartland of enforced individuality, sentenced to a lifetime of solitude.

7

EXTREME BEHAVIOR

MORALITY VERSUS CELEBRITY IN THE AGE OF SPECIAL

A MAN DRESSED in ripped fatigues lurches out of the bushes brandishing a chainsaw. The crowd falls back. He raises the revving weapon above his head. He's about to lobotomize a fourteen-year-old girl. Her screams cut through the mist, echoing similar shrieks and cries. At the last minute, friends pull her away. The man melts into the shadows.

The scene is Halloween Horror Night at Universal Studios' Islands of Adventure theme park. I'm somewhere between SuperHero Island and Jurassic Park. Actually, I'm not sure where I am. Thick fog billows in front of me. Shrieks and cackles create a disorienting cacophony of sound. The light on this hot Orlando October night is dim. I can see a few feet ahead. Occasionally, couples or groups come into view, arms interlocked as they take tentative steps into the gloom. I scan the shifting array of shapes. Are any hostile?

I'm surprised at how real the Horror Night seems. The theme park—normally child-friendly and bright as an airport even at nine o'clock at night—is gloomy and menacing. Ghouls work the gallows at the entrance. Up ahead, I hear squeamish gasps and groans. I soon find out why. I'm among the cringing as I march resolutely through clinging knee-high foam. There are haunted mazes and houses, creepy displays, high-tech horror extravaganzas. But the real scares come from the old-fashioned peekaboo. An anonymous mass murderer steps out of the bushes. Everybody screams. It's like being immersed in a cheesy horror movie. You know what's coming, but you can't help being surprised.

As I wander through the park, I think about the fact that there are upwards of ten thousand people here, each paying the premium price of sixty U.S. dollars to have the shit scared out of them. And this is only a single evening of Horror Night's three-week run. In other words, we are talking about two hundred thousand people signing up to be terrorized. Though there are many teens and university students in the crowd, they are not the only demographic. I see middle-aged couples, gaggles of thirty-something women on a night out, and even the occasional senior citizen. The night is for almost anyone who wants to be scared—and some who don't. I come across one little girl who is crying. Horror Night is not for children. Kids don't need such elaborate set-ups; they can get scared by just lying in bed and staring at the black crack where the closet door hasn't quite closed.

When a skeleton woman wielding a scythe creeps up behind a group of us and I'm simultaneously jostled from behind, my shoulders tighten. Did I, too, let out a little yelp? Ostensibly, there's nothing that will actually hurt me at Halloween Horror Night. But with thousands of attendees and hundreds of "scarecters" dressed as chainsaw massacrers, skeletons, and zombies, you never know. What if someone a bit, well, unhinged decided to join the party tonight? Nobody else seems nervous. I keep looking behind me. I think of the Maryland sniper, who has been terrorizing the region of greater Washington, D.C. A sniper could be anywhere. He could be here. There seem to be an inordinate number of dark empty corners and menacing crannies where someone could hide. I keep asking myself: *C'mon Hal, are you really scared?* Well, yes and no. Mostly no. I raise the plastic beer bottle to my lips and take a gulp.

Immersion to the Max!

Barraged by pop culture and its insistence on seize-the-day instant satisfaction, we are increasingly frustrated by the tedium of everyday life. The primary way we respond to this frustration is by finding ways to further immerse ourselves in the pop culture of fun and heightened self-actualization. *Here we are now!* we cry as we plunge ourselves into the movie theaters, theme parks, casinos, laser-tag war games, and virtual-reality arcades of the ever-more-rapacious entertainment industry. *Entertain us!*

Being entertained these days, though, often means being in the action, part of the show, immersed in the quasi-reality of pop. The screens have to be bigger, the sound louder, the action more enticing. If the seats move, if scents are released, and if objects jump off the screen and into our laps, all the better. The more our lives seem mundane and dull compared with what pop promises us they could be, the more we demand that pop culture finds us ways to make fantasy reality by putting us *right in there.*

Halloween Horror Night puts us right in there. Gets as close to the feel of actually being stalked and terrorized as, theoretically, we would want to be. Wandering through the Halloween Horror Night fog listening to the cries of delighted terror, I keep thinking: *Why are we here?* Surely real life is scary enough. It wasn't that long ago that terrorists crashed planes into the heart of New York City. As I write this, Toronto police are scouring the city for the murderer and rapist of a ten-year-old girl. But we'll still pay sixty bucks for a pretend stalker to leap out of the bushes as we pass. We're looking for a shock, a thrill, the next most exciting thing. Why?

Those of us who are shut out from actually participating and making meaning through localized cultural exchange depend mainly on prefab fun to legitimize our lives. As a result, the conformist individualist wants—needs—constant stimulation and satisfaction. Only partly able to establish identity by having a place in a community and being able to reach our peers through the electronic mediums of communication—the tentacles of mass culture—we seek other ways to get into the action and reaffirm our desire to be noticed. We do as we are told; we give ourselves over to the world of pop and invite it to make us feel *special*. This is who we've become: people who cannot sit still, people who desire ever further immersion in the spectacle.

To answer our demand for recognition, entertainment has to become more interactive, more immersive, more intense. Keep upping the ante, and we'll keep coming back. Horror Night is scary, and with the use of live actors to provide "real" thrills, it is closing in on the ultimate—a displaced parallel entertainment reality, the equivalent of Star Trek's holodeck, only with sets and actors creating the fantasy. New entertainment concepts often focus on virtual-reality scenarios that allow us to explore our (implanted) fantasies without repercussions. Adventure sports and war-zone travel takes this one step further: Here we have "real" scenarios where the thrill comes from knowing that there is a very good chance we could get hurt, caught, or even killed. Horror Night merges the parallel universes of virtual reality and adventure/travel, in the hopes that the combo will satisfy our desire for heightened feeling, for dramatic surges of emotion, without actually exposing us to any real and potentially litigious danger.

But Horror Night doesn't fully satisfy. The sun comes up the next day, and everything seems normal again. We stagger into the bathroom, have a look at ourselves in the mirror, utter a collective groan. We feel dulled and distanced, unengaged and, worst of all, un-entertained. That's why the age of the individual is also the *age of extremist behavior*. For an ever-increasing number of people, the harder we work to proclaim our individuality—whether it's through participating in ever-more-extreme pop-culture immersions or radically rejecting those programs altogether—the more extreme we have to get. A desire for opportunities to articulate our individuality is the legacy of a pop culture that then tries to satisfy such a desire with ever-more-immersive attractions. These attractions are so extreme and over the top that they make it even harder for us to imagine anything we can do in our daily lives that can match that level of intensity. Thereby, we feel even more devalued and distanced from our normal selves. And therein lies the trap: With even our sanctioned mass culture becoming ever more violent and extreme, what is left to do that will shock and horrify and thereby proclaim I'm-Specialness? If you go to work like a good boy, you are labelled boring. But how far does the good boy need to go to shake off the aura of Corporate Ken and achieve the status of *bad*?

Extreme culture usurps the territory of extremity in real life. Where even modestly weird behavior would have once been enough to get us excommunicated, drowned as witches, or at least ostracized, today wearing tattoos and piercings, or becoming a Satanist, paganist, exorcist, or even a grown-up with an elaborate collection of dolls still in their boxes can actually have the reverse effect and make you friends. The more extreme culture gets in order to satisfy our urge to be immersed and entertained, the more extreme real-life antics meant to attract attention also become. It's a loop—extreme acts in real life must then be converted into extreme entertainment, which leads to another round of real-life extremists trying to enter pop culture by being even more extreme than what they see on television. As a result, mainstream culture's insistence on specialness becomes an insistence on extremity. Every night on TV we are treated to a roster of bad cops, rapists, murderers, and maniacs. What's a real-life extremist supposed to do to get on TV these days?

Author Michael Bracewell writes of the nineties as a decade trapped in a cycle of "boredom and craving for one-shot celebrity, prompting a culture of 'to the max,' which was spun to keep raising the pitch of its own superlatives. (Ultimate Terror! Ultimate Destruction!)" And yet, the more extreme culture becomes—Halloween Horror Night, however momentarily and genuinely frightening, is just the tip of the iceberg—the more difficult it is to be invited into the world of pop culture and recognized purely on the basis of one's extreme behaviors. "Just what would people be prepared to do to get their little nugget of celebrity?" asks Bracewell. "Throughout the second half of the 1990s, the answer to this—not surprisingly, perhaps—would be 'absolutely anything.'"

Today it's conformist to kill in a flamboyant fashion, to commit grievous crimes of supposed passion, to excise your modesty in order to mine your fleeting minutes of fame to the hilt. Each action demands and compels a more extreme counteraction. No wonder public explosions of rage seem more common. The sniper taunts the police, leaves tarot cards, and makes sure the camera crews know all about it. The media-savvy serial killer and the video-camera-toting high school mass murderer are both taking "standard" extreme measures within the I'm-Special framework: They are trying to find a way to get noticed and recognized.

I am not saying that violent pop culture causes people to be more violent. Rather, since we live our lives in a perpetually beckoning but always exclusionary pop world that tells us we are special but allows us very little in the way of articulating our specialness, many of us turn to extreme acts as a predictable response—a way to get noticed. This is not necessarily pop culture's fault, but rather the pop-culture *industry's* fault. Extreme action gets noticed on TV but only the first few times. Then something even more extreme has to take place before its perpetrator can enter the gates of fame. All of this is because we are, essentially, shut out from making meaning through established models of community. The system that creates the new conformity causes us to want in. Badly. And we'll do whatever it takes to get there.

Escape from the Theme Park

Orlando. You might think that Los Angles, Tokyo, London, Hong Kong, or even Toronto would be the best place to explore the way we are increasingly immersing ourselves in the movies, TV shows, video games, and pop music that dominate our culture. But it was Orlando that drew me—center of unabashed fun; sinkhole meeting ground where theme hotels, massive entertainment complexes anachronistically dubbed *parks*, and the beleaguered working stiffs of the middle class indulge themselves in an orgiastic frenzy of manufactured good times. Orlando is where a significant number of North Americans go to relax, line up, take it all in. Orlando is a good place to test the theory that pop culture is becoming more extreme and immersive in order to meet our increasing demand to be recognized on an individual basis for our specialness.

I stay at the Hard Rock Hotel on the Universal Studios theme park "campus." This particular Hard Rock Hotel is supposed to replicate a California mansion once owned by a Don Henley–type rock star with a memorabilia fetish. That explains the oversized stucco look and the glass cases containing, among other things, a 1972 Elvis Vegas jumpsuit. At the Hard Rock, pop music is played in every hallway and lounge. It dominates the huge pool and there are even speakers underwater so you can rock while you dunk.

The Hard Rock Hotel is a reminder that a great many vacations are no longer about travel or even tourism. How many places can we go that are authentic, unsullied, free of Coca-Cola and Mickey Mouse? The majority of people, anyway, are losing interest in authenticity. They want more of the fake. These days, vacations and escapes are about extending the entertainment experience, making that night at the movies last a week. If we are to live in a fake world, then we will embrace that fake world by making it *our special* world. In talking to fellow vacationers, I discover that the primary goal of this bunch of travelers is neither to lie passively in the sun nor to discover a culture different from their own. We have come for one reason only: to be entertained.

At the original Universal Studios theme park, I take in Beetlejuice's Graveyard Revue. There are women dressed in cleavage-revealing black leather. There is a Frankenstein and a Wolfboy. Beetlejuice trolls the audience picking out people to make fun of, and introduces the various lame songs. Beetlejuice is intent on audience participation, constantly leading us through pat exercises in which we are instructed to yell this or that. The audience is palpably unenthusiastic, offering up minimal response to Beetlejuice's throaty entreaties. I sit down next to a man in his seventies who lives in Florida and visits Universal Studios several times a year. He tells me that he always goes to the same shows. Doesn't he get bored? "It's better than sitting on the couch watching TV with my thumb up my butt," he says.

Blunt but insightful, this fellow sums up theme-park Orlando. We are here for a more enticing and elaborate entertainment experience that doles out our prepackaged fun in biggie sizes. In an era where entertainment defines who and what we are, it is not surprising that what we want are better and bigger entertainments, preferably with a personalized dimension. And yet there is an accompanying sense of purposelessness and futility. Over a small container of watery clam chowder (four dollars), I talk to an overweight, pallid couple from Chicago. They seem apologetic for being caught in the midst of the theme park. They tell me that Walt Disney World is better, that the Epcot light show is the best thing they have ever seen. Ever. "But," the man says sadly, "the prices are outrageous." "They gouge you," his wife agrees. Typically they go to the mountains or someplace quiet for vacation. Both of them are wearing earplugs. The man complains about the noise. "We're having a great time," his wife snaps at him. "Let's try to make this a positive experience."

We sign on for entertainments that affirm we've been somewhere different while immersing us in the cultural tropes we've already come to know and anticipate. A pop-culture vacation won't stress you out, because you've seen it all before, but it won't bore you either. This is louder, brighter, faster—better than a thumb up the butt.

It is clear from the passive, grudgingly offered responses that the audience is bored with Beetlejuice, a show so filled with burlesque imagery and ribald humor that twenty years ago it would have been considered inappropriate for family entertainment. The more entertainment culture becomes steadily immersed in our everyday lives, promising us a great time all the time, the more difficult it is to treat us to something new, different, and better than what we've had before. We want entertainment that can meet our demands— for better, quicker and faster, but also for immersion and at least the sense that we are fully empowered participants, each of us special, each of us a perpetually rising star.

Theme hotels like the Hard Rock are a good example of how this works. Why shouldn't we be entertained even while we wait to check in? Hooters Air, a spinoff of the cleavage-and-buffalo-wings bar chain, offers flights between Atlanta, Newark, and Myrtle Beach, and each plane is guaranteed to contain two busty, tank-top-wearing, short-shorts-adorned Hooters babes, who don't function as flight attendants, but simply ride the plane offering "entertainment and customer service." Similarly, all three of the relatively new hotels on the Universal complex promise a different "entertainment" experience. One hotel is built to look like an Italian seaside village, one to reflect a Bali, South Pacific, vacation. But the most popular of them all is my temporary home, part of the Hard Rock chain. The rock 'n' roll theme permeates your stay; you can get a wake-up call from previous rock-star guests of the hotel. A freshly painted banister warns you away by quoting the Police: "Don't stand so close to me." Sitting in the lobby, I listen to a live recording of the Violent Femme's "Blister in the Sun" and stare at a portrait of Mick Jagger, his mouth gaping open like a caught fish. The Hard Rock Hotel, as with all permutations of pop, sells a version of individuality and rebellion. It says: Be who you are, do your own thing, but pay for it with your credit card and please no swearing, there are kids staying here. At the poolside bar, they play an Eminem video, the theme being how much the bad-boy ranter hates his mother. The dirty words are bleeped out. Next to me, Mom orders a burger and virgin margarita for her son, puts it on her room bill. The boy looks distinctly unimpressed. Stares blankly at the screen. Even here, in the midst of total and constant stimulation, he is obviously bored.

Why wouldn't he be bored? All the way to Florida, but he is still on the outside looking in. For the entertainment makers, the answer to the boy's bored stare is simple: bigger theme-park complexes with steadily more immersive attractions.

In early 1995, this particular outskirt of the city was pretty much empty, with the exception of a single, aging Universal Studios theme park, an afterthought that tourists visited on their way out of Disney World. But a mere four years later, there were three huge hotels, a refurbished Universal Studios park, and a new adjacent park, Islands of Adventure, with the highest tech rides found anywhere. Sitting in the middle of the theme parks and the hotels is a new restaurant-shopping complex called City Walk. All of this aims to provide an edgier, more adult counterpart to Disney's toddler fantasy. It's also tangible evidence that immersive entertainment is growing by leaps and bounds.

Canals and lush, groomed garden paths connect the Hard Rock Hotel to City Walk, which despite its name is anything but urban. The walk features a collection of name-brand venues—including Jimmy Buffet's Margaritaville, Emeril's Restaurant (the celeb chef again!), and a giant NBA City Restaurant—mixed in with innumerable gift shops and a thirty-screen movie theater, providing a combination that can hardly be said to replicate even the most pasteurized downtown. This is a collapsed version of suburbia, minus the parking lots and the necessity of driving up and down the strip. Here you stroll instead of cruise, which permits you to maximize your entertainment experience by using the ample on-site takeout-margarita windows and beer kiosks. And since you don't have a truck waiting, any purchases you make at the gift centers can be left behind to be delivered later to your on-site hotel. It seems perfect, but there's a downside: More than one person I spoke to complained about *all that walking*.

City Walk is designed to immerse. You can stand in the middle of it and see nothing but pop culture—pop restaurants, pop gift shops selling pop products, pop bars promising a fake Mardi Gras or pseudo-Caribbean cruise, a giant movie theater, and, of course, the two theme parks standing on either end of the City Walk like all-knowing, all-enticing pyramid tributes to the gods of fun. Spend more than a day or two here and you start to lose sense of things outside the theme-park world. You become used to the constant noise. You become inured to the bright lights and crowds. You start to think that Emeril's Restaurant might actually have decent food.

I can't sit still. I'm in motion, moving back and forth between hotel bar, theme park 1, City Walk, theme park 2, hotel pool, and hotel bar. A few days into my trip and I am a desensitized wanderer, constantly on the lookout for fun. The complex is designed in such a way that you never have to leave the complex.

I don't leave the complex.

The more we demand participation, the more difficult it becomes for the technicians of fun to satisfy us. Mass entertainment is invariably passive because money is made when millions of units and millions of people move relatively quickly (thus passively) through the same set of experiences and rides. The Men in Black ride outfits us with guns and invites us to shoot at aliens as we lurch through in automated cars. Basically a giant video game (and let's not forget that video games sell better than any other entertainment product), it is probably the most popular attraction at Universal Studios. Over in the adjoining Islands of Adventure, the high-tech Spiderman ride reigns supreme, with its mixture of traditional pop-out thrill surprises and the latest in virtual-reality special effects. It is hard to imagine any more immersive, extreme thrills that can still accommodate hundreds of thousands of people a day.

At the hotel bar I talk to a London-based set designer who worked on *The Mummy* and *The Mummy 2*. He is in town to consult with Universal about the Mummy ride that is currently in development. He seems ambivalent about theme parks, defends them and Hollywood movies as just harmless mind candy, but then goes on a rant about the Americanization of a country like Thailand and how local culture is disappearing there. I point out that when local culture disappears, it is replaced in large part by pop-culture products like *The Mummy*. He agrees, but insists that the larger process isn't his fault or responsibility. He has to go, he is being taken out to dinner by theme-park execs. Watching him leave, I think of media critic Todd Gitlin's assertion that what the mass media give us is the "promise of feeling"—feeling divorced from opinion. "We may not know how we feel about one or another batch of images," writes Gitlin, "except that they are there."

Despite, and because of, their ultimate role in creating homogeneous societies, the theme rides continue to evolve and search for ways to give us the sense that we have integral roles in the action.

The future of entertainment is clearly specialization, personalization. This is obvious from the theme park's newer attractions—
Spiderman and Men in Black—and from the audience's boredom
when it comes to old-fashioned shows such as the Beetlejuice
revue. Back at the theme hotel, there is more evidence of entertainment culture searching for new ways to extend and "extreme" the
experience. In conjunction with Halloween Horror Night, Hard
Rock has created a "Halloween Suite," a specially decorated,
cadaver-inclusive horror room. A framed portrait of ghoulish
shock-rocker Marilyn Manson hangs on the foyer wall, but other
than that, the two-room suite's decorations are strictly ersatz-
Gothic. The sitting room contains a spiderweb-enshrouded coffin;
ceiling-to-floor shelving filled with dust-covered jars trapping eyeballs and bugs; and scattered Victorian-looking medical imple-
ments. The bedroom is all old furniture and fusty fixtures, though
the TV and clock radio remain, somewhat spoiling the illusion. So
what's the deal with the Horror suite? Well, couples who rent out
the room for a night (at US$568, double the cost of a regular room)
have bought themselves a first-class, one-of-a kind haunting.

Scott, on loan from the Universal Studios special-effects department, shows how it all works. The lights go out. Footsteps, groans.
A glass jar shatters. The sounds intensify as the steps get louder.
Then a swirling noise, like a strong wind. Candles flare. Lights
flicker. The bed shakes, the dresser rattles. The haunting ends in an
outpouring of silly string, supposedly covering the (by now) cow-
ering occupants of the bed. The haunting, technically excellent,
lasts less than five minutes. The suite is occupied three to four
nights a week, sold as a package with the Halloween Horror Night
experience. The scare is short-lived, but coming as it does at two or
three in the morning, the anticipation is surely extensive. One gets
the sense that the couples who stay don't really care about dura-
tion—the idea is to amp up the fun by attaining the ultimate contradiction: unique *and* prepackaged; safely extreme fun. Certainly
nobody seems to be complaining. A second Horror Night room has
been opened to meet market demand.

DESPITE ALL THIS EFFORT to take us to the next level of fun, nobody over age twelve at the theme parks seems able to muster up anything like unabashed enthusiasm. The crowds, abundant even in a slow time of year, are patently sluggish, clapping lethargically and leaving before the final act in order to beat the lineup sure to form at the next attraction. Talking to three high school kids who travelled several hours to attend Halloween Horror Night, I ask what draws them to this particular extravaganza. "We go every year," one says. "It's something to do," another remarks. At the epicenter of fun: resignation and ritual.

I am reminded of a scene in the great Japanese film *After Life*. In it, the recently dead are asked to choose a single memory they can bring with them to the afterlife. To assist them, the dead are met by counselors. At one point, a girl reveals her memory to her counselor. She happily describes a ride on a theme-park roller coaster. The counselor cringes and asks if she is sure that is the memory she wants. The counselor also says that many of the kids who pass through choose a similar memory. Is that *really* the memory she wants? She sends her charge back to her room to think about it.

It's a telling scene because it speaks to the false reality of the park experience. Do we really want our memories to be given to us by disillusioned set designers with a love-hate attraction to the way their work is reshaping the world? Of course not. We want our memories to be personal, unique. But the more we seek precrafted entertainment as the primary focus our lives, as a way to give the meaning to our lives that pop promises us our lives should have, the more our memories are shared, colonized, implanted. And the more deadened we feel thinking about the fun we had yesterday, the keener we are going to be to experience more fun, different fun, *better* fun. Entertainment seeks out further and further extremes to keep us engaged and immersed in the pop dream. Each entertainment trend must erase the past, outdo itself, place us entirely in the all-encompassing present of our self—if only for a moment.

Extreme Plus! Upping the Ante

We find the trend to extremity even in the theoretically sedate art films of Europe. The French film *À ma soeur! (Fat Girl)* was banned in Ontario for its depiction of a plump thirteen-year-old having sex with the man who has just murdered her mother and sister. ("Banned in Ontario!" ads for the film proclaimed in other parts of Canada.) While some defended the movie as a feminist director's poignant exploration of adolescent girlhood, others wondered about a seemingly pointless violent ending sure to garner the kind of attention that a "poignant exploration of adolescence" would not. Sticking with France, the film *Irreversible* sent people fleeing the theater when it opened in Cannes. Apparently a depiction of one man beating another's head in with a fire extinguisher was just a bit too real. The film also includes a nine-minute rape scene. In Japan, a wildly popular film was *Battle Royale,* a brutal blood-bath featuring a class of thirteen-year-olds who are condemned to an island, assigned weapons, and instructed to kill each other while the rest of the country enjoys the spectacle on TV. The most poignant moment comes when a boy tries to protect a girl from danger. Unfortunately, the girl thinks he is trying to kill her, so she shoots him. As he dies, he moans a last proclamation of love. "But," the girl cries, playing the gruesome scene for laughs, "he never even called me!" The teenage girl killer from *Battle Royale* would later be cast in Quentin Tarantino's *Kill Bill*, Tarantino's way, no doubt, of giving props to a movie whose plot-free destruction mirrors his own epic slaughterfest. Explains U.S. film critic David Thomson: "We've reached the point where there is excessive pressure to show us what we haven't seen before, with or without—but increasingly without—dramatic or narrative support." "There's no moral," agrees heavy-metal-dude-turned-director Rob Zombie, commenting on his B-movie debut *House of 1,000 Corpses,* the DVD of which features a grotesque clown host verbally abusing the viewer with every foul word in the English language in the course of demanding that we press play and start the feature. "There's no upside," Zombie says, "it's morally corrupt."

But forget the movies. Again, TV does it with less style and artistic pretense, but with far more penetration into our daily lives and collective consciousness. So-called reality TV is where the real extreme entertainment can be found. *Fear Factor* shows us vats of bugs poured over people's heads, or contestants chewing (and puking up) rotten sheep's eyes. *Cops* and its legions of imitators show us bloody arrests, rampant profanity. We can see cancer operations, women giving birth, meticulously recreated tragedies. A short-lived TV show honed in on the "flaws" of regular people, then showed us step-by-step how plastic surgery would correct their physical blights and change their lives. The evening before her surgery, Stacey looks boldly at the camera and announces, "This is the last night that I'm going to look like me." Thousands of applicants signed up to be considered for the ABC series *Extreme Makeover*, not to be confused with the Fox network's version *The Swan* or other even lower-rent shows based on this premise. The popularity of these shows, both with viewers and eager participants, is not only evidence of the new conformity and the pop-inspired notion that you can and should reshape the narrative of your life through techniques as extreme as surgery, but is also evidence of the increasingly virulent strain of extreme individuality that the new conformity is giving rise to. In an era where everybody is special, you have to go the extra mile. You have to, as Geraldo once did, have on-camera live liposuction in front of your studio audience.

Gross sells, and so does anger, outrage, and evil. Extreme emotion expressed in extreme ways. The goal of this kind of entertainment is what one critic describes as the creation of "pure and unrelated presents in time." In other words, entertainment will do whatever is necessary to rescue us from the mundane realities of daily life. If nothing I've said so far surprises you or even seems all that extreme, well, that's just the point, isn't it? In 1967, Seattle underground newspaper *Helix* reported on a new band called the Doors. Wrote an excited reporter: "Their style is early cunnilingual with overtones of the Massacre of the Innocents. An electrified sex slaughter. A musical blood-bath . . . if they leave us crotch-raw and exhausted, at least they leave us aware of our aliveness." This has always been the project of pop: to give us a sense of aliveness amid a reductive system of anonymous power subsources reducing us to various categories of crowd. In '67, pop pointed to a new way to be; it felt fresh, wild, liberating. Today it is hard to imagine even the most naively enthusiastic campus journalist penning a similar concert review. The Beatles, Elvis (Presley), and Jim Morrison had kids swooning, screaming, and fainting in their day. Today they seem quaint and friendly compared with Eminem, who, on the DVD version of the fictionalized retelling of his life *8 Mile,* includes a video/song about all the (mostly naked) "bitches" who want but can't have him. (Suddenly wholesome, the rapper has since announced his retirement from music so he can focus on raising his daughter and reuniting with his ex-wife, whom he has remarried.)

Entertainment keeps searching for that next fainting moment. In Las Vegas in the summer of 2003, Montreal's Cirque du Soleil opened its show *Zumanity*, which the troupe billed as "erotic cabaret." A *New York Times* writer called the production a "mainstream entertainment that features among its acts a sadomasochist prison scenario, a drag queen who channels Billie Holiday, and couplings in configurations across the sexual range." Or how about the Russian teen duo Tatu, whose manager Ivan Shapovalov, a former psychiatrist, came up with what one rock commentator describes as the duo's "teen lesbian shtick" after noting the boom in "lolita porn" in his homeland? Meanwhile, U.S. illusionist David Blaine locked himself in a clear plastic box that was then hung over London's Thames River and sat there for forty-four days. Starving yourself to death for attention proved successful—a quarter of a million people visited the site of the stunt.

And still, none of this is particularly groundbreaking these days. As Tom Beaujour, the editor of rock magazine *Revolver,* is quoted as saying:

> If anything, rock stars have become too respectable for their own good. Rock has been around for so long that, unless you're unhinged, you're not doing anything counter-cultural

or even adventurous by being a rock musician—or even a hard rock musician. That trail has been blazed. You don't get beat up on the street for having long hair and tattoos. Everyone has tattoos.

Indeed, Michael Atkinson, a professor at Memorial University in St. John's, Newfoundland, concludes in his book *Tattooed: The Sociogenesis of a Body Art* that far from being a rebel custom, tattooing is increasingly popular with women, who, according to his estimates, now make up something like 65 percent of tattoo customers. Most, he notes, get tats that emphasize traditional ideas of femininity—goodbye forearm skull and crossbones, hello navel butterfly. No surprise that tattoos are now commonplace, given their popularity with sports stars. "You don't have a tattoo, you're the strange one," points out Malik Rose of the San Antonio Spurs. He is referring to the fact that in the 2003 season, upwards of 70 percent of players on the National Basketball Association teams sported tattoos.

There are now magazines devoted exclusively to once-fringe behavior, from tattoos and piercing to communicating with aliens or becoming a sex slave. *Vice,* a free monthly magazine that began in the early nineties as an irregularly printed newsprint indie serving the mean streets of Montreal, made its reputation as a potty-mouth tome for the post-literate. Articles celebrate all manners of extreme behavior: "Vice's Top Ten Criminals of All Time," "My Mom Shot Me," "A Guy Who Was on Acid for a Whole Year." Naturally these masterworks cried out to become a book—*The Vice Guide to Sex and Drugs and Rock and Roll,* which begins with an introduction that references editor Suroosh Alvi's former heroin habit, editor Shane Smith's drinking problem, and how the boys screwed ad reps—"old balding dogs with horrible tits"—and chilled out at peep shows while on their way to the top. All this published not by some underground outfit but by HarperCollins.

It takes a particular brand of cynicism to profitably run an extreme culture outfit. Richard Metzger manages an entire "extreme" empire, with his disinfo.com brand including a website, books, and a TV show.

One visit to his popular website yields Metzger interviewing a performance artist on "why she sewed her vagina shut," plus an artist on serial killers, and a philosopher discussing the "coming biological apocalypse." Metzger cynically and blatantly preys on the I'm-Special cravings of a pop-infested populace. As he says in an interview: "I like to encourage deviance wherever I go and make a buck in the process." He clearly knows who his audience is and why they are attracted to this prophet of the perverse. These days, he says, when so many kids are buying tattoos and piercings at the local shopping mall, what used to be the ultimate nonconformist statement "signifies nothing. Well, if it signifies anything, it's the 'I want to be different—like everybody else' mentality. Pathetic."

It may be pathetic, but it's also Metzger's bread and butter. We want to be noticed (like everybody else), and we're careful students of those who have the balls to take the extreme path toward recognition. Metzger himself is following in the path of a noticeable "underground" trend that can be traced from the eighties pattern of turning nihilism into pop via the auspices of cultural outlets such as the still-popular RE/Search, publisher of journals and books celebrating, among other things, the body modifications of "modern primitives," the life and times of pain-embracing performance artist Bob Flanagan "supermasochist," and fun with bodily fluids.

The Dark Side: Killing the Cat

How far would you be prepared—or allowed—to go to be special?

Serge Moscovici argues that our society is "an institution which inhibits what it stimulates." He speaks of a society that "invents prohibitions together with the means of transgressing them." However immersive pop is, the one thing it does not and cannot allow is true access. The profit-mongering gatekeepers keep us at bay, replacing interpersonal communication with ever-more-extreme pseudo-participatory entertainments. Entertainment today stimulates then inhibits us.

Inhibited by what stimulates us—the pop imagery that becomes ever more extreme—we shouldn't be surprised that our attempts to access pop culture and claim our I'm-Special birthright will also become more extreme. Pop culture, as we've seen, is all about preaching transgression and rebellion for the greater good of you. We want to make the pop theme real. When pop culture and neo-traditional communities fail, we search for other ways to satisfy our need. In many cases, we turn to extreme transgression. We behave badly and reap the "rewards" of notoriety and celebrity. As Margaret Atwood wrote in her sci-fi dystopia *The Handmaid's Tale,* "People will do anything rather than admit that their lives have no meaning."

But would you eat rotting sheep eyeballs? Or marry a total stranger, expose your flabby thighs to the scalpel, change your name to Dunlop-tires? Or maybe, like Larry Corcoran, vacation at the sites of mass tragedies? Corcoran drove the thirteen hours from Boston to Columbine so he could be at the high school on the one-year anniversary of the massacre. Corcoran's already been to Waco and Oklahoma City. "Maybe I am intruding a bit," he tells a reporter. "But it seems like in this country, whenever there's a tragedy, there's a tourist attraction. I'm not the only one." When pop and life merge into the new conformity, we start to feel entitled to engage in what-ever antic brings us pleasure, makes us feel special. Corcoran is just one of many who get off on seeming to transgress. But with more and more people joining him on the *sites of tragedy tour,* even this sick pop kink begins to feel inhibited, just another part of a pop culture that allows anything except real participation.

Using extreme behavior to articulate specialness is a tactic with a growing following, particularly among younger generations. Writes teen psychologist Ron Taffel: "We are seeing a new kind of teenager embedded in a far more raw, intense and pervasive youth culture than ever before."

Jesse Power was a twenty-one-year-old Toronto art student who wanted to do something really special for a final project. He came up with a brilliant solution: A video of a black-and-white domestic cat being tortured. That ought to get their attention. Indeed, it did. And a cruelty to animals conviction to go with it. After the video was screened, police raided his loft, and they found the dead cat and videos "including one that showed the men slash the cat's throat, repeatedly stab it with dental tools and then disembowel the short-haired cat with a straight knife." (Note: Powers had two accomplices, but it was his art project.) Powers initially defended himself by claiming that the video was a commentary on how badly we treat animals. This is the kind of deluded thinking that the new conformity perpetuates: What I'm doing must be right, because it is about *how I feel*.

Gratuitous violence portrayed as a way to protest violence. The strategy of momentary extremity to call attention to a moment in time is increasingly appealing to anyone seeking mainstream attention. Creating a pop moment through preplanned acts of (extreme) spontaneity allows individuals to take advantage of a world in which the cameras are always ready, trained on whatever is about to happen.

Is it any wonder that the once unheard-of phenomenon of fans randomly attacking sports figures while they are on the field has become yet another commonplace occurrence? The most infamous of these incidents was the stabbing of tennis teen Monica Seles in the middle of a match. Since then, as a *Sports Illustrated* commentator puts it, "there has been a fundamental shift out on fandom's fringe . . . today's intruders want to be part of the show." Before William Ligue Jr. and his teenage son violently assaulted and permanently injured a major-league baseball coach standing next to first base, Ligue called his sister to make sure she was watching the game on TV. "People want to be noticed, and they'll spend the night in jail just to get their name in the paper," says Boston University Professor Leonard Zaichkowsky, who has studied fan behavior for fifteen years. "Getting noticed" is no longer achieved by the age-old tradition of racing across the pitch in the nude. Today, stabbings and beatings are more likely to get you your fifteen moments. After all, no fewer than *five* people ran onto the SkyDome turf in the ninth inning of the summer of 2003 Toronto Blue Jays' game against

Baltimore Orioles. The perpetrators were arrested and charged with mere trespassing, and who remembers them?

The distinction between using violence as a way to critique society versus employing violent or radical acts simply for their shock value and as a surefire way to get noticed has become blurred. Just as the "news" of a celebrity's arrest on rape charges spills over to an interview with the celebrity's wife on *Entertainment Tonight,* so too does the ongoing merger between real and fake create moral and ethical dilemmas and turn every action into a popularity poll. French novelist Michel Houellebecq writes in his novel *The Elementary Particles:* "Having exhausted the possibilities of sexual pleasure, it was reasonable that individuals, liberated from the constraints of ordinary morality, should turn their attentions to the wider pleasures of cruelty." Houellebecq makes connections between the Marquis de Sade, the devolvement of the pleasure-seeking hippie movement into Charles Manson's "family," and the Viennese Actionists of the fifties who, not unlike Jesse Power, filmed their torturing and gutting of animals for later exhibition in art galleries. Houellebecq equates all of this human activity to the pursuit of pleasure and power, noting that "Actionists, beatniks, hippies and serial killers were all pure libertarians who affirmed the rights of the individual against social norms." In other words: Put into practice and taken to its extreme, the right to individuality is the right to claim pleasure for oneself regardless of the consequences. Since pleasure today is garnered from achieving celebrity, the right to individuality at any cost becomes the right to special, regardless.

THE EERIE OVERLAPPING time frame of the Maryland sniper attacks and my visit to Halloween Horror Night finds a neat parallel in the relationship between murder and celebrity. We pay to be terrified, and crave the feeling of being alive that supposedly comes out of proximity to death. Is it any surprise that there are those who confuse the fantasy with reality and figure that if that's what we want, such excitement can be easily provided?

The disaffected duo who terrorized suburban Washington did so seemingly without ideological or political inclinations. It just gave them a rush to drive around and shoot people. A letter left at a crime scene begins "Call me God." There was, at the time, some debate regarding whether this letter was left by the killer(s) or an enthusiastic fan. Looking back now, we can see how little it matters. Someone left the handwritten note (police now attribute the document to one of the two killers). The note was there to deliberately titillate the media, further reinforcing the fact that seventeen-year-old Lee Boyd Malvo and his ersatz stepfather John Allen Muhammad had nothing to gain from their activities. What did they want? What were they trying to prove? We'll probably never know. We don't even know if their motivation was really nothing more than the opportunity to be noticed and feel special. But we do know that they left notes and messages taunting the police ("p.s. your children are not safe anywhere at anytime") and consequently ensuring that the media would lurch from one frenzy to another so long as the spree continued.

Not surprisingly, the letter and notes mirror previous serial killers and their attempts to court media favor with catchy monikers and pithy trademark "styles." David Berkowitz, who killed six in New York in the mid-seventies and earned immortality in the Spike Lee flick *Summer of Sam,* wrote a famous note to a police detective: "I am a monster. I am the 'Son of Sam.'" A former FBI profiler who interviewed Berkowitz after his arrest later reported that the Son of Sam found it a "stimulating thing for him to see the letters in the paper." This same profiler notes that for an "inadequate loser" like Berkowitz, getting his deeds and his words in the paper becomes his only "way of imposing power and control over society."

Lawrence Bittaker, who tortured and murdered girls in southern California in 1979, encouraged media coverage by dumping a mutilated body on a lawn. In prison, he signed autographs "pliers Bittaker." Clifford Olson, who raped and killed at least eleven children in British Columbia, apparently begged to be referred to by the name of the fictional sadistic murderer genius Hannibal Lecter.

The Los Angeles "Night Stalker" Richard Ramirez reportedly said to one of his victims, "You know who I am, don't you? I'm the one they're writing about in the newspapers and on TV." When Paul Bernardo and Karla Homolka raped and killed young girls (including Homolka's sister), all the activities were meticulously recorded on videotape. Naturally, the infamous duo are now the subject of several books and a feature film. Write Jack Levin and James Allan Fox, professors at Northeastern University in Boston: "Becoming a popular culture celebrity is an important part of the motivation that inspires serial killers to continue committing murder." Can anyone doubt that Theodore Kaczynski—the Unabomber—was inspired by the media attention he received? He promised to stop killing if *The New York Times* and *The Washington Post* would run his lengthy essay on the evils of technology. Although Kaczynski was turned in by his brother, his plan would have to be called "a success" in public relations terms: He branded himself a celebrity, and got his message out into the world in a big way. PR companies spend millions trying to achieve the same effect. All Kaczynski had to do was kill and maim. And let's not forget that Eric Rudolph—the man accused of planting a bomb at the 1996 Atlanta Olympics, killing one and wounding 111, not to mention blowing up several abortion clinics—inspired two country-and-western songs and a top-selling T-shirt bearing the words "Run Rudolph Run." A $1-million reward offer from the government went unclaimed. He was finally apprehended in 2003, much to the dismay of his "fan base."

Serial killers aren't the only ones motivated by celebrity. So-called rampage killers are also clearly concerned with their legacy. Most of these killers are basically committing a kind of attention-getting, media-friendly suicide. A study of 102 rampage killers in the United States, starting with the first case in 1966 (Charles Whitman killing 14 people from his position atop a tower at the University of Texas) showed that not a single one of the perpetrators made an escape and most—89—never even tried to leave the scene. Why leave if the point is for you to gain glorious recognition as you bask in the ultimate rush of taking other people's lives?

As rampage killers became more sophisticated, we started to see more deliberate plans for courting celebrity after death. Eric Harris and Dylan Klebold shot and killed thirteen people at Columbine High School in April 1999, then killed themselves. They were teenagers, fully versed in the lore of extreme celebrity. They left behind videos of themselves preening with firearms. Harris also left a journal making sure that his actions would not be misunderstood: "I want to leave a lasting impression on the world, and goddamnit, do not blame anyone else besides me and V [Klebold] for this." After reviewing the videos left behind, Jefferson County's deputy district attorney, Steve Jensen, said: "It's obvious that these guys wanted to become cult heroes of some kind." As Michael Moore noted famously in his Oscar-winning anti-gun documentary *Bowling for Columbine,* the two boys, perhaps anxious to seal their legacy as cool customers, went bowling the morning before they shot up their cafeteria. (Actually, there is debate about this: The cops say the boys didn't go bowling, but Moore says witnesses place them at the alley.)

A similar incident three years later saw nineteen-year-old Robert Steinhauser kill sixteen at the Johann Gutenberg high school in Erfurt, Germany. Composed and well-liked, Steinhauser was the opposite of the Columbine boys, who were bullied and reviled. Steinhauser had gotten himself expelled from school while the Columbine kids endured their bullying and plotted revenge. Completely different personalities and scenarios, but one thing remains the same: Steinhauser and the Columbine duo believed that extreme behavior would enshrine them in pop culture for perpetuity. "One day I want everyone to know my name and I want to be famous," Steinhauser told a schoolmate not long before his murderous rampage.

Sometimes destruction is avoided because it's enough for the perpetrators to achieve a certain recognition and attention and then go on with what is left of their lives. In an apparent copycat incident, a teenager brandishing a pistol took hostages in another German school in October 2002. He demanded one million dollars in ransom but ended up exchanging hostages for a pizza and a cellphone before finally letting everyone go and revealing that the pistol was a fake. This would-be kidnapper didn't want to die before he could be notorious. He was wearing a bulletproof vest. Such antics continue to inspire others. A Swedish sixteen-year-old was detained in spring 2004 after a hunting rifle and bomb-making chemicals were found. An accompanying online diary detailed plans that centered around a high-school massacre meant to, as a news report says, "imitate the 1999 massacre at Columbine High School."

"The condemned man," notes Michel Foucault, "found himself transformed into a hero by the sheer extent of his widely advertised crimes." Knowledge that they will inevitably become figures reproduced in the entertainment world means that serial and rampage killers increasingly seem to be acting out a predetermined pop ritual. Why does it seem as though the sniper duo just *had* to leave their "Call me God" note? Paradoxically, to not do so would be to deviate from the way it is supposed to be. Even if the killer does not leave a "memento" these days, one can be sure that no gruesome deed will go unchronicled. Though Karla Homolka and Paul Bernardo are not able to write a tell-all book about their crimes (nor peddle the videotapes they predictably recorded), a lurid tell-all account of their crimes was a bestseller, and at least one individual has been arrested for posting banned footage on the internet. Meanwhile, Montgomery County Police Chief Charles Moose, who presided over the Maryland sniper investigation, signed a US$100,000 deal with a publisher to write an insider account of the police hunt for the killer, and is reported to be a consultant on, naturally enough, the movie version of events. When Moose lost an appeal to an ethics board that ruled he could not profit from his work as a government official and would have to return the advance and consulting fees, he promptly quit his day job and signed up with a California speakers' agency.

The anthropologist Francis Hsu made a convincing connection between deviant violence and the rise of individualism. "Achievement and violence in fact spring from one common denominator: rugged individualism." In pondering this connection, he points out that "all creativity is a form of deviation, a departure from the norm." In an era where departures from the norm are the norm, where being "creative" has come to be understood as being noticed, and being noticed as the highest pinnacle of achievement, Hsu sees more and more of us being driven to succeed (i.e., articulate our individual special creativity) "without regard for established rules." He writes of the individualist being "driven to treat all other human beings as things, to be manipulated, forced or eliminated if they happen to get in the way of his forward march." Hsu finishes by presciently warning that "our society will continue to generate more geniuses and star performers who will excel in diverse fields, but it will also relentlessly foster more deviants and criminals whose anti-social creativity will reach more alarming proportions."

The bridge between individualism and extreme behavior is the ideology of special. Taunted by a pop culture sensibility that relentlessly celebrates greedy billionaires, we crave recognition of our special existence and receive only ever-more-intense bouts of momentary instantaneous entertainment to satisfy us. Invited, urged, and commanded to rebel against the system to gain access to the system, many are beginning to do so. But what happens to a society in which everyone's a rebel?

8

REVOLUTION REDUX
THE END OF INDIVIDUALITY?

L ASQUETI IS A TINY DOT on the edge of the Pacific, the barely noted island home to 350 people. Sitting in the middle of the Strait of Georgia to the west of mainland British Columbia and reached via a small passenger ferry from much larger Vancouver Island, it seems far away from the whirling confusions of life. Here is simplicity and isolation, the embodiment of the dream so many of us harbor to drop out and tune in to a different frequency: the squall of seabirds flying low as they scavenge for a snack, the continual arrival of the surf against the primeval coastline, the wind through the giant firs, whose green boughs sway majestically in the winter breeze.

If there's anywhere left to run away from or rebel against the mounting pressures of the new conformity, it is here. I take the ferry over. The boat is fundamentally different from the usual ferries that serve the other Gulf Islands. Walk-on passengers only. Some might argue that the island is too small to support a car ferry, but the overall effect is to discourage day trippers and tourists from putting the island on their destination agenda. Lasqueti Island, which has deliberately declined electric hookup (residents voted against it), inspires such theories. This is a place that conveys a distinct commitment to preserving its isolation.

The water is calm and the strong wind cool and fresh. There are ten or so others on the ferry with me, all of them island residents dragging home everything from sacks of rice to bags of laundered socks and underwear. Just surveying the supplies packed into the ferry gives you a sense of the sacrifices that living on an island with no electricity and running water demand. Though most residents of Lasqueti have generators (and plumbing systems that rely on those generators), there is still much that needs to be either done by hand or dragged into the nearest small town, a typically provincial burg that fades into the distance as the ferry chugs me toward this tiny outpost.

Soaking up the fierce breeze is Morgan, an intense man in his early forties. Morgan runs a small sawmill on the island, and he moved from Vancouver to Lasqueti in the eighties, when around one hundred thousand dollars fetched him a 160-acre plot. Before moving out to the island, both he and his wife were working in a fish-processing plant. Morgan scans the receding horizon and speaks with a bitterness that belies the seeming calm of his life. He talks about the conformity of mainstream society and points at Vancouver Island, from whence we came. He talks about having to send his kids to live on the bigger island so that they can go to high school. He says they are having trouble making friends in high school, "trouble socializing" is how he puts it, and attributes this to the fact that "they aren't interested in making superficial friends." He notes that "on the [smaller] island you make friends for real; it's an entirely different way of life."

Morgan moved to Lasqueti with the intention of becoming a furniture maker. That dream has yet to be realized. He's always busy just surviving and never seems to have time to work on his craft. He tells me that he thought he'd have more free time on the island, but he ends up expending a lot of effort just living in an environment where all the luxuries of modern life have to be maintained by do-it-yourself schemes. Still, he can't imagine moving back to Vancouver, and, he notes, if he did, he'd never be able to afford anything but the most generic lodgings, a far cry from his vast spread. Even out in Lasqueti,

Morgan is impatient with the trappings of ordinary life. On summers and weekends, he says, you sometimes have to wait in line to get the ferry. He says it as though he can't believe it, ruefully spits it out as if he has just tasted something bad. Does the self-reliant life lived on Lasqueti translate into people being less susceptible to the conformity from "over there"? Morgan isn't sure. He says that if he could, he would move even further off the grid. "But," he says, "there are some things I'm not willing to give up."

The ferry pulls into Lasqueti. Supplies are dragged into the backs of barged-in pickups and with the uncertain rumble of old engines, the residents are gone, swallowed into the swaying forest that faces us. As we walk up from the boat, there is a beaten-up hotel on one side, closed for the season. On the other side, Karen runs a small diner, which features a counter and four stools, and is the island's only restaurant. Karen serves up a tasty muffin and tells me that she recently moved to Lasqueti from Salt Spring, a much bigger Gulf Island with more than ten thousand year-round residents, multiple daily car-ferry service from several ports, and the feel of a tourist resort. Karen worked at the Salt Spring Island hospital for twenty-four years. She watched the island "being taken over by yuppies" and finally decided to bail out. "It's really hard to make a living here," she notes. "You have to be more in touch with the earth and yourself, more creative in your work."

In front of Karen's diner, a leathery man named Frank is settling down to the task of turning a piece of wood into a paddle. Frank lived in Yukon for twenty years, then spent the subsequent decade living on his boat, scavenging, and working oyster beds. These days, he lives on Lasqueti and beachcombs; he tells me he can get three hundred dollars for a prize tree stump, twice that if he turns the stump into a coffee table. Frank shows me a picture from an old how-to manual, probably printed in the fifties. It's a diagram of a flat, dock-like boat. Frank plans to build a similar scow this winter to facilitate his beachcombing.

Nobody I meet is all that keen to talk about the future. I encounter young Jim while still on the ferry, when he comes out on deck to admire his motor-powered dirt bike. He says he can ride it around the island without a license, no problem. He tells me that his family has one channel on TV, so he doesn't watch much, prefers his bike, hanging out with his friends. Jim's had the same friends since kindergarten, which isn't surprising because the school has only two classrooms: kindergarten to Grade 3, and Grades 4 to 8. Does Jim wish there were more people to talk to, maybe some new girls to meet? He breaks into a shy smile, puts his hands in his pockets. It isn't all isolation, Jim notes. Whenever the family goes into town for supplies, he gets to pick out a DVD. He's bringing home *Men in Black 2*, and something tells me it will get plenty of viewing. In the near future, Jim will have to leave the island to complete his schooling. Is he worried about that? Jim's smile fades. "Well," he says, "I don't know." The rains will stop soon. There are familiar roads to re-explore in the dappled sunshine of quiet spring. Old enough to appreciate what he has and young enough not to know to worry, Jim has a simple and all-encompassing take on island life. He has nothing to rebel against and enough distance from the world of mass culture to not feel as though he should be rebelling just for the notoriety. Jim lives in a tiny community, has never felt what it is like to be anonymous. In a short time, he'll be thrust into a different world. The boat pulls up, and he wheels his dirt bike down the ramp.

Searching for the Originals

"I came here to write and lead a private life," retired novelist Jane Rule wryly notes about her life on another of the two-hundred-plus Gulf Islands. "But gradually you get involved in the community." So it is with many of the rustic loners who come—as they still do—to the cluster of islands mere hours from the bustling metropolis of big-city Vancouver searching for escape and a less-acquisitive version of the good life. So it goes on my own trip through the Gulf Islands of British Columbia—I came to find the last rebels, the genuine individuals clinging to their revolutions.

But, gradually, I realized that what I was looking for no longer exists. Even tenacious individualists like Jane Rule are eventually consumed by what is going on around them, the necessary constraints of socialization in a world where solitary physical and mental spaces are increasingly difficult to come by.

Rule lives on Galiano Island. It's a lush verdant blob of land with two restaurants, a post office, and a healthy resentment directed at those landowners who want the right to clear swatches of their lots and put up giant vacation homes. She is as unique a person as you'll find on this earth, and yet she shares with many residents of these British Columbia islands the conflicting urges that are coming to define rustic life in the twenty-first century. On the one hand, there is the urge to escape, to find a spot where no one knows or cares who you are, and disappear. On the other hand, there is the growing realization that such spots are increasingly either endangered, swooped up like mice in the talons of rich absentee owners who rarely find the time to visit, or suddenly subject to some new legislation and governed as parsimoniously and ignorantly as many of our most crowded cities. You come to escape and be on your own, but you eventually discover that all the threats to your escape necessitate working together with your neighbors. In such circumstances, disappearing may no longer be possible.

I am cruising the islands with Grant Shilling, at the time editor, along with his partner, Mary Alice, of the *Gulf Islands Gazette,* a.k.a. the *GIG* (now, sadly, defunct). Ostensibly, we are delivering the *GIG* to its far-flung empire of islands—large and small, friendly and standoffish. But just as importantly, this is Shilling's time to reconnect to his world, drop in on old friends (some of whom are literally aged, but all sharp as the axes they once used to carve enclaves for themselves out of the rainy forest). These bimonthly delivery trips are also an opportunity for Shilling to pursue a new passion: surfing the West Coast. His book *The Cedar Surf*—about riding the waves in British Columbia—is in a second edition. For Shilling, surfing is another way to get closer to a region he loves for the way it beckons him: part salvation, part responsibility. In his early forties, Shilling is the weather-beaten, muscle-bound, six-foot-plus, slow-drawling epitome of the islander. But dig a little deeper and you'll find that, like most people living on these islands, Shilling is not exactly what he seems to be. He is, in fact, as unlikely a Jew from the Toronto suburbs as you will ever come across. He made his way from the East to Vancouver and finally to the islands, where he fell in love with the land and, though he wouldn't necessarily admit it, maybe even the people. From his year-long stint living hermit-like on a tiny island off the small coastal town of Tofino, to his tenure on Galiano Island working odd jobs, to his current set-up in a cottage on a hill overlooking the bay leading into one of Salt Spring Island's four ports, Shilling has sought and wrestled with the twin demons: escape and community, freedom and entrapment.

As we drive and ferry from Vancouver Island's Fanny Bay to lush Hornby Island, Shilling introduces me to the characters and figures that make this unique and beautiful region more than just another tourist destination. These are the people I've come to meet. Like Shilling, they are the true individualists, rebels who refuse to conform to any notion—whether of conformity or originality. Like Shilling, they are wrestling with the reality of the new conformity, struggling to preserve a sense of unique identity in an age when the rebel— especially the rebel—is as ubiquitous and prepacked as they come.

In Fanny Bay, a small outpost that lies on the east coast of the large Vancouver Island and has the feel of a suburb, we drop in on George Sawchuk, a grizzled former logger. Sawchuk is famed for having converted the woods behind his house into a giant sculpture garden replete with glorious wood carvings all done by his own hand. When the province tried to stop Sawchuk's designs on its land, local pressure forced it to back off. The sculpture garden remains. German backpackers and neighborhood kids stop by, the tourists pausing in Sawchuk's garage studio, the kids looking for a handout of Sawchuk's famous home-baked cookies. Sawchuk takes us into the studio, shows us a tree stump with a tap protruding. Above the tap, a clock methodically ticks off the seconds. The message is clear: How much longer can we keep abusing the planet?

Sawchuk spent his younger years as a logger and he's pretty much done it all, including a solo show at the Vancouver Art Gallery in 1989, which he has now come to regret. "Worst of all," he says, "you become an artist. Better to remain an individual." As he grows older, Sawchuk has become more and more focused on this idea of remaining true to yourself at all costs. Once, when a gallery exhibiting his work asked him for an artist's statement, Sawchuk wrote: "I do what I do not because I want to be some sort of hero for the underculture, but to survive as an individual with an identity. People often ask why do all this. The answer I give is, 'What does one do when you are too old to work and too young to die?' It is a nice way to fill in the interim."

Sawchuk is serious—not glib. In an age when people increasingly seem to be floating through life, awaiting death in tastefully decorated prisons, he reacts the only way he knows how: by continuing to assert his primal existence, the stuff of his life, that which makes him want to survive—his identity as a singular unit. "We're losing our individuality today," he says. Sawchuk puts artists right in the middle of what he calls "the cloning process." He speaks vehemently about the art world: "You become a hero, you're in a circle, you're not an individual any more. Artists talk and get together, they become part of the pot of stew."

But isn't there any way to be an individual *and* an artist? Sawchuk describes the local college's art show. "I viewed the show, I looked around and it was shameful, there's nothing there. You can't blame the students. Ninety percent of them have never missed a meal, been cold, slept on the ground, never had any real life experiences, never bled. So how can you expect them to have any real material?"

The same could be said for a lot of the citizens of Western countries. The majority of us have never gone hungry, have never truly suffered. Does that mean we can't be real, we can't have something to say?

"When I lecture I say, 'Don't think you're going to go out in the real world with your brushes and chisels. Go out into the world, live and suffer a little, then if it takes ten years or whatever, you go back.' I tell them now that you made the escape from the womb, don't just go crawling into another one."

Eschewing the life of the artist, Sawchuk no longer sells and rarely exhibits his work. "All my sculptures go to the camp out back." Sawchuk prefers to live on his pension and his disability payments. But even he has not been totally able to avoid the trap of consumerism and contradiction. He was featured in an ad campaign for a long-distance company. The campaign appeared all over the province in billboards, newspapers, and on television. "They drove up in a fancy German car, yuppie types, but nice guys. They took a lot of pictures. Then they came back and they stayed around all weekend. I was never so happy to see them leave. I told them I hate corporations and I hate telephones and they said, 'That's all right George, just don't say it on camera.' Centerfold in *The Globe and Mail, National Post, Vancouver Sun,* sixty different newspapers. I'm not selling telephones, never once do I say the world *telephone.* They came back and gave me a couple of thousand dollars. People say I sold out and I say maybe I have but I've got enough to pay my phone bill for two years and you've got to pay your bill out of your pocket."

Why did the phone company look to Sawchuk? The Telus ad features Sawchuk staring out at passersby. A caption says, "Sing your own song George." Over Sawchuk's mussed hair, a single word: "Original."

Can a straight-talking logger with socialist sensibilities who reinvented himself as an artist shill long distance without being compromised? Perhaps that's what true individuality is all about these days—an ability to shift and change and take advantage of circumstance without abandoning a core truth and confidence. While we were visiting Sawchuk, he was musing over what piece to send to a local gallery that claimed to be putting on a show meant to challenge conventional sensibilities. Sawchuk was considering a piece he'd been sculpting: a Bible with a knife stuck in it.

Few can force themselves to suffer. We can't choose to leave home still a boy, wander the backwoods, work as a logger in the days when logging meant heading off to the forest and cutting down trees by hand—a dangerous business, you could easily lose a life or a leg. Maybe that's why most of the professional creators working in Western countries today seem to lack gravitas, seem to be complaining just for something to do, just because it's the next move in playing the game. Sawchuk has a moral certainty that suggests he refuses to play the game. Things have gone wrong with the world, but Sawchuk remains stalwart. He survived the British Columbian woods, so he'll bloody well survive the Vancouver Art Gallery and the phone company. Selling out would have been capitalizing on the billboard ads to promote his image and his work. Sawchuk didn't do that.

Walking Forward Backward

George Sawchuk responded to potential fame by retreating. For a lot of the people I meet in these parts, the answer has been escape. Rebellion becomes *not* doing something. This is most certainly because when *everyone* is a rebel, refusing to conform to pseudo-rebellion seems to be one of the few ways we can actually step outside the system. In the age of the new conformity, of the pseudo-individual, of the serial-killer celeb, can there be genuine dissent? If individualism has become conformity, how can we assert the opinions of our true unique selves without evoking the cliché of special and buying into the pseudo-extremes of pop-culture sensationalism? If George Sawchuk is deemed fit for a long-distance commercial, who has not been drawn into the drama of that mass-dispensed oxymoron, semi-specialness? If even extreme acts of violence now seem *de rigueur* and made-for-TV, then what act could convey genuine dissent, true individuality? As Shilling and I drive through the Gulf Islands and then backtrack across the twisting mountain road from Fanny Bay to the burgeoning resort town of Tofino on the other side of Vancouver Island, I stare out at the gorgeous fog-dipped landscape—complete, at times, with clear-cuts as dramatic as swatches of giant firs. I keep coming back to this question: If everything is allowed, if everyone is special, if conformity and individuality are equally encompassed into the system that consumes and regurgitates all human activity as a form of (pop) product, then is genuine individual identity essentially doomed?

George Sawchuk tells us that to establish identity and have something to put on the blank canvas we all imagine filling, we have to first get out into the world and suffer. Today's university students sign up for a summer of tree planting, a year long stint in the Peace Corps, a weekend of labor for Habitat for Humanity. They come back to their parents' comfortable manses acting as if they'd just parachuted into Baghdad on a solo mission. True escape requires more extreme measures. While *Gulf Islands Gazette* editor Grant Shilling routinely accelerates the teetering van into steep blind curves, he tells me about the *year* he spent on an all-but-deserted island off the coast of Tofino. He survived on rice and mussels he collected from the shore. He smoked a lot of pot. There was another squatter on the other side of his island, and every month or so, they met up at one of their camps. With no rent and nothing to buy, the days passed slowly. It was quiet. Very quiet. "I still can't look at mussels," Shilling says.

From Sawchuk's perspective, Shilling earned his stripes, his right to write about the grizzled elders such as Jane Rule who came to these islands in the sixties and seventies without a plan or a safety net, without a down payment on a luxury cottage with a view of the coast and no fewer than five sunroofs, guaranteed. And it's true. Like Sawchuk's evocation of art as a way to continue to assert primal identity, Shilling's journey was no mere cliché of adventure, but a search for something different, for a way into the center of a single human being's nature, sprung from the trap of society and mass culture.

There are few deserted islands left to colonize. The Gulf Islands were once full of hippie squatters living under tarps in the trees. Today, the former-hippie residents, now comfortably ensconced, grumble equally about the kids draped in tie-dye sheets who stagger half-dead into town looking for handouts, and the rich foreigners who tear down modest cottages to build huge vacation mansions they rarely visit.

The idea of the land shrinking is not just a metaphor for the shrinking opportunities we have to assert our identity. It is also a very literal phenomenon that I encounter repeatedly while travelling through the Gulf Islands. On Hornby Island, we stop in on Jerry Pethick, another sculptor, but one who at the time was still involved in the contemporary art scene. A giant robot figure he made entirely of empty champagne bottles has recently been exhibited overseas. An elaborate sculpture project for the City of Vancouver is underway when I visit. Pethick and his wife and son moved to Hornby in the early seventies and spent their first two summers living in a cave. With their children grown, Pethick and his wife reside in a sprawling series of shack-like cottages all connected by a weathered wood boardwalk. He built the complex himself. Over a lunch of cheese and bread and homemade preserves, Pethick talks about being visited recently by a provincial compliance officer who informed him of changes to the laws regarding construction. Now, Pethick complains, they say you need insurance to guarantee construction, and you have to register with the province, for a fee of course. This effectively drums out the island tradition of slowly building your own home or casually contracting out your services to erect a home for someone else. DIY replaced by costly professionals. If Pethick was moving to Hornby today, his method of building up a homestead and studio one shack at a time would be illegal. "All you can do is fight it," he says, shaking his head. Pethick thinks that you could still come to the islands and live in the woods, drop out of society. But he says that the kids today aren't prepared for the sacrifices, and they don't know how to subsist in the woods. He admits that the island is no longer the space it was—cheap hippie haven providing refuge to artists and dropouts alike. "The island is aging," Pethick tells me sadly. "No young people are coming."

Pethick no longer sculpts on Hornby Island. The summer after our meeting, he died of brain cancer.

Unlike Pethick's beloved Hornby Island, the Vancouver Island town of Tofino is booming. It has transformed, from an all-but-ignored low-rent retreat on the far corner of the isolated coast of a huge island into a world-renowned scenic destination with resorts and vacation complexes and more on the way. With its organic food co-ops, community bakeries, and tiny tie-dye shirt shops, it exudes the superficial specialness that emerges when locality is superimposed on a region that is increasingly dependent on the displacements of tourism. Shilling and I meet up with Ralph, an old pal of Shilling's from his wilder years. Ralph is in his forties, an imposing figure with a big beard and thick, black horn-rimmed glasses. His house sits on prime Tofino beachfront real estate, and he's been living there on the cheap since 1979. Up to a few years ago, he believed that he would spend the rest of his life in that house, attuned to the slow rhythms of the Tofino tide. Lately, though, he's begun to reconsider. He feels oppressed by the commercialization he's witnessed over the past five years. We sip coffee and he talks menacingly—though jokingly—about "a terror campaign against the out-of-towners." Ralph muses out loud about what it might look like. "Bullets through windows, emptying their gas tanks, stickers on their doors saying 'Go Home.'" Recently, Ralph was offered almost half a million dollars for his land. He talks about how the pressure to sell out and move somewhere cheaper is decaying the community. If all the residents decamp to make way for rich absentee owners, what will be left of the town he once knew? Ralph has never really had a steady job and works intermittently as a painter, builder, and jack of all trades. His most recent venture is a plan to cash in on the tourist market and open a surf shop. Why would he cater to the tourists he hates?

Ralph admits that his need to feel part of his community on an ongoing basis is stronger than his disgust for "out-of-towners." If he's not going to sell out, he needs to assert his place in what's left of the town in some other way. In that respect, his decision to open the surf shop is not unlike George Sawchuk's decision to become a sculptor: Both are rebels seeking ways to cling to what they see as genuine individuality, recognition that comes not from reinventing one's narrative via evermore-extreme antics but from sticking to one's hard-fought principles; neither are motivated by finances, but, rather, by the pressing and evermore-difficult desire to assert identity and presence. Angry and sarcastic, Ralph still wants to hold on to the diminishing sense that he lives in a place where he is recognized, where people know who he is and what he is about. "I feel ridiculous," he says, "living a white-trash lifestyle in a house worth half a million dollars." Ralph finishes his coffee and tells us a final story: "When I was in England," he says, "I went into this small pub in a tiny village and all the old men in there said, 'Fuck off, we don't want you here. The tourists and the young kids go to the other pub in the next village and that's the way we like it.' Now if we in Tofino had done that since day one, we would have been all right."

Leaving Ralph and heading out to one of Tofino's gorgeous beaches, Shilling tells me about his own reservations: He hates the built-up Salt Spring and longs for Galiano Island, the much smaller and less-developed island he and Mary recently left. But, as the Lasqueti diner proprietor Karen noted, Salt Spring has more opportunities for those who need to make a living. Once, Shilling thought he could disappear, live off the land. As the land shrinks, even this garrulous figure finds himself pulled into compromise. "The world has separated from individuals," writes Keith Tester in *Moral Culture*, adding:

> And it has experientially become increasingly like a seamless web of overlapping institutions with an independent existence. These institutions together seem to cover the whole world and all possibilities and opportunities within it, leaving individuals with the choice of either accommodation . . . or exit.

Power to the People?

"Accommodation or exit" may sound unduly grim to many of us. After all, aren't there still those who fight the system and even manage the occasional victory? To evoke present-day rebellion is to

demand some accounting of the so-called anti-globalization movement, which is often compared to the counterculture of the sixties
that fueled a good deal of migration to the Gulf Islands. When the
"Battle in Seattle" protest occurred in 1999 on the occasion of a
meeting of the secretive World Trade Organization, everything
from CNN to *Adbusters* magazine to a barrage of underground press
zines and websites announced that here, at last, was a twenty-first-
century answer to the age of civil disobedience, flower power, and
Aquarius. Here was the center of genuine rebellion, perhaps even the
great hope for a new flowering of true individuality. Not unlike the
fervor of the sixties, today's anti-globalization movement pits the
young against the ossified, lays claim to a moral high ground, and
flirts with violence, danger, and martyrdom. Here is rebellion and
dissent, not only possible but underway in our own lifetime.
However, as we move further into the millennial age, this supposed
flowering of civil disobedience seems to be withering. Though
protests continue, they also continue to get smaller and less effective,
and they are more likely to become mired in competing claims for
media attention and pointless outbursts of random vandalism. What
happened? Where did this new generation of authentic rebels go?

When agitators stage massive protests in order to get mainstream coverage, they are welcomed as momentary entertainment
fodder: Pop culture covers the protests like a *Star Wars* movie; the
protesters are invaders, and the leaders are under siege. Or vice
versa: The protesters are the rebels swathed in white, the leaders
are the Evil Empire breathing heavily through their ominous masks.
Either way, there is very little discussion of the substance of anti-
globalization claims, amid the detailed analysis of troop movements, tear gas, and which parts of the summit fence have been
penetrated. Each protest brings with it a kind of mass-media-
imposed déjà vu futility—since pop culture has already had its
wide-scale revolt of young people (they called it the Sixties), this
new round of protests is treated like a second performance, not as
vibrant or interesting as the first. It is reported on TV with all the
excitement of a summer repeat.

When activists try to get the word out about the cause on their own, using websites, videos, zines, and pirate radio, the line between chronicling dissent and using one's status as protester to enter the pop world and further an I'm-Special agenda is a thin one. The 2001 protest at a globalization meeting of world leaders in Quebec City, Canada's largest protest ever, gave birth to a number of independent encapsulations of the event. Two books emerged in a timely fashion: *Resist!* published by Halifax's Fernwood Books, and *Counterproductive,* put out by Montreal micro-press Cumulus. Both feature a mixture of first-hand reports from the front lines and fervent rhetoric against global capitalism. But much of the writing suggests that the protesters are feeling the I'm-Special vibe. Jennifer Bennett starts her "Anishinaabe Girl in Quebec" essay in *Resist!* with the sentence: "The best vacation of my life began Wednesday night, April 18th, 2001, at 10 pm, the day after my twenty-third birthday." A volunteer medic follows up in *Counterproductive* with the pronouncement: "Going to Quebec City was, without a doubt, the craziest, most dangerous, most fun experience I've ever had." This kind of commentary, unfortunately, plays into the hands of cynics such as Jean Chrétien, prime minister of Canada at the time, who told the Montreal newspaper *Le Devoir* before the Quebec City Summit of the Americas: "They say to themselves, 'Let's go spend the weekend in Quebec City; we'll have fun, we'll protest and blah, blah, blah.'"

Chrétien's obvious contempt for democratic protest aside, he had a point: How many of the mostly middle-class Westerners who protested at the anti-globalization rallies of the early millennial period were in attendance at least as much *to be there* as to "work for change"? At Quebec City, there were all-night parties, bonfires under overpasses, booze and drugs aplenty. This is, in fact, probably not that different from the Sixties, a movement that began with parallel battles to oppose systemized racism in the United States and the war in Vietnam, and ended in a confusing swirl of contradictory cultural antics, many of which were more about fun than commitment to any cause. "It wasn't really a deep-seated sense of pacifism or outrage toward the military," said one counterculture activist who is quoted in writer Abe Peck's book about the sixties social revolution. "It was more like 'here's a chance for me to get back at parents, government, cops, society, culture, you name it. Them — the big guys, the people in control.'"

Among the three film/video projects released not long after the Quebec City protests is the twenty-minute video assemblage of footage put out by the Toronto Video Activist Collective (TVAC). In the TVAC video, protesters variously chant, attack the giant four-thousand-meter security fence surrounding the summit, lurch away blinded by tear gas, and dance defiantly to the beat of drums under the watchful eyes of the police. It is clear from this video that the protesters descended on the demonstration with fingers poised over the record button. The overall effect is, again, not to communicate any sense of what these protests are about or who they are meant to ultimately assist, but to convey notions of self-empowerment and DIY culture: *We are here, we did something, we me me me we.*

The fact that none of this material is memorable in the least reminds us of the way pop culture has colonized extremity. The sixties had Abbie Hoffman, who could shock us with entreaties to violate the laws of property by calling his manifesto *Steal This Book.* Today, mainstream and popular singers, artists, and writers celebrate murder, mayhem, rape. Petty theft seems mundane when every character, from B-movie detective Shaft to Eminem's "Slim Shady" to even the fictional liberal president of the United States played on TV by a pedigreed actor, is against the state, against the system. Comments Gustin Reichbach, a former sixties radical who is now in the downside of his fifties and a New York State Supreme Court justice: "The counterculture of 30 years ago is the mainstream today. Our success shifted the parameters of what constitutes a counterculture." That is, dissident culture and even dissident protest is now mainstream. Since nothing is shocking, we can never challenge the precepts of mainstream society through an aesthetic that aims to jar passive spectators out of their mindless habits. To try to organize a spectacle is to do a service for the corporate pop-

culture world, which demands a series of spectacles that it can endlessly overshadow and turn into product. And when protesters go
it alone, producing indie media, they find themselves shut out of
the mainstream's capacity to fetishize and aestheticize, and unable
to reach that wider audience that is essential to activate any kind of
change. Moreover, they find themselves slipping into I'm-Special
mode, creating their own mini-spectacles featuring you-know-who
at the center.

The failure of the anti-globalization movement to figure out how
to use the contrivances of mass media—either indie or corporate—to harness a groundswell of resentment into a genuine
worldwide movement perhaps accounts for the frustrating way that
these protests seem to degenerate. Like many who are sympathetic
with the aims and goals of anti-globalization, I cringe every time
such protests end up in pointless battles with the police, who have
become expert at keeping protesters far away from the fat cats who
conduct the business of world trade; inevitably, the action then
moves on to become even more pointless mini-riots featuring
smashed windows, vandalized luxury automobiles, and infighting.
"You can't protest against violence and poor treatment and then go
do it yourself," notes one activist interviewed by *The Globe and Mail*
after being randomly arrested following a summer 2003 protest
against a World Trade Organization meeting in Montreal. And yet I
also sympathize with the degeneration: When you're shut out from
having your say, relentlessly prevented from making all-too-valid
points about the majority left out of the world economy, why *not*
break a few windows?

While in discussion with one anti-globalization activist, I ask if
she considers herself a rebel. "Whether I consider myself a rebel or
not has absolutely nothing to do with my political activities,"
Heather Maxwell explains via email from Halifax. "It is not about
rebellion. At the risk of sounding like George W. Bush, it is about
justice. Since childhood I have always questioned and spoken out
against what I felt was unjust. Somewhere along the line I got the
radical idea that every person in the world has the right to food,

shelter, health care, education and dignified work and so far no one has been able to talk me out of it. As long as resources are unevenly distributed none of us will be free and I will have no choice but to speak out. That is the point."

At the same time, "speaking out" seems ever more complex and compromised. As the self-help language of pseudo-individuality creeps into anti-capitalist sentiments, rebellious political initiatives seem to devolve into fragmented micro-groupings of like-minded enthusiasts who use radical politics as a way to reinvent themselves and affirm their specialness. Having been back in Canada for a year and a half after spending a few years in Mexico, Maxwell tells me that, until the previous week, she was working with a street newspaper, but the funding ran out so she was now volunteering with a street paper and preparing for the Medical College Admission Test (MCAT). She was considering travelling to the United States, Colombia, or Mexico again for a year while she applied to medical school.

Committed, yet filled with wanderlust and all the while planning a professional career. I can't help but wonder if activists like this have more of the rebel in them than they would admit. I've observed firsthand the way activist communities provide a niche and a recognition that is not unlike that of pop-culture communities. I've seen youths arrested for taking over an abandoned building—action they ostensibly took to protest a lack of affordable housing—hugging and high-fiving each other as they emerged from jail. They were clearly exuberant. Why? They had achieved nothing except a paragraph in the paper and legal hassles. But in their minds they had also accrued real evidence of their personal commitment to rebellion, to the cause. While waiting for their accused offspring to be released, I watched annoyed liberal parents wring their hands in frustration. How to yell at your kid for wanting to do something to help others? And yet the parents seemed to sense that altruism was not the sole motive behind their children's actions. The line between the pop-culture-infused desire for individualistic adventure and commitment to the cause becomes blurred.

We are all invaded by the new conformity. Are Western activists who temporarily subsume themselves in the causes of other poorer countries in some way also seeking further excitement, more extreme scenarios that can break through the doldrums of regular life? How much of one's dedication has to do with the I'm-Special imperative? Getting arrested in Canada is impressive, but risking death in Colombia is way more exciting. Yes, there are many activists who are truly committed to the struggles they engage in and have no interest in excitement, thrills, or getting noticed. And certainly, I would not want to suggest that, say, the motives of Mexican farmers infuriated by the falling price of corn and reduced to throwing chunks of concrete at the police while the big players enjoy a Cancun buffet can be in any way explained as anything other than rage at their inability to make a living as a result of an uneven playing field. At the same time, there are also those well-off, Western-born momentary deviants who stormed the barricades at the Quebec City Summit of the Americas, using what they call activism in their quest to get deeper into the world of images and refractions, that instilled need for pseudo-rebellion that is so much a part of the new conformity. McDonald's burns, the Starbucks window is shattered, the digicam records, and the people who are supposed to benefit from this wait for their lives to get better, work for pennies a day, and dream of Big Macs.

Say It All Together Now: Resistance Is Futile

Without the capacity for rebellion, we are reduced to quasi-automatons living in a fake democracy of focus-grouped consensus. In 1969, at the height of the sixties movement, Theodore Roszak described the world he foresaw should the "resistance fail." He writes in his book *The Making of a Counter Culture:*

> Above all, the capacity of our emerging technocratic paradise to denature the imagination by appropriating to itself the whole meaning of Reason, Reality, Progress, and Knowledge will render it impossible for men to give any more to their bothersomely unfulfilled potentialities but that of madness.

Lacking methods to register our dissent, without real access to the mass media to speak to each other, we fall prey to what sixties pundits called the *technocracy,* that giant Foucaultian web of dispersed knowledge-power nodes, each one of them propping up the next, but none of them actually under the control of any particular person or branch of industry or government. "And for such madness," Roszak predicts, accurately foreshadowing the likes of executive confidante Charmaine Semon and teen therapist Karyn Gordon, "humanitarian therapies will be generously provided."

Pseudo-rebellion blurs into passivity. We start to think that seeing a film or videotaping a protest is the same thing as actually striking a blow against the evil corporation, tantamount to rejecting the latest ultra-convenient polluting apparatus in favor of some benevolent alternative. Again and again, we see our cultural products actually incorporating this idea of rebellion against the corporate status quo into the storyline.

Today, so many are rebels because a posture of rebellion puts us on course to arrive at our intended destination: pop fame or at least momentary mass-culture recognition. And so rebellion is predictable. We expect it as an aspect of every entertainment product, viral carrier of the pop theme. "These are hard times for individuality," Luc Sante writes in *The New York Times,* continuing:

> Even if you engage in some kind of radical piercing, like encasing both eyebrows in tight rows of small rings, and by this means emphatically announce to the world that you are not employed in middle management at a Fortune 500 company, you are hardly doing something unprecedented.

In fact, Sante points out, the opposite is the case: Adopting this radical look "virtually insures that you've taken notice of all other humans in your town or on your travels who have done the same."

From the moment marketeers perceived that dissent itself was saleable, worthy of being bottled as a scent and sold back to customers anxious to be sniffed out as dangerous, rebellion became posture. An email news release touts teen band Untamed from

Guelph, Ontario. Apparently it has been chosen by Rock Hard Cosmetic Company to represent a "brand new shade of soft pink with purple fluorescent shimmer." The lipstick will be called . . . Untamed. And so it goes, this seemingly innocent colonization and adaptation into commercial life of every word, gesture, symbol, and posture that might suggest spontaneous freedom or dissent. It's the slow chipping away at our right to uphold particular values in particular ways. In the process, there is a change in our perception of the possibility of having real positions on real issues of importance to us. Everything becomes a smokescreen. Everything real disappears. Just stand there and frown. Content is reduced to image. True individuality becomes another market brand.

We live in a culture where everything is permissible, everything is celebrated, everything is an option on the quest for special, even those things that are against the law (but relentlessly celebrated nevertheless). A culture in which it is no longer possible to author genuine dissent is a dying culture. I see our pop-culture system creating, as Georg Simmel writes, an "age which feels that all cultural forms are like exhausted soil, which has yielded all it can but which is still entirely covered with the products of its earlier fertility." Society needs to have boundaries. To live, as we do, as a culture of wannabe rebels is to live in a society dangerously without limits. Without a way for us to fall off the edge, we have no way to rebel or challenge the accepted order. The result is exhaustion, stagnation, erosion, decline, hopelessness.

The anger, despair, futility, and resistance through retreat I found in the Gulf Islands wasn't really a surprise to me. I had sensed it, known it since the first time I felt the urge to be bigger than I am, to do something great, to be recognized. Gradually, I realized the urge was fake, implanted by pop's theme, transparent and pathetic. And yet the urge is as real as the people I met in British Columbia— "old souls," Grant Shilling calls them, alluding not necessarily to their age but to the sense that they are displaced from their true time, people clinging to an individualism born of conviction and experience when the best the mass-culture-dominated world can hope for is to catch a really wild ride at the theme park. Those old souls also feel the urge to be recognized, to be known for who they are. Theirs is the anger not of the usurped but of the redundant. There seems to be little left for them to do but disappear.

Is an intense redundancy all we have left to make known our discontent? In such a scenario, John Lindh is a rebel and amateur warzone correspondent Ken Hechtman a conformist everyday thrill-seeker. To engage in a Lindh-like rebellion is to subvert your personhood, to deliberately be less than you can be. Giving up on opportunity and freedom—whether you are George Sawchuk shunning artistic fame or John Lindh memorizing the Koran—becomes a mute articulation of anger. There's a kind of anti-rebellion rebellion here, a rejection of the dominant social order that demands in-your-face antics and radical exhibitionism. In our world, such is the state of iconoclastic individuality. The true act of revolt against the system is a kind of disappearing act. Rebellion is found in George Sawchuk's shed: Sculptures that could earn him hundreds of thousands of dollars await placement in an anonymous forest. As places like Tofino and Salt Spring become tourist havens, those who originally sought them as retreats move further out to even more remote outposts. Like the last two birds desperately searching for a safe place to make their nest, the last of these authentic individualists, untouched by the I'm-Special mantra, are clearly losing their environment slowly and methodically. They are being pulled in, politely asked to compromise, subtly forced to alter their lives to fit the precepts of the new conformity. All that vitality and spirit forced into hiding. Are we ready to disappear into the I'm-*not*-Special era? Performing a stunt without cameras ready to capture the achievement? I'm not sure we can do it.

And if we did, who would notice?

Most of us are taking the seemingly inevitable path of least resistance: We are advancing on the shifting parallel reality of pop culture, anxious to convert connectivity and its compromises into opportunities for reinvention and entry into the pop world. Chat rooms, instant messaging, movies, tunes, TV shows, online video games, an endless array of mall stores. This is the life of our rapidly aging young people. For current and future generations of pop-culture-bred new conformists, the urge to rebellion will come not from a desire and inability to escape mass culture's looming presence, but from the realization that something prevents them from truly entering the pop dream. The need to go deeper is always met by rippling reflections, perpetual invitations. The kids, taking their cue from the adults, want more than just invitations. They are infused with ideas around rebellion and dissent. But they find no way to articulate those dreams. At the extreme, such frustrations spill over into school-cafeteria shootings or, less portentously, radical devotion to backyard wrestling. Either way, these rebellions end up absorbed and reinvented, become part of the endless narrative that is mass culture, become part of the individuality-spewing pop theme. After all, the West is no longer vast, untamed, an expanse to be explored and defined by cowboys, pilgrims, spiritualists, gold seekers, hippies, artists, freaks, rustlers, hustlers, revolutionaries, and outlaws. Manifest destiny and the myth of expansion, so intertwined with our conceptions of rebellion and individuality, is at an end. Tofino was once isolated, a distant beach-strewn paradise buffered from society by cold waves and steep forest ranges. But these days it is nothing more than the end of the road. And if you don't feel like driving there, you can fly in and rent the beachfront mansion a couple doors down from winsome soprano crooner Sarah McLachlan's. It's a vacation as easily arranged as activating a Gold card.

THE TRANS-CANADA HIGHWAY officially ends at Tofino. This is surely a neat commentary on the state of our culture's fascination with the notion of frontier. Think about it: You can drive no further. The old ways of life are gone. But we are still trying to define ourselves using old precepts, old ideas. We need a new way of understanding what individuality is. Trapped between the extremes, we long for escape, a place where we are not constantly torn between emotionally unstable pop stardom and emotionally unfulfilling regular life.

Where is the place in which we were at once recognized just for being ourselves and gently encouraged to decide for ourselves who and what to be?

Our society changes, and we do not necessarily have the tools to evolve with it. We seek to evoke old ways and understandings, even as we lapse into depression resulting from inconsequence, from our difficulty accessing what we have been told is our inalienable right: the freedom to tell our story and have it *heard*.

Back on the eastern side of Vancouver Island, on our way to one of the ferry gateways that will return us to the tiny Gulf Islands, Grant Shilling and I pass a surprisingly crowded strip mall: A&W, Boston Pizza, Cactus Club. We could be anywhere. Shilling presses down on the gas, eager to escape to the long cedars and empty beaches flanked by monster vacation homes and tiny artist shacks.

CONCLUSION

ON MY OWN AT THE END OF THE ROAD

O N A CBC RADIO discussion about media coverage of the second U.S.-led war on Iraq, I congratulate the media for their success in creating widespread apathy. With their profusion of call-in shows, reporters on the front line, and breathless accounts of any protest gathering consisting of more than ten people, the overwhelming sense was that of the average person having a voice. We were stifled by our apparent opportunities for input. The lines were jammed with callers eager to reflect on Saddam Hussein, the Palestinian-Israeli conflict, the imperialist evil of the United States, or the benefits of war. Protests that started as the first bombs dropped fizzled within a few short days to nothing. It was as if twenty-four-hour news coverage had robbed the anti-war movement of its momentum—though protests were large in some cities, they were one-time events, and they never really caught on. Huge protests in the first few days that quickly faded in the face of blanket news coverage gave viewers the impression that people were out on the streets en masse. Since the anti-war movement was having its say on TV, there was the sense that others could sit back and just watch. Thus, media-generated apathy: blanket coverage of relatively small protests that, mixed with interactivity via call-in, leaves the overall impression that somebody somewhere is doing something.

A day after my comments on the radio, I received an email from an angry listener. Heather Maxwell of Halifax (mentioned briefly in the last chapter) condemned my detached analysis and wrote: "Even though there are a large number of passionate committed people we cannot do it alone. So Hal, get off your butt, stop making excuses, start thinking about something other than your own comfort, and GET INVOLVED!!"

Was Maxwell right? Was I just another snide know-it-all commentator clinging to my clever specialness to avoid commitment to any real involvement in a cause that might make the world a better place? What makes some middle-class denizens of urban North America so compelled to GET INVOLVED, and others so individually apathetic?

Like me, Maxwell is obviously concerned about the decline of real community and the rise of false individuality. And the point she makes is an important one. Individuals are, essentially, powerless. Only communities can truly effect change in society. The more pretend-individualism infiltrates our behavior and lifestyle, the less we are able to band together and throw out an ineffective government, boycott the products of a destructive company, start a school based not on standardized testing and proclamations of self-esteem but on creativity and commitment to learning. But the view that Maxwell articulates so well seems to deny our shared pop-culture heritage. I cannot ignore the fact that I don't want to band together; I want to be the lone rebel, the dangerous outsider, the solitary hero. Perhaps I need to relinquish my dream of solitary, restless rebellion, subject of almost all the pop culture I have been exposed to since birth. But, alas, I seem unable to.

I used to believe that the answer to the problem of a generic mass culture (and the voicelessness and passivity it creates) was to form alternative systems of personal technocracies—an entire other indie medium living like a parasite embedded in the guts of the corporate entertainment structure. That process has, in some ways, begun, with millions taking to the internet and announcing their presence, millions of others making zines, CDs, pirate radio shows, comics, books, all on an independent basis. I believed that this parallel parasitic personal media system would eventually break down the artificial barriers that prevent us from reclaiming mass culture and effecting meaningful change. The ubiquity of the pop theme insisting that we are all special, coupled with the insurgent arrival of ever-more-individualistic and available technologies (from the photocopier to high-speed internet), would inevitably yield a quasi-revolution of creative action ending the monoculture once and for all. The transformation would come, I thought, when creativity emerged once again as an ordinary, normal, everyday aspect of ongoing life. When it became an ordinary act for individuals to record their own albums, sew their own clothes, make their own movies, tell their own stories. When, as Václav Havel has written, "culture . . . is, once again, perceived as the air we breathe."

The transformation has not come. Despite ever-more-available personal technologies, the system continues to hold its own, killing anything that threatens the pop-culture monopoly, drawing us into ever-more-irresistible spectacles, transferring all dissent into an endless array of options that cleverly create a patina of democratic input. We are alone together, reduced to endlessly trying to replicate the feeling of community that individuals once took for granted.

So what went wrong? I think that I, and many others, have perhaps underestimated the allure, power, and sheer intoxication of pseudo-special in the age of enforced individuality and collapsing community. The time has come to recognize just how much of what we have considered genuine rebellion over the past hundred or so years has really been ersatz articulation of Special conforming to the norms of ersatz individualism. We can no longer dismiss the pattern of political, cultural, and even personal agitation being consumed by a system that seems to have a way to embrace and embody every desire and possibility.

Maxwell wants me to just get up and go, but I think first people have to become far more sophisticated about the forces and mechanisms of a society that turns every act and gesture into an articulation of the new conformity of specialness. Only when we recognize the trap we are in can we even begin to start figuring out how to get free ourselves. The world needs people like Maxwell, people willing to fight the injustices and inequalities of global capitalism. But at the same time, we also have to recognize the contradictions that occur when we start demanding that we have a voice—even if it's on behalf of others. Since we live our lives in a pop-culture sphere but are denied true access to the mechanisms of the mass media, we are constantly at odds with ourselves. We want in for a variety of political, social, aesthetic, and personal reasons. But we don't always know exactly why we want in, and what we want in *to*.

We want more, not less. We want in, not out. At the same time, it would be ingenuous in the extreme to say that throwing open the gates of mass culture and giving us all our own TV stations and movie theaters would produce the answer to the problems of a narcissistic society of wannabe stars drowning their aspirations in a sea of serotonin enhancers, retro cocktails, and divorces, never mind the voiceless, the poverty-stricken, and/or the desperate who are so in need of justice. A much-expanded, open-access pop-culture system that caters to individuals instead of corporations will only sow more confusion, not less. Rebellion against what? Against whom? We have become our own enemy.

This doesn't mean that even those who are the middle-class denizens of rich power-hungry societies don't have a real grievance against "the system." Would Eric Harris and Dylan Klebold and their victims still be alive today if the Columbine duo had been able to enact their revenge fantasies on their own weekly half-hour TV show? My answer: Most definitely. Deluded youngsters whom the new conformity tricked into the fractured world of celebrity by every means possible, they nevertheless had a legitimate complaint: "The system" promised them everything and gave them nothing. What did they want? More of the same, only with them in the picture. Would it have been so hard to give them that?

I'm not going to give up on the idea of reclaiming mass entertainment culture, of making the technology available for anyone and everyone to have their own TV show, songs, poems, radio stations, etc. By personalizing, colonizing, and restating pop culture, we are reclaiming technology, forming new types of communities, and actively positing a new, and better, present-future. We have to recognize that no matter how much nostalgia for the old ways we exude, there are no old ways left: We live in an interconnected world whose single law is that of constant mutation and reinvention. In this environment, what is traditional life? Where is it? There is only a voided struggle of individuals against a faceless, self-perpetuating "system" that generates grids of power masquerading as meaning. We can rage against those interlocking systems of power, but little will change. We are, and will continue to be, compelled by the world we live in to continually (re)assert our individual identities and reinvent our communities. As long as we are stuck simply defending our right to tell our own stories and form our own communities and localities, what are the chances we will be able to truly help others in their struggles? Since we cannot avoid the demands society now makes on personhood, we must, instead, insist on truly realizing those demands. We have to continue to insist on our everyday right to creativity *and* the right to speak to each other through the mass media. Here I do not refer to the imitative creativity of backyard wrestling and Elvis impersonation, but to the creativity that has always separated human beings from beasts: the creative impulse of storytelling that gives our individual lives and separate communities personal and communal meaning. In clinging to the inherent creativity of humanity, we cling to the hope, however distant and naive, that as technology gives more and more of us access directly to each other's stories, songs, diaries, and artwork, gradually a new conception of individuality will emerge, one that is based less on being seen on TV and more on *being*.

At the same time, we are now seeing new possibilities made accessible through technological advances usurped by the vast arenas of pseudo-interactivity, pretend spirituality, and, worst of all, ersatz community. With a flip of a switch we can join all manner of electronic and pop-culture communities. And these communities, a rebuttal to Robert Putnam's assertion that in the future we will all be "bowling alone," are not necessarily a bad thing. But the more they become stand-ins for meaning and accomplishment—the more they ask that participants exchange individuality for specialness—the less likely it is that these kinds of communities can help us balance the need for personal recognition with the need for collective meaning. Pop-culture communities inspired by and dependent on the mass entertainment system for their existence can only ever be an attractive panacea to the problems of an I'm-Special world.

Ultimately, what we need is a conceptual methodology that will allow us to balance happiness with duty, the need for recognition with the need for self-recognized limits on the efficacies of egotism. We need a new way to understand the self within the context of our new global systems of mass production and increasing opportunities for individual creativity played out in endless swaths of self-same suburbs. Before we can get up and do, we must find this formula. Otherwise our "doing" may well end up having the exact opposite effect it intended, just as the CBC's all-day call-in show and constant coverage of the protests against the second Iraq war ended up dampening discord against the U.S.-led invasion.

What will this new model encompass? How will it manifest itself? Who will articulate it? Once, our neo-trad souls cry, there was such a world. Where has it gone?

Like every theorist, scholar, and pundit I have encountered on my journey to the heart of the new conformity, I have presented a handful of ideas in this book, but nothing likely to shake up assumptions and truly challenge the status quo. Unsatisfying, heretical, and downright unspecial as my lack of an instant solution may be, I do not lay claim to a new prototype (the key to divorce, diet, self-esteem, stock markets, fishing, cyberspace) that can fuse the inherent human need for the dignity of stability and recognition with the allure of displaced pop culture and its promise—the beckoning beacon of fame.

But a lack of a definitive answer doesn't mean I'm suggesting we give up. Recognizing and understanding the new conformity of special is a huge step toward moving forward. We need to move into the systems that have led us to the new conformity. We need to understand them and use them to not only get what we want— more us, for better or worse—but to start to understand why we want what we want. The ongoing struggle to reclaim individuality is not some feel-good program of Brush Dance self-actualization. Ultimately, the future depends not on what we can do to make our-selves feel momentarily better, but on going beyond temporary stop-gap measures. We must learn to take an active role in our own sublimated desires. We can no longer afford to settle for anything less than what we have been promised. As Michel Foucault has said, "It is not to awaken consciousness that we struggle, but to sap power, to take power."

DESPITE ALL MY MISGIVINGS and because of the malleable center of my pop-corrupted identity, part of me still believes that if I look hard enough, I'll find a way to reconcile individualism and deserved recognition with its corruption into the virus of special. There must, I believe, be a way to prevent us from simply dropping out, disengaging from a system that seems best at sapping our power when we think we are at our most powerful—protesting injustice, sculpting a block of wood into a poignant symbol, joining together with our neighbors and praying to a higher power. My brother, Orthodox Jewish conservative, remains a good friend, someone I can turn to for advice and companionship. We are different in many ways, but at our core we want similar things: a society of honesty, creativity, individuality, and communality. Because our many differ-ences lead to such core similarity, I occasionally allow myself to wallow in the optimistic idea that uniting to form a society that encompasses the needs and beliefs and hopes of feckless rebel critic Hal, his conservative neo-trad brother, and justice-seeking anti-capitalist Maxwell is not impossible.

In my darker, more realistic moments, I cannot deny that we are moving further into the realm of a fake individuality shaped by the pretend interactivity of the focus group, the poll, the *Idol* vote, the video game. Most of us unconsciously embrace the shift from creativity to interactivity, desiring more than anything to *feel* noticed in an anonymous, lonely era. Since my coming of age in the shopping malls of suburban North America, I've been unable to resolve the conflict within me: the desire to be known in a superficial I'm-special way versus the need to articulate who I am and what I stand for in a manner that runs counter to the all-encompassing precepts of fame and fortune, style and surface flash. Is there a middle ground, a way to be powerful without being susceptible to the suction of the system? I went looking for a way to enact that miniature triumph, that personal rebellion. I did not find it.

And yet, I persist. After all, rebellion implies change, possibility, newness. And at the heart of humanity is this urge for new experience, new patterns, expanded truths. It is not because I am filled with misanthropic horror that I sought to document the rise of the new conformity. On the contrary: It is because I am filled with awe and wonder, boggled by what we have collectively and individually wrought. Infused—by God, by pop culture, by permissive parents with conservative tendencies (infused, that is, by some combination of genes and social engineering and cosmic mystery)—with the idea that individualistic free thought is our great gift to ourselves, I am compelled not to turn away. I refuse to reject the collective possibilities of pop culture. At the same time, I refuse to embrace a global mass sameness that leaves the bulk of us pretending to be the one thing the system will never let us be: really and truly special. And so, like many others, I must continue to search for a way out that is also a way to get further in. I'd invite you to come with me, but . . . well . . . you know. I kinda think I should do this on my own.

REFERENCES

Introduction

Brush Dance website. http://www.brushdance.com (accessed May 22, 2003).

1: Hello, I'm Special

Ballard, Chris. "That Stomach Is Going to Make You Money Some Day." *The New York Times Magazine,* August 31, 2003.

Barnes, Brooks. "Don't Just Sit There . . . Do Something!" *The Wall Street Journal,* August 6, 2005.

Beck, Ulrich, and Elisabeth Beck-Gernsheim. *Individualization.* London: Sage, 2002.

Bellafanta, Gina. "Young and Chubby: What's So Heavy?" *The New York Times,* January 26, 2003.

Bellah, Robert, et al. *Habits of the Heart.* Berkeley: University of California Press, 1985.

Bracewell, Michael. *When Surface Was Depth.* Cambridge, MA: Da Capo Press, 2002. (Includes Michael Collins quotation.)

Bunn, Austin. "Not Fade Away." *The New York Times Magazine,* December 1, 2002.

Cernetig, Miro. "How Bronfmans Fell out with Corporate Sun King." *The Globe and Mail,* July 2, 2002.

Critser, Greg. "New Front in the Battle of the Bulge." *The New York Times,* May 18, 2003.

Dillon, Sam. "For One Student, A College Career Becomes A Career." *The New York Times,* November 10, 2005.

"Dropping Logos That Shout, Luxury Sellers Try Whispers." *The New York Times,* September 15, 2002.

Egan, Jennifer. "Love in the Time of No Time." *The New York Times Magazine,* November 23, 2003.

Ellmann, Richard. *Oscar Wilde.* London: H. Hamilton, 1987.

Homer-Dixon, Thomas. *The Ingenuity Gap.* Toronto: Vintage Canada, 2001.

Hsu, Francis L.K. *Rugged Individualism Reconsidered.* Knoxville: University of Tennessee Press, 1983.

Kates, Joanne, and Mara Kates. "My Child Is Starving Herself to Death." *The Globe and Mail,* January, 25, 2003.

"Marketing Hits and Misses." *Sales and Marketing Management Magazine,* July 2001.

"Meeting and Greeting in the Capital of Plastic." *The New York Times,* May 5, 2002.

Mickleburgh, Rod. "The Rapper, the Teacher, the Scandal." *The Globe and Mail,* May 7, 2003.

Mitchell, Alanna. "Extra Lettuce, Hold the Mayo, and Pile on the Information." *The Globe and Mail,* January 8, 2004.

Morris, Bob. "Hi I'm Your Waiter and This Is Reality" *The New York Times,* May 11, 2003.

Orenstein, Peggy. "Where Have All the Lisas Gone?" *The New York Times,* July 6, 2003.

Palahniuk, Chuck. *Choke.* New York: Doubleday, 2001.

Polgreen, Lydia. "Night out for 3 Friends Ends in Heroism and Mourning." *The New York Times,* March 2, 2003.

Reed, Christopher. "Backyard Wrestling for Fun and Glory, Not Cash or Gore." *Broken Pencil,* no. 17.

Rozhon, Tracie. "Reinventing Tommy: More Surf, Less Logo." *The New York Times,* March 16, 2003.

Schor, Juliet. *The Overspent American.* New York: Basic Books, 1998.

Schuler, Corinna. "The Civic-Minded Sex King." *Walrus,* February 2004.

Shalit, Wendy. *A Return to Modesty.* New York: Free Press, 1999.

Silcoff, Mireille. "Custom Fitting." *EnRoute,* January 2003.

"Sizing Up Teenagers." *The New York Times,* October 13, 2002.

Smith, Craig. "Risking Limbs for Height, and Success, in China." *The New York Times,* May 5, 2002.

St. John, Warren. "Young, Single and Dating at Hyperspeed." *The New York Times,* April 21, 2002.

Stone, Gary. *Elvis Impersonator Webring.* http://hometown.aol.com/gstone2814/index.htm.

Taffel, Ron. "Wall of Silence." *Psychotherapy Networker,* May/June 2001.

Talbot, Margaret. "Why Isn't He Just the Cutest Brand Image Enhancer You've Ever Seen." *The New York Times Magazine,* September 21, 2003.

Twitchell, James B. *Living It Up.* New York: Columbia University Press, 2002. (Source *Wall Street Journal* poll.)

"VA Legislators Driven to Win More Speciality Plates." *The Washington Post,* January 4, 2003.

Walker, Rob. "The Marketing of No Marketing." *The New York Times Magazine,* June 22, 2003.

Wente, Margaret. "Who's Too Fat?" *The Globe and Mail,* February 18, 2003.

Whyte, William H. *The Organization Man.* New York: Simon and Schuster, 1956.

2: Alone Together

Barna Group, "Rapid Increase in Alternative Forms of The Church Are Changing the Religious Landscape." http://www.barna.org, October 24, 2005.

Barber, Benjamin. *Jihad vs. McWorld.* New York: Balantine, 1996.

"Barks of Praise." *The Globe and Mail,* August 13, 2003.

Barry, Dan. "Scandal and Social Change Leave Irish Church Adrift." *The New York Times,* April 7, 2002.

Beck, Ulrich, and Elisabeth Beck-Gernsheim. *Individualization.* London: Sage, 2002.

Bellah, Robert, et al. *Habits of the Heart.* Berkeley: University of California Press, 1985.

Chafets, Zev. "The Rabbi who Loved Evangelicals (and vice versa)." *The New York Times,* July 24, 2005.

Dueck, Lorna. "Practise What You Preach." *The Globe and Mail,* January 1, 2004.

Galt, Virginia. "More Firms Offering Flex-Time Option." *The Globe and Mail,* August 11, 2003.

Grossman, Cathy. "Charting the Unchurched in America," *USA Today,* March 7, 2002.

Harding, Katherine. "Beer at Work a Frothy Issue." *The Globe and Mail,* December 4, 2002.

Hitt, Jack. "A Gospel According to the Earth." *Harper's,* July 2003.

Jang, Brent. "Births Decline Again." *The Globe and Mail,* September 27, 2002.

Kaplan, Robert D. *An Empire Wilderness.* New York: Random House, 1998.

Lehmann-Haupt, Rachel. "Need a Minister? How about Your Brother?" *The New York Times,* January 12, 2003.

Lewis, Michael. "The Artist in the Gray Flannel Pajamas." *The New York Times Magazine,* May 3, 2000.

Lyall, Sarah. "With Approval, Europeans Opt Not to Marry." *The New York Times,* March 24, 2002.

Smith, Graeme. "God at the Touch of a Screen." *The Globe and Mail,* April 12, 2003.

Swainson, Gail. "Elvis Priestley Rocks His Pulpit." *Toronto Star,* January 12, 2004.

Vansittart, Katherine. "Akared States." *The Globe and Mail,* November 27, 1999.

Yourk, Darren. "Marriage Numbers Decline Sharply." *The Globe and Mail,* November 20, 2003.

———. "Young Not Wedded to Marriage." *The Globe and Mail,* July 11, 2002.

3: Everyone's a Star

"And the Oscar Does Not Go To." *The New York Times,* March 23, 2003.

Barber, Benjamin. *Jihad vs. McWorld.* New York: Balantine, 1996.

Beck, Ulrich, and Elisabeth Beck-Gernsheim. *Individualization.* London: Sage, 2002.

Bracewell, Michael. *When Surface Was Depth.* Cambridge, MA: Da Capo Press, 2002.

Chapman, James. "Are You a Celeb Worshipper?" *This Is London,* May 14, 2003. http://www.thisislondon.com.

Gitlin, Todd. *Media Unlimited.* New York: Metropolitan Books, 2001.

Gray, Tim. "Report Shows Internet Spending Jumps", internet-news.com, June 14, 2005.

Hechtman, Ken. *www.straightgoods.com,* December 4, 2001.

Kapica, Jack. "TV Loses Ground to Net: Study." *The Globe and Mail,* May 13, 2003.

Klosterman, Chuck. "Celebrities Are Just Like You and Me." *The New York Times Magazine,* December 15, 2002.

Lesly, Philip. *The People Factor.* Homewood, IL: Richard D. Irwin, 1974.

MacDonald, Gayle. "The Road from Nowhere." *The Globe and Mail,* February 22, 2003.

Menon, Vinay. "Why We Like to Watch." *Toronto Star,* August 3, 2002.

Mirapual, Matthew. "Why Listen to Pop When You Can Mix Your Own." *The New York Times,* August 20, 2001.

Schor, Juliet. *The Overspent American.* New York: Basic Books, 1998.

Simmel, Georg. *On Individuality and Social Forms.* Chicago: University of Chicago Press, 1971.

"Social Studies." *The Globe and Mail,* November 25, 2002.

St. John, Warren. "Trying Hard to Get Free, via Rap on Your Own CD." *The New York Times,* March 3, 2002.

Taffel, Ron. "Wall of Silence." *Psychotherapy Networker,* May/June 2001.

Wolfe, Alan. *Moral Freedom.* New York: Norton, 2001.

4: Crowd Control

Ahrers, Frank. "Fiercely Top 40." *The Washington Post,* April 7, 2001.

Baker, Chris. ".hack Attack." *Wired,* October 2002.

Barber, Benjamin. *Jihad vs. McWorld.* New York: Balantine, 1996.

Bellah, Robert, et al. *Habits of the Heart.* Berkeley: University of California Press, 1985.

Black, Debra, and Robin Harvey. "Stigma of Depression Finally Gone." *Toronto Star,* June 6, 2003.

Boehelrt, Eric. "Radio's Big Bully." *Salon,* April 30, 2001.

Carr, David, and Lorne Manly. "At Star Crazy Magazines, the Brand's the Thing. *The New York Times,* March 10, 2002.

Cernetig, Miro. "One Big Mac, Hold the Imperialism." *The Globe and Mail,* April 10, 2001.

_____. "Starlet Fever." *The Globe and Mail,* August 19, 2000.

"City TV Now Available in Assorted Cultures." *The Globe and Mail,* March 21, 2001.

"Condominium Development on the Fringes of St. Petersburg." *The New York Times,* July 13, 2000.

Considine, J.D. "Reaching out to the Multitasking Modern Teenager." *The New York Times,* March 2, 2003.

Elliot, Stuart. "Advertising's Big Four." *The New York Times,* March 31, 2002.

"Foreign Distillers Seek to Slake India's Thirst." *The New York Times,* May 5, 2002.

"From the Airwaves to the Streets." *Adbusters,* January/February 2001.

Gordon, Karyn. *Analyse Yourself.* Pickering, ON: Castle Quay Books, 2002.

Hardison Jr., O.B. *Disappearing through the Skylight.* New York: Penguin, 1990.

Harmon, Amy. "Star Wars Fan Films Come Tumbling Back to Earth." *The New York Times,* April 28, 2002.

Hirschberg, Lynn. "Who's That Girl?" *The New York Times Magazine,* August 4, 2002.

Hogan, Patrick Colm. *The Culture of Conformism.* Durham, NC: Duke University Press, 2001.

Hollywoodreporter.com. May 7, 2004.

Holson, Laura M. "Why Hollywood Loves to Repeat Itself." *The New York Times,* May 11, 2003.

Homer-Dixon, Thomas. *The Ingenuity Gap.* Toronto: Vintage Canada, 2001.

Kirkpatrick, David. "Shaping Cultural Tastes at Big Retail Chains." *The New York Times,* May 18, 2003.

Mydang, Seth. "Oh Blue Eyed Thais, Flaunt Your Western Genes!" *The New York Times,* August 29, 2002.

Nelson, Chris. "Lip-synching Gets Real." *The New York Times,* February 1, 2004.

Peoplecards.net (accessed 2002).

Rachel. *iwannabefamous.com,* August 5, 2003.

Salaman, Julie. "Looking Back at the Bonfires, Personal and Professional." *The New York Times,* June 16, 2002.

Scott, A.O. "An Outsider Who Isn't out Far Enough." *The New York Times,* March 24, 2002.

Siegler, Chris. "A Wasteland of the Airwaves." *Punk Planet,* no. 52, November/ December 2002.

St. John, Allen. "I'm on the Olympic Team? Bummer!" *The New York Times Magazine,* January 27, 2002.

Turner, Chris. "Geek No More." *The Globe and Mail,* May 24, 2003.

Twitchell, James B. *Living It Up.* New York: Columbia University Press, 2002.

Whyte, Murray. "Life after Moses." *Toronto Star,* April 27, 2003.

Wong, Jan. "It's a Global Party, Thanks to Santa." *The Globe and Mail,* December 24, 1999.

5: "Who Else Is Me?"

Beck, Ulrich, and Elisabeth Beck-Gernsheim. *Individualization.* London: Sage, 2002.

Birnbaum, Pierre. "Mass, Mobilization, and the State." In *Changing Conceptions of Crowd Mind and Behaviour,* ed. Carl F. Graumann and Serge Moscovici. New York: Springer-Verlag, 1986.

Cantril, Hadley. *The Psychology of Social Movements.* New York: Wiley, 1941.

Ewen, Stuart. *PR!* New York: Basic Books, 1996.

Firkins, O.W. "The Cult of the Passing Hour." *The Atlantic Monthly,* May 1914.

Forgas, Joseph P. *The Social Mind: Cognitive and Motivational Aspects of Interpersonal Behaviour.* Cambridge, England: Cambridge University Press, 2001.

Foucault, Michel. *Discipline and Punish: The Birth of the Prison.* New York: Vintage, 1995 (originally published 1977).

Kaplan, Ben. "Making the Bands." *The New York Times Magazine,* November 5, 2000.

Le Bon, Gustave. *The Crowd.* Dunwoody, GA: N.S. Berg, 1968 (originally published 1896).

Lyon, David. *Postmodernity.* Buckingham, England: Open University Press, 1999.

Moscovici, Serge. "The Discovery of the Masses." In *Changing Conceptions of Crowd Mind and Behaviour,* ed. Carl F. Graumann and Serge Moscovici. New York: Springer-Verlag, 1986.

Parks, Tim. *Adultery and Other Diversions.* New York: Arcade, 2000.

Rey, Jean-Michel. "Freud and Massenpsychologie." In *Changing Conceptions of Crowd Mind and Behaviour,* ed. Carl F. Graumann and Serge Moscovici. New York: Springer-Verlag, 1986.

Shalit, Wendy. *A Return to Modesty.* New York: Free Press, 1999.

Simmel, Georg. *On Individuality and Social Forms.* Chicago: University of Chicago Press, 1971.

_____. *Simmel on Culture.* London: Sage, 1997.

Tarde, Gabriel. *On Communication and Social Influence: Selected Papers.* Chicago: University of Chicago Press, 1969.

Tester, Keith. *Moral Culture.* London: Sage, 1997.

6: The Search for Home

"Angry Country Folk Flood London." *The Globe and Mail,* September 22, 2002.

Bailie, Ericka. "A Week in the Life of Ericka Bailie." *Broken Pencil,* fall 2000.

Barber, Benjamin. *Jihad vs. McWorld.* New York: Balantine, 1996.

Beck, Ulrich, and Elisabeth Beck-Gernsheim. *Individualization.* London: Sage, 2002.

Colapinto, John. "The Young Republicans." *The New York Times Magazine,* May 25, 2003.

Cross, Michelle. "Dear E-Diary" *Broken Pencil,* fall 2000.

Cunco, Michael. *American Exorcism.* New York: Doubleday, 2001.

Ewen, Stuart. *PR!* New York: Basic Books, 1996.

Fountain, John W. "Exorcists and Exorcisms Proliferate across the U.S." *The New York Times,* November 28, 2000.

Friedman, Thomas L. "The Two Domes of Belgium." *The New York Times,* January 27, 2002.

Galanter, Marc. *Cults.* New York: Oxford University Press, 1999.

Hayt, Elizabeth. "Surprise, Mom: I'm against Abortion." *The New York Times,* March 30, 2003.

Himelfarb, Ellen. "Britons Get Their 15 Minutes of Farm." *The New York Times,* March 2, 2003.

Hitt, Jack. "A Gospel According to the Earth." *Harper's,* July 28, 2003.

Kaplan, Robert D. *An Empire Wilderness.* New York. Random House, 1998.

Lyon, David. *Postmodernity.* Buckingham, England: Open University Press, 1999.

Morris, David, and Gary Langer. "Same Sex Marriage." ABC News website, January 21, 2004. http://abcnews.go.com.

Moscovici, Serge. "The Discovery of the Masses." In *Changing Conceptions of Crowd Mind and Behaviour,* ed. Carl F. Graumann and Serge Moscovici. New York: Springer-Verlag, 1986.

Putnam, Robert D. *Bowling Alone.* New York: Simon and Schuster, 2000.

Schor, Juliet. *The Overspent American.* New York: Basic Books, 1998.

Shalit, Wendy. *A Return to Modesty.* New York: Free Press, 1999.

Simmd, Georg. *On Individuality and Social Forms.* Chicago: University of Chicago Press, 1971.

Soloway, Colin, et al. "A Long Strange Trip to the Taliban." *Newsweek,* December 17, 2001.

Saunders, Doug. "John Lindh's Hip-Hop Youth." *The Globe and Mail,* January 30, 2002.

St. John, Warren. "Dating a Blogger." *The New York Times,* May 18, 2003.

_____. "Dot-Commers on a Mom and Pop Track." *The New York Times,* August 11, 2002.

Wilkinson, Jack. "Pennefather Heeds Her Calling." *The Atlanta Journal-Constitution,* April 6, 2003.

7: Extreme Behavior

Anderssen, Erin. "Fatal Attractions." *The Globe and Mail,* May 22, 2000.

"As You Were." *Harper's,* February 2002.

Atwood, Margaret. *The Handmaid's Tale.* Toronto: McClelland and Stewart, 1985.

Battle Royale. Director Kinji Fukasaku. Japan, 2000.

Bosman, Julie. "Short-Shorts at 35,000 Feet." *The New York Times,* March 23, 2003.

Bracewell, Michael. *When Surface Was Depth.* Cambridge, MA: Da Capo Press, 2002.

Caldwell, Rebecca. "Shock, Schlock, Corpses Galore." *The Globe and Mail,* April 1, 2003.

"Chief Moose Appeals Panel Ruling on Sniper Book." *CNN.com* (accessed July 10, 2003).

Conlogue, Ray. "A Film Too Sick for Cannes." *The Globe and Mail,* March 14, 2003.

Considine, J.D. "Boogie Nights." *The Globe and Mail,* May 7, 2003.

Fessenden, Ford. "They Threaten, Seethe and Unhinge, Then Kill in Quantity." *The New York Times,* April 9, 2000.

Forgas, Joseph P. *The Social Mind: Cognitive and Motivational Aspects of Interpersonal Behaviour.* Cambridge, England: Cambridge University Press, 2001.

Foucault, Michel. *Discipline and Punish.* New York: Vintage, 1995 (originally published 1977).

Gitlin, Todd. *Media Unlimited.* New York: Metropolitan Books, 2001.

"Hostage Taker at German School Surrenders." *The Globe and Mail,* October 18, 2002.

Houellebecq, Michel. *The Elementary Particles.* New York: Vintage, 2000.

Hsu, Francis. *Rugged Individualism Reconsidered.* Knoxville, TN: University of Tennessee Press.

James, Caryn. "Plain Folks Surgery Is Ugly TV." *Toronto Star,* December 12, 2002.

Kaplan, Robert D. *An Empire Wilderness.* New York: Random House, 1998.

La Spirale. http://www.laspirale.org (accessed June 6, 2000).

Levin, Jack, and James Alan Fox. "Making Celebrities of Serial Killers Elevates the Threat." *USA Today,* October 23, 2002.

Lyon, David. *Postmoderniry.* Buckingham, England: Open University Press, 1999.

"Man Shot Dead at Gas Station in Virginia." *The Globe and Mail,* October 9, 2002.

Mckenna, Barrie. "How a Fugitive Turned into a Folk Hero in Appalachia." *The Globe and Mail,* June 6, 2003.

Morrison, Jennifer. "Cat Mutilators Face Doggy Power." *Toronto Sun,* March 25, 2002.

MSNBC. "Harris and Klebold Wanted to Be Cult Heroes According to Videotapes," November 11, 1999.

Price, S.L. "When Fans Attack." *Sports Illustrated,* April 28, 2003.

Robinson, Jennifer. "Young Women Break Taboos with Tattoos." *Toronto Star,* June 24, 2003.

Roszack, Theodore. *The Making of a Counter Culture.* New York: Doubleday, 1968.

"Swedish Teen Accused of Planning Massacre." *The Globe and Mail,* May 25, 2004.

Taffel, Ron. "Wall of Silence." *Psychotherapy Networker,* May/June 2001.

Trebay, Guy. "After Nice, a Return to Vice." *The New York Times,* June 8, 2003.

Wise, Mike. "Rugged Individualism: Tattoo-Less Arms." *The New York Times,* June 8, 2003.

Zwolinski, Mark. "Unruly Fans Run Amok at Jays Game." *Toronto Star,* June 26, 2003.

8: Revolution Redux

Chang, Jen, et al. *Resist!* Halifax: Fernwood, 2002.

Ha, Tu Thanh. "More Than 200 Arrested after WTO Protests." *The Globe and Mail,* July 29, 2003.

Leland, John. "A Movement, Yes, but No Counterculture." *The New York Times,* March 23, 2003.

Palladino, Luca, et al. *Counterproductive*. Montreal: Cumulus Press, 2002.

Peck, Abe. *Uncovering the Sixties*. New York: Pantheon, 1985.

Roszak, Theodore. *The Making of a Counter Culture*. New York: Doubleday, 1969.

Sante, Luc. "Be Different! (Like Everyone Else!)." *The New York Times Magazine,* December 12, 1999.

Simmel, Georg. *Simmel on Culture*. London: Sage, 1997.

Tester, Keith. *Moral Culture*. London: Sage, 1997.

Conclusion

Havel, Václav. "The Culture of Enterprise." *Walrus,* February 2004.

"Intellectuals and Power: A Conversation between Michel Foucault and Gilles Deleuze." http://www.csun.edu/~hfspc002/foucB3.html#power.

INDEX

HAL NIEDZVIECKI'S writings about culture have appeared in newspapers and magazines across North America. He is the founder and current fiction editor of *Broken Pencil: the magazine of zine culture and the independent arts* (www.brokenpencil.com). Niedzviecki is the author of the short fiction collection *Smell It* and the novels *Lurvy* and *Ditch*. He is also the author of *We Want Some Too: Underground Desire and the Reinvention of Mass Culture*. His most recent novel, *The Program*, was published in 2005. For more information about his work, visit www.smellit.ca.